# irreverent

# guide to

# Paris

4th Edition

By

Alec Lobrano

HUNGRY MINDS, INC.

**a disclaimer**

Please note that prices fluctuate in the course of time, and travel information changes under the impact of the many factors that influence the travel industry. We therefore suggest that you write or call ahead for confirmation when making your travel plans. Every effort has been made to ensure the accuracy of information throughout this book and the contents of this publication are believed correct at the time of printing. Nevertheless, the publishers cannot accept responsibility for errors or omissions or for changes in details given in this guide or for the consequences of any reliance on the information provided by the same. Assessments of attractions and so forth are based upon the author's own experience and therefore, descriptions given in this guide necessarily contain an element of subjective opinion, which may not reflect the publisher's opinion or dictate a reader's own experience on another occasion. Readers are invited to write to the publisher with ideas, comments, and suggestions for future editions.

Your safety is important to us, however, so we encourage you to stay alert and be aware of your surroundings. Keep a close eye on cameras, purses, and wallets, all favorite targets of thieves and pickpockets.

**Published by HUNGRY MINDS, INC.**

909 Third Avenue
New York, NY 10022

ISBN 0-7645-6564-8
ISSN 1085-4711

Interior design contributed to by Tsang Seymour Design Studio

**special sales**

For general information on Hungry Minds' products and services please contact our Customer Care Department within the U.S. at 800-762-2974, outside the U.S. at 317-572-3993 or fax 317-572-4002.

For sales inquiries and reseller information, including discounts, premium and bulk quantity sales, and foreign-language translations, please contact our Customer Care Department at 800-434-3422 or fax 317-572-4002.

Manufactured in the United States of America

# what's so irreverent?

It's up to you.

You can buy a traditional guidebook with its fluff, its pro-motional hype, its let's-find-something-nice-to-say-about-everything point of view. Or you can buy an Irreverent guide.

What the Irreverents give you is the lowdown, the inside story. They have nothing to sell but the truth, which includes a balance of good and bad. They praise, they trash, they weigh, and leave the final decisions up to you. No tourist board, no chamber of commerce will ever recommend them.

Our writers are insiders, who feel passionate about the cities they live in, and have strong opinions they want to share with you. They take a special pleasure leading you where other guides fear to tread.

How irreverent are they? One of our authors insisted on writing under a pseudonym. "I couldn't show my face in town again if I used my own name," she told me. "My friends would never speak to me." Such is the price of honesty. She, like you, should know she'll always have a friend at Frommer's.

Warm regards,

*Michael Spring*

Michael Spring
Publisher

# contents

**INDEX** **222**

# Central Paris Neighborhoods

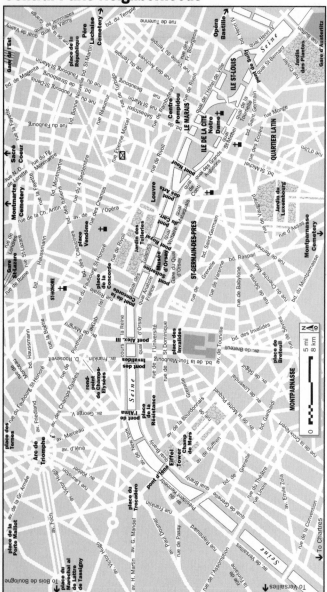

# you
# probably
# didn't know

**Where do you think you're going?...** No major city in the world is as wantonly misperceived as Paris. People get all moony-eyed about the place just looking at their airplane tickets, fantasizing about romantic sidewalk cafes (with accordion music in the background, of course), incredible food at fancy restaurants, and perhaps a stolen kiss from a new *amour* while leaning against the side of an idyllic bridge on the Seine. Ah, Paris. Pure romance, right? Well, maybe and maybe not. The city inarguably offers a beautiful backdrop for hand-holding and secret trysts, and being a foreigner there makes it all that much more romantic. But the cold truth is that Paris is a staid, grandmotherly city with a highly conventional, bourgeois sense of decorum and an aging population that mostly lives alone. (Singles make up more than half of all Parisian households.) Take a seat in the Parc Monceau on a sunny afternoon and you'll be more likely to observe a strict code of conduct than rampant displays of public affection. If Gene Kelly were to dance down the street at night the way he did in the movies, he'd likely be reprimanded for public drunkenness. Real Paris is not Hollywood Paris, and that is part of what makes it so lovely for most visitors. The city's unbending reverence for tradition keeps its treasures of art, architecture, and classic cuisine alive. But if you're looking for reckless romance or cutting-edge anything, you're likely to be disappointed. The best fashion designers are imported; the restaurant scene (and the food) is much more innovative in San Francisco, New York, and London; the art scene is completely moribund; and when was the last time you saw a play by a contemporary French playwright? So why come to Paris? Because it is Paris, of course! And it is, quite simply, the best place in the Western world to absolutely luxuriate in sepia-tinted pleasures in a 19th century atmosphere.

**Is it true that the French hate American culture?...** Do you really care? It's not as though French people are going to stop you in the street and hold you responsible for past episodes of *The Brady Bunch*. And if you mistake the upturned nose of Parisian waiters (or underpaid shop clerks) as a specific snub, you're wasting your energy. That whole attitude is merely a pose, and no one knows that better than the French themselves. The truth is, most young French people harbor a passion for American culture—at least the version they've soaked up from movies, TV, and pop music. In fact, if you meet up with any Parisians under the age of 25, don't be surprised if they throw themselves at you just because you're American. They dress up in full hip-hop regalia and flock to McDonald's and Burger King, not to mention the Hard Rock Cafe and Planet Hollywood. The wonderful thing is that while decked out in American drag, they still act totally French, kissing their friends on the cheeks upon arrival and departure and observing French table manners to the letter.

**Why do people answer me in English when I've spoken to them in French?...** For many people a trip to Paris is a chance to go live with the wreckage of once seemingly pointless high school French classes. So why is it that when you summon up your courage and say, "Je prends l'omelette au fromage, s'il vous plait," the waiter replies, "Do you want it with salad or fries?" This reflexive linguistic upstaging might be a help if you don't know "oui" from "non," but it's really off-putting when you've made the effort to go local. So why do they do it? Partly because your North American accent is just too good a target to resist a putdown, and partly because they're showing off that they're not schnooks either—to wit, "Hey, man, I can speak English, too." More and more

French do speak English, and occasionally, an Anglo reply is actually well-intended, but curiously for a country that spends millions propigating its language around the globe and that even has a Ministere de la Francophonie—a cabinet-level post devoted to ensuring the use of French around the world—the locals are pretty bluff when you make the effort. So get used to it, or learn Spanish or Japanese instead.

**Why do the French smoke so much?...** French cigarettes carry a health warning, too, and French lungs contract cancer as easily as American ones, but the relaxed attitude towards smoking is part of the ferocious Gallic devotion to the pleasure principal. To their credit, they'll fiercely defend anybody's right to have a good time, even if it includes that most evil of weeds, and there's also an indirect rebuke to what they see as characteristically excessive and draconian American anti-smoking campaigns.

**Is Disneyland Paris worth a visit?...** Only if you're a die-hard fan of Mickey (pronounced Mick-kay in French) or want the boofo experience of a truly weird cultural hybrid. Franco-American has almost never been more spaghetti-O than it is on the wind-swept plains of Marne-la-Vallee, where the park is located. Other reasons to go might be that you've got the tots in tow, are feeling homesick, hate Florida or have never been to California, but don't snub Mona Lisa to see Donald Duck.

**Why is that guy staring at me?...** The French don't hesitate to stare openly, whether in admiration or condemnation (it's often difficult to tell which is which). You might as well get used to it and stare back. In the Métro, for instance, a woman may study another woman closely, checking out her clothes, hairstyle, makeup, and accessories. This is probably a compliment; she's making mental notes of things to copy. And though French people try not to stand out from the crowd in public, they take great pleasure in seeing someone else do it, and they'll stare unapologetically at anything unusual—an accident, a shouting *clochard* (street person), a man in an ape suit, a woman with purple hair. Go ahead and gawk with them.

**No, really, he's hitting on me...** A species of French males called *dragueurs* (literally "dredgers") especially like to pick up female American tourists. Some women find this amusing, others merely find it annoying. In any either case, *dragueurs* may be persistent, but they're almost never dangerous. Some try to charm you with their French accents, while others get right to the point: "Bonjour. Would you like to sleep with me?" If you would, the appropriate answer is, obviously, "Oui." If not, the internationally accepted negative response, "No," usually works, especially if you add an evil stare. And don't worry about being rude. (You are, after all, in Paris, where rude is a sport if not an art form.) As in any city, a woman alone is often a target; most French women don't go out by themselves in Paris, not even to dinner. To make sure you'll feel comfortable in restaurants, make reservations in advance; most restaurateurs are solicitous of single female diners. You'll probably have no problems in a cafe or restaurant during the day.

**Why you might as well leave your watch at home...** Do not mistake the French for the Swiss. Precision is not a passion in Paris, and time is certainly not of the essence. Never mind what the TV guide said; the shows will come on when it is convenient. And if the photo shop says that your prints will be ready at 10am on Tuesday, it means nothing. Maybe they'll be there, maybe they won't. (Don't expect an apology, either. *C'est la vie.*) Many shops, museums, and galleries close at lunchtime (as do some unlikely places such as supermarkets and large electronics stores). And French restaurants have an annoying habit of being closed only when you most want to eat, like on Saturday night. Sure, the restaurateurs know they could make more money if they stayed open on Saturday evening, but they don't care. It's more important for them to get out of town on the weekend for rest and relaxation. Are you totally irritated yet? If so, take a deep breath and try to think calm thoughts. After all, isn't it refreshing to be in a place where the dollar (or the euro) isn't worshipped above all else?

**How to deal with surly waiters...** On the other hand, though you may linger until you are old and gray (especially if you are in a hurry for your check), don't even think about service with a smile. It is simply not part of the French vocabulary. Waiters are rude and that's that. You can try being polite, but it will probably have little or no effect. So do as the French do: Join the attitude war. Unfortunately, in Paris, in-your-face is what works.

**How to talk your way into a club...** Don't try it. Paris nightclub bouncers are redoubtable. Once a bouncer has refused you, you have to prove you're royalty to get in (and even that might not work—the bouncer's pride might be hurt because he didn't recognize you). Don't show up dowdy or scruffy unless you're famous. The best way to get into the most *branché* (trendy, literally "plugged in") night-clubs is to arrive in some sort of flamboyant costume. Unaccompanied men hardly ever get in because there's always a shortage of women; beautiful women, especially tall American models, are a sure open sesame. On the other hand, many gay bars and nightclubs refuse to admit women at all.

**How to talk your way into a fashion show...** If you're not a lucky invitation-holder, getting past the gorillas at the gate into Paris's haute couture and *prêt-à-porter* shows is nearly impossible. The key word here is "nearly." Truly dedicated garment groupies have been known to arrive ahead of time at the location of their favorite designer's show and, looking irresistibly pathetic, ask everyone heading inside if they have an extra invitation. This actu-ally works sometimes, but don't count on it for the really hot shows, such as John Galliano (Dior), Alexander McQueen (Givenchy), Dries Van Noten, or Jean-Paul Gaultier. Your best bet, of course, is to have an influential friend who is willing to give you an extra invite. Check with the Chambre Syndicale de la Couture (tel 01 42 66 64 44) for the location of particular shows.

**Where to catch some rays...** The moment there's a ray of sunshine (a rarity in this gray city), no matter how chilly it is, Parisian sun worshippers flock to the banks of the Seine, where you'll see nearly naked bodies sprawled on every available stretch of concrete. Okay, so it's not the Riviera, but it ain't Hoboken, either. Feel free to join them. The area near the Tuileries Gardens is a gay cruising ground, as well.

**Why you should hoard those 50 centimes pieces...** They are the key to relieving a bursting bladder. Forget those *pissoirs* Henry Miller loved so much—today Paris is dotted with ugly, pre-cast cement toilets, awaiting your two-franc deposit. Don't get freaked out if the seat is wet; the whole toilet is automatically ster-ilized with boiling water and disinfectant after each use. Your other alternative is to march into a busy cafe and brazenly head for the WC without ordering anything. If someone stops you, say you're going to use the pay phone (almost invariably next to the john).

**What is a zebra?...** A band of striped pavement across a street is called a zebra crossing, and French law stipulates that a driver must stop for pedestrians who have started to cross in front of them. Ha! When they see you trying to cross the street, French drivers will show no signs of slowing. If you keep going, they may swerve to avoid you, they may stop (unlikely), or they may just run you down. The French don't have the right to bear arms as Americans do, so this is one of the few means available to them to commit homicide. Don't tempt them.

**Can't they see I'm walking here?...** Even long-time Yankee expats are still amazed that Parisians, unlike American or other northern European city dwellers, wander down the street as though they had it all to themselves. If some sidewalk hog is blocking your path, a stiff, "*Pardon!*" usually does the trick.

**How to see the sights without taking a tour bus...** The 95 bus passes the Paris Opera, the Louvre, and the Palais Royal, then crosses the Seine and goes through Saint-Germain-des-Prés and on to Montparnasse. All it costs is a bus ticket, which you buy from the driver when you board.

**How to get a taxi at 2am...** That's the witching hour, when many bars close, the Métro is no longer running, the Noctambus provides only infrequent bus service (see Hotlines & Other Basics), and many taxi drivers are on their way home to bed. The best way to avoid a long walk home is to book a taxi in advance: call **Taxis Bleu** (tel 01 49 36 10 10), **Taxi G7** (tel 01 47 39 47 39), or **Alpha Taxis** (tel 01 45 85 85 85). Otherwise, head for a bar or club that stays open all night and grab a taxi discharging new arrivals.

**It's Sunday. Where the hell is everybody?...** Pressure from still-powerful unions has kept the French "blue laws" in effect. Unless they sell food, stores aren't supposed to open on Sunday, though many small boutiques do anyway. In the **Marais**, almost all the shops are open on Sunday. Many boutiques around the **rue des Abbesses** in Montmartre are also open on Sunday, and the area also has some wonderful specialty food shops open in the morning. Many museums are open, but they'll be crowded. Instead, visit one of the many atmospheric food markets—the **Marché d'Aligre** (don't miss Le Baron Rouge wine bar), and the markets on the **rue Mouffetard** and the **rue Montorgueil**. Or check out the enormous flea market at Porte de Clignancourt, skipping the usual cheap leather jackets and cowboy boots and bee-lining for the antique stalls. Have a drink (the food is too bad to contemplate) at **Chez Louisette** in the Vernaison section of the market and soak up the local color—accordion players, Edith Piaf imitators, and the palm-reading Gypsy lady.

**It's August. Where the hell is everybody?...** Nearly the entire city goes on vacation for the whole month of August. Many restaurants will be closed—most small businesspeople would rather close down than trust their business to an outsider. (If your heart is set on eating in a particular restaurant, check whether it will be open; see Dining.) The upside of August in Paris is the wonderful calm that descends on the city. The streets, normally choked with traffic noise and pollution, become blessedly empty. It doesn't get completely dark until about 11pm, and the larger cafes do stay open. The Eric Rohmer film *Le Rayon Vert* gives a wonderful feeling for Paris in August, when it feels more like a lazy provincial city than a world capital.

**Why you shouldn't mind if someone calls you a Bobo...** Relax, it has nothing to do with how you get your kit off and with whom; "Bobo" means bohemian-bourgeois, which is what yuppies have morphed into now that the y-word has become such an embarrassment and so many of them have grown old enough to get important editorial jobs, and so defend themselves.

**Why you shouldn't spend too much time in Saint Germain...** Paris really has changed, and if you honestly want to discover the city beyond the most seriously shop-worn tourist cliches in the book (not this one, of course), you're not going to do it sitting around in overpriced Left Bank cafes surfing the garbagey conversations of other American college students, British divorcees, Australian backpackers, or, for Parisians that most alarming of all foreign species, honeymooners from Texas. Saint Germain is all about luxury shopping these days—witness the Louis Vuitton, Chanel, and Cartier boutiques—so if you want to re-enact Audrey Hepburn's role in *Funny Face* (she plays a naïve, intellectually ambitious bookstore clerk)—head for Menilmontant (it's partly in the 11th arrondissement, partly in the 20th) or Batignolles (17th arrondissement); this is where the wild things are. And if you really want to groove a cool, young French scene hop the train to Rennes, in Brittany, or Marseilles for the weekend; both are truly happening in places in a way that Paris isn't for the most part.

accomm

# 1

# odations

Paris used to be
the capital of fan-
tastically hideous
floral wallpaper.
Almost all of its
hundreds of
cheap, family-run

hotels offered heart-stopping examples, as any veteran of a backpack-and-stale-baguette student trip to Paris knows. Their heating and plumbing systems presented such puzzles as, "How can I wash my face in a two-inch-deep basin without hitting my head on that beam?"

At the other end of the scale, in *les palaces*, whippet-like men with pencil mustaches once made a life's work out of exponential nastiness, guarding acre-sized black-and-white marble lobbies against the blight of your presence. If you got past these guard dogs, your room upstairs invariably had a crystal chandelier, a lot of gilt Louis-something furniture, a very slow-dialing telephone on a short cord, and a flummoxing handheld shower that forced you to bathe on your knees.

The $20 triangular room with fluorescent dahlia print wallpaper is gone forever—but Paris still offers a broad choice of comfortable, well-located hotels with lots of local charm for around $60 to $80 a night. Many of them have been modernized and are run by such chains as the very-good-value Libertel group. Even the palace hotels are enhancing and augmenting their amenities (witness the spectacular underground health club at the glitzy **Ritz**, of all places). Finally, painful though it may be, many Parisian hoteliers have accepted the inevitable and learned to speak English—and even how to smile.

If stairs are difficult for you, be sure to ask when you book whether the hotel has an elevator. Few Paris hotels are well equipped for travelers with disabilities (even if there is an elevator, there's often a half-flight of stairs that must be mounted). In addition, bathrooms in Paris can be ridiculously tiny and cramped. Be very specific about your needs when booking. *Paris Ile-de-France Pour Tous,* an informative book on the accessibility of hotels, museums, etc., in the Paris area, is available by mail for 12.20 euros (CNRH 236 bis, rue de Tolbiac, 75013; tel 01 53 80 66 66).

Note that the value-added tax, or TVA, and service are included in all hotel room prices and that tipping is not necessary unless someone has done some very special favor for you.

### Winning the Reservations Game

Paris is one of the most popular tourist destinations in the world, so always book a hotel as far in advance as possible, at least four to six weeks if you can. You may be able to find a room after you arrive, but it probably won't be exactly what you want and may be much more expensive than you'd like.

It's easier to find a room in November, December, July, and August than at other times of the year, when events like fashion shows, trade fairs, conferences, and the Le Bourget air show keep hotels—even modest ones—full. **Ely 12 12** (tel 01 43 59 12 12, fax 01 42 56 24 31; 9, rue d'Artois, 75008 Paris) can usually get a room for you even when the whole town is booked up. The service is free. The **Paris Office du Tourisme** (tel 01 49 52 53 54, fax 01 49 52 53 00; 127, ave des Champs-Elysées, 75008, www.paris-touristoffice.com) also has a hotel booking service. **Paris-Séjour-Réservation** (tel 01 53 89 10 50 or 01 53 89 10 59; 90, ave des Champs-Elysées, 75008 Paris, www.gconline.com/parispsr/) can find you an apartment complete with towels, sheets, and maid service for a stay of seven days or more. A free classified advertising publication called **France-USA Contacts**, or FUSAC (in Paris: tel 01 45 38 56 57, fax 01 45 38 98 94; 3, rue Larochelle, 75014; in the U.S.: tel 212/777–5553, fax 212/777–5554; Box 115, Cooper Station, New York, NY 10276; www.fusac.com), carries ads for short-term apartment rentals or apartment exchanges. If all else fails, and you arrive in Paris without a reservation, the Office du Tourisme has desks at the airports, train stations, and the Eiffel Tower. The pickings might be slim and you might not get a hotel in the area you prefer, but you never know—you might get lucky.

**What to do with a bidet**

*Bidets are indispensable to the French. So first off, it's pronounced "bee-DAY." And it's for washing you private parts after using the toilet or engaging in, ahem, certain other acts. The French have long been an international standing joke for their lack of personal hygiene, but they're finally getting into the habit of the daily wash-up (although they still use the smallest amount of soap per capita in Europe). They're even beginning to use deodorants, as you can tell from the slightly less pungent air in the Métro in summertime. In retaliation, the French—who consider Americans hypersensitive in matters of cleanliness—get a good laugh out of watching Yankee tourists encountering bidets in their hotel rooms. Some Americans use it to wash out their underwea; others think it's handy for soaking swollen feet after hours of heavy-duty sightseing.*

INTRODUCTION | ACCOMMODATIONS

When you reserve, ask about special rates, including corporate or weekend packages, which are offered by many large or pricey hotels. Most hotels lower their rates, sometimes considerably, during their low season (July through August and November through December).

## What the Rating Stars Mean

All French hotels are rated with a star system, ranging from no stars to four, plus four-star deluxe. Though the stars will give you an idea of the relative luxury and price of the hotel, they relate more to technical criteria such as room size and the number of electrical outlets than they do to Old World charm.

It's important to note that the star ratings directly affect the tax rates of a hotel. Some of the most delightful properties have two stars strictly because the owners don't want to raise their property taxes. The French themselves regularly stay in two-stars, where they know they'll get a clean, comfortable room with a private bath.

Many small, inexpensive hotels with no stars or one star don't have toilets or even showers in the rooms, although a sink and a bidet are generally provided. At this level, it's also unlikely that your sheets and towels will be changed daily. If you don't mind scooting down the hall in a bathrobe, you can save a lot of money by staying in these hotels. Some of them are actually comfortable and pretty.

A number of hotels have a range of prices that depend on the size and amenities of different rooms. Rooms with a bathtub rather than just a shower, for example, will cost a bit more, as will rooms with twin beds instead of a double bed. And you may be expected to pay extra for a room with a view or a balcony. Again, if you have a preference or would rather not pay for extras, say so when you book.

## Is There a Right Address?

If you're more interested in hanging out in Algerian Rai clubs than in doing the Louvre, look for a room around the Bastille. If you want to have plenty of room for your matching Louis Vuitton luggage, need a safe for your jewelry, and need to be close to the couture houses for your fittings, you'll want to pop for a grand hotel. If this is your 12th visit, you might enjoy staying in one of the outlying neighborhoods to sample more of the daily life of the city. First-timers are generally happiest in and around Saint-Germain-des-Prés on the Left Bank, where the local charm veritably screams Paris. Just make sure your hotel is in a district well served by public transportation—when choosing between two similar hotels, go with the one near a Métro stop that's served by several lines instead of just one.

Left Bank or Right Bank? The way Paris is getting gentrified, there's not so much difference anymore. These days the Left Bank is about as bohemian as Betty Crocker, having become more the bastion of the liberal Parisian bourgeoisie than a center of radical thought. But it still *looks* like the Left Bank, the one part of town that wasn't ruthlessly modernized in the 19th century by Baron Haussmann, master of the grand boulevard.

Almost all the grande dame hotels are located on the Right Bank off the **Champs-Elysées** and near the **place de la Concorde** (8th arrondissement). These palaces cost a fortune, but the same area has many of the city's most luxurious boutiques. Heading east along the Seine, you come to **Châtelet** and **Les Halles** (1st arrondissement), two of the city's major pulse points, with lots of car and foot traffic, cafes, bars, restaurants, and clubs. It is a McDonald's–Pizza Hut–KFC cluttered haven for lounging suburban youth, junkies, and assorted young blood on shopping sprees, but it's an easy walk to the **Centre Pompidou**, the Marais, the Ile-de-la-Cité, and the Left Bank. Hotels here run from tiny no-stars on the side streets running off the Les Halles shopping center to big, brassy, commercial chain places.

The maze-like medieval **Marais** (3rd and 4th arrondissements) is home to gorgeous 16th- and 17th-century architecture, funky little bars and restaurants, and a cosmopolitan character. Here, Hasidic Jews rub shoulders with Paris's vibrant gay community, and chic French *mamans* wheel their Dior-clad babies past Asian wholesalers. Hotels tend to be reasonably priced and romantic, if a bit idiosyncratic, with the odd water-pressure problem or slanting floors. The demand for rooms in the Marais far outstrips availability, so if you have your heart set on this quarter, book extra far in advance.

If you want to indulge a long-nurtured desire to sleep near Mona (Lisa, that is), there are fancy hotels near the **Louvre** and **Palais-Royal** (1st arrondissement) and the **Eiffel Tower** (7th arrondissement; see listings below). The former is a busy area in the monument-studded but traffic-clogged center of town; the latter, a rather staid residential area. The **Opéra Garnier** (2nd and 9th arrondissement) is another hopping part of town well served by reasonably priced hotels; this area has been colonized by the resident Japanese population and is popular with Asian visitors, so bet on plenty of good, cheap sushi bars and Korean barbecue restaurants on the busy side streets.

The Left Bank's **Saint-Germain-des-Prés** neighborhood (6th arrondissement) is chic, beautiful, and centrally located.

There's a large concentration of small hotels overflowing with charm, some very expensive and others surprisingly cheap. A more bohemian choice is the **Latin Quarter** (5th arrondissement), the lively student district that's home to the **Jardin du Luxembourg**, the **Musée de Cluny**, and lots of inexpensive restaurants and hotels. The **Montparnasse** area (14th and 15th arrondissements), formerly haunted by writers and artists such as Hemingway and Picasso, is now extremely sedate and a bit out of the way for most tourists.

Hotels continue to pop up in the booming **Bastille** (11th arrondissement) area surrounding the relatively new opera house, where crowds flock to wannabe-trendy restaurants, bars, and nightclubs. There's a lot of automobile traffic, but you'll be on line 1 of the Métro, which makes access to other parts of town fairly easy. If you want to be closer to nature than to Notre-Dame, you might choose a hotel in the swanky 16th arrondissement near the **Bois de Boulogne**. This is a great location for joggers or those seeking tranquillity, but don't expect much in the way of street life or nightlife, aside from the odd mauve-haired baroness promenading a Chanel-swathed Fifi at midnight. **Montmartre,** a quaint village in the 18th arrondissement, still has steep, atmospheric cobbled streets where neither tourists nor trendoids congregate. For those who can sleep through the noise, its Abbesses area features a lively nightlife scene that now reaches down to **Pigalle**.

# The Lowdown

**Overrated...** Since the George V became the Beverly Hills style Four Seasons George V and the Plaza Athénée and the Meurice got multimillion dollar makeovers, the **Crillon** is starting to look like granny in tattered panties. The restaurants and bar here are great, but rooms need work. Glossy magazines have drooled all over the **Hôtel Costes** ever since it opened, but the fact is that they pull such nasty attitude that unless you're Gwyneth Paltrow or an internationally famous fashion photographer or magazine editor, you'll get the same small overpriced rooms they fob off on the wannabe fashion buyers who are they're real clientele.

**Palaces: le top...** The biggest, grandest hotels, which the French refer to as *palaces*, are the ultimate in luxury, as only the French know how to do it. And as you'd expect, they fall into the top price bracket. Each room in the **Hôtel le**

Bristol—considered by some to be the best hotel in France—is furnished in Louis XIV or Louis XV splendor; the bathrooms are dressed in white Carrara marble, and some of its suites open onto grand terraces. A glass-enclosed swimming pool on the sixth floor was designed by a hotshot naval architect who worked for Onassis, and the hotel's enormous garden, a rarity in the center of Paris, is large enough for meditative strolls. The opulent, old-world **Raphaël** in the tony 16th arrondissement is one of the last of the great hotels—after all, how many have a real Turner painting in the lobby? The bedrooms are especially large, and some have hidden alcoves behind the dressing rooms where maids used to iron for their masters and mistresses. If you can afford it, it's the perfect place for an illicit afternoon—the setting is so wonderfully staid and proper that it cries out for naughtiness. The gallery at the **Plaza Athénée**, with potted palms, crystal chandeliers, and plush furnishings, is the ultimate rendezvous spot, especially for tea in the afternoon or preprandial drinks. The rooms and suites are decorated in Louis XV, Louis XVI, and Regency styles, with nary a false detail. The colonnaded **Crillon** attracts modern-day royalty such as Michael Jackson, Madonna, Meryl Streep, and Tom Cruise, but in earlier times its prime site—looking right out on the place de la Concorde—might have given certain monarchs the heebie-jeebies: Louis XVI and Marie Antoinette were guillotined here during the French Revolution. The **Four Seasons George V** is the newest of all the Paris palaces following a makeover so thorough that you might as easily be in Dallas as Paris. Still, the service is efficient and American "Have-a-Nice-Day" style friendly, the restaurant Le V is superb, and this luxury chain probably serves up the most comfortable beds (special editions Simmons jobs) to be found anywhere in the world, plus there's a sexy little health club with all kinds of massages, sauna, steamroom, and pool. Business travelers also congregate in the 1st arrondissement at the weathered **Inter-Continental**, between the place Vendôme and the Tuileries Gardens. Its Belle Epoque banquet room, the Salon Impérial, a fantasy in gold leaf and crystal, sets the opulent style for the whole hotel. Starwood's takeover of the **Prince de Galles** was a happy conclusion after a series of ups and downs for this *palace* near the Champs-Elysées whose Art Deco interior has been refurbished and facilities modernized. The rooms are prettily decorated with Toile de Jouy fabric and some original bathroom mosaics, worthy of a Roman bathhouse, have been preserved.

**Palaces: les flops...** Right next to the Opéra Garnier is the **Grand Hôtel Inter-Continental**, where the eccentric American millionaire James Gordon Bennett once asked Henry Stanley to go off to the wilds of Africa in search of Dr. David Livingstone. Built in 1862, the Grand underwent an unfortunate modernization in the spirit of the Pompidou 1970s. Its new owners, Inter-Continental, have put a lot of effort into correcting that mistake, and now it's restored to much (but not all) of its former glory. Despite its swell location just on the edge of the place Vendôme, the **Vendôme**, an opulent ultra-luxury boutique hotel, is the right address only for anyone too cheap to travel with his or her body guard. The little videophones that let you see who's at the door lead one to suspect it's an ideal setting for shady dealings of various types, and the decor is so studiously Louis-something that only the Beverly Hillbillys would be impressed.

**Palaces: over le top...** The **Ritz**, on the place Vendôme, is everything you would expect it to be—and worse. Like a character from an Inspector Clouseau movie, if the uniformed doorman doesn't like the way you're dressed, he won't let you into the lobby. (Hint: Tell him you have a rendezvous in the bar with Anthony Delon, the model and son of actor Alain Delon. This works very well to get past velvet nightclub ropes, too.) Do go for a drink at the bar just for the hell of it, and don't forget that Marcel Proust was nourished by take-out beer and *frites* from the Ritz while writing *Remembrance of Things Past* or that Marlene Dietrich used to sit on the edge of the bathtub in Hemingway's room there and sing to him while he shaved.

**Best decor for travelers allergic to gilt and cherubs...** If you feel like splashing out on some really classy digs with deep dish comfort, the **Hotel Lancaster** is an elegant, intimate little gem that was recently renovated with impeccable townhouse decor just off the newly revived Champs-Elysées. Marlene Dietrich lived here for years, and if it was good enough for her, then it's surely good enough for you. Left Bank hotels often get lost in a bower of cutesy Anglo-French floral prints that should be confined to the nightgowns of adolescent girls, which is why the stately **Hotel d'Aubusson** is a great new bet. You can clock a couple of the real namesake tapestries without even leaving the premises, and this place has a sumptuous, vaguely medieval atmosphere that comes from ancient beamed ceilings, silk damask, and real antiques. Also on the Left Bank, the **Montalembert** offers up a nice mix of contemporary design and Deco, although rooms are a bit small. Directly across the street from the new Bastille opera house is the **Pavillon Bastille**, a town-house hotel with a distinctive bright-yellow and deep-blue decor softened by blond wood and black-and-white floor tiles. Even the flowers in the bathrooms conform to architect Jean-Pierre Heim's color scheme, though each room is somewhat unique.

**For those who hate surprises...** Paris has several chain hotels that provide what are referred to as "international standard" in-room amenities—cable TV, direct-dial phones, minibars, hair dryers—and International Bland decor to match. Some of them, however, have a little extra, like the **Holiday Inn** on the place de la République, which has the advantage of being located in a handsome 19th-century quadrangular building that takes up an entire city block. The glass-sheathed **Paris Hilton** may be right next to the Eiffel Tower, but it's as American as Pop Tarts: Built in 1966, it has everything you were always afraid to leave home without. (There is one indubitable French touch, though: The hotel accepts cats and dogs in the rooms and coffee shop and even provides food for them.) The Méridien chain has two hotels in Paris. The **Méridien Etoile**, near Porte Maillot, is ugly as sin but has a very good restaurant, Le Clos Longchamp, plus outstanding live jazz concerts in the lobby every night. The high-rise **Méridien Montparnasse** has lofty views and tip-top business facilities. And if you want to stay safe, but go a tiny bit French, the **Ibis** chain is the French equivalent of the Holiday Inn, with about 20 locations around town offering characterless but clean, comfortable rooms at low rates.

**Cheap sleeps...** It's still possible to get a room for $60 or less in Paris, but don't count on luxury, or even a private toilet or shower (though a private sink is fairly standard). Still, slumming it doesn't mean you have to stay in a slum:

Many of the city's most budget-friendly hotels are located in hip areas. Bouquets of rather dusty fake flowers sum up the decor at the tiny **Hotel de Lille**, but it's a stone's throw from Louvre and the Palais Royal, and so perfectly situated for anyone planning a lot of heavy-duty museum-going. The carpeting's a bit worn and the Toulouse Lautrec prints may bring back visions of your teenaged bedroom, but this place is squeaky clean and very inexpensive, so book well ahead in advance. The tiny **Hôtel de Nesle**, snuggled down in the atmospheric Saint-Germain-des-Prés area, has plenty of character and a rather bohemian atmosphere. The main drawback (and it's a biggie) is that no reservations are accepted: You have to call in the morning to see whether a room is available that night, and they don't take credit cards. In the Marais, the **Grand Hôtel Jeanne d'Arc** lies just off the restaurant-lined place du Marché Sainte-Catherine. It's a fabulous deal for this area, so book well in advance. The **Style Hôtel** is off the beaten track, but it's near Montmartre and very inexpensive, spacious, clean, and pretty, with a little garden for warm-weather breakfasts. Rooms in the main building have bathrooms.

**Cheap sleeps *sans charme*...** You might expect to pay through the nose to stay in a 400-year-old hotel a few steps away from Notre-Dame, but the **Henri IV** is one of the cheapest around. The rooms are small and basic, with very thin walls, and the shower and toilet are a trek down the hall for most. Still, it's clean, and you may luck into a room with a view. Book far in advance, though—the Henri IV is always full of backpacking Americans. **Vauvilliers**, located next to Les Halles, Paris's glaringly flourescent underground shopping mall, is a clean, no-frills, low-cost hotel with a no-nonsense *patronne*. The lobby of the Left Bank's **Rive Gauche** is utterly lacking in taste and the street can be noisy, but the small, serviceable rooms are kind of cozy. Finally, it might be a kick to stay in a hotel on a street named after "bad boys," the rue des Mauvais-Garçons. There's only one hotel that fits the description, the very inexpensive **Grand Hôtel du Loiret**. It's in the Marais, where even charmless rooms are in demand, so reserve in advance.

**Where Oscar Wilde slept around...** Oscar Wilde died broke and complaining about the wallpaper in a room at **L'Hôtel**, but don't read a description of his last moments or you may not *want* to spend a night in his painstakingly restored death chamber. Today Mick Jagger stays at this luxurious and eccentrically baroque Left Bank landmark. In Wilde's earlier, better days, he rested his head at the **Quai Voltaire**, where he resolutely ignored the great views of the Louvre and the Tuileries across the Seine. Despite a past guest roster that also includes Wagner, Baudelaire, and Sibelius (now there's a combination), the rooms here are reasonably priced, not to mention pretty.

**Where to finally get started on that novel...** You can hardly sign a credit card slip in a Paris hotel without feeling a tingle of inspiration from some other literary ghost. The early 18th-century building where the great French novelist Stendhal once lived is now a romantic, four-star hotel near the tony place Vendôme. Each chamber at the **Stendhal** is individually decorated with rich fabrics and period furniture, and Room 52 pays homage to the author's *The Red and the Black*. Voltaire, Sainte-Beuve, and Victor Hugo used to carouse at the **Relais du Louvre** when it housed the Café Momus, inspiration for the second act of Puccini's *La Bohème*. The venerable Left Bank **Angleterre** has improved greatly since Ernest Hemingway tripped drunkenly up its broken stairs. Formerly the British embassy where American independence was officially recognized, it has also logged less obstreperous author-guests, including Washington Irving and Sherwood Anderson. Expatriate authors have also long been associated with the **Lenox Saint-Germain**, a small Left Bank hotel with snug rooms, a great bar, and names like T.S. Eliot, James Joyce, and Ezra Pound on its guest register. Joyce also stayed at the **Lutétia**, the large Art Deco hotel near Montparnasse, where negative reviews of *Finnegans Wake* threw him into a funk. Other creative types—from Jean Cocteau, Pablo Picasso, Henri Matisse, André Gide, and Josephine Baker to Marcello Mastroianni and Christopher Lambert—have logged time here.

**Where to paint like Pissarro...** At the lavish **Hôtel du Louvre**, a 19th-century luxury hotel located smack in between the Louvre and the Palais-Royal, you can stay in the room where Impressionist painter Camille Pissarro transformed his window view into one of the best-known works of the 19th century.

ACCOMMODATIONS | THE LOWDOWN

**If I can see the Eiffel Tower, I must be in Paris...**
The walls of glass that sheathe the 1960s-modern **Paris Hilton** betray an otherwise heroic attempt to make American travelers feel as if they never left the States. If it weren't for the kiss-close view of Gustave Eiffel's engineering wonder, guests tucking into their salads or pizzas at their oh-so-trendy new California-style restaurant (an improvement of the former ghastly and embarassing "Hi, Sheriff" type Western steakhouse) might think they were in, well, Cleveland. For a real eye-opener, appreciate the Hilton's soaring neighbor from the hotel's rooftop bar. Across the Seine near the Champs-Elysées, the palatial **Plaza Athénée** has a few rooms with balconies affording views of the tower. Film director Francis Ford Coppola's favorite stop, the large Art Deco **Lutétia**, near Montparnasse, has some long views of the tower from an unusual Left Bank perspective. If you're willing to go for broke, you can also score a view of the Eiffel Tower from rooms or suites on the southern flank of the **Four Seasons George V**.

**Other rooms with a view...** Oscar Wilde said of his view across the Seine from the **Quai Voltaire**: "Oh, that is altogether immaterial, except to the innkeeper, who of course charges it in the bill." Oscar be damned, it's a heavenly sight. If anything could beat a view across the Seine, it'd be a view from the middle of the Seine, on the ever-so-chic Ile Saint-Louis. The surprisingly homey little **Lutèce** has dynamite views from some rooms, at moderate prices. The **TimHôtel Montmartre**, a totally affordable hotel on a quiet, tree-lined square in Montmartre, has sweeping views of *tout* Paris, including close-ups of Sacré-Coeur, from its top floors. Terraces on the upper floors of the **Parc Saint-Séverin**, in the Latin Quarter, let you gaze out over Left Bank rooftops and the deliciously creepy gargoyles of Saint-Séverin church—vistas that certainly make up for the hotel's lack of period charm. Also in the Latin Quarter, the restful and newly renovated **Grands Hommes** offers top-floor perspectives of the Panthéon, where Voltaire and Victor Hugo, among others, were laid to permanent rest. For somewhat plusher accommodations, try the antique-laden **Left Bank Saint-Germain**: The back rooms offer swoony views of Notre-Dame and the rooftops of Paris. If it's outright luxury you want, though, you'll have to pop for the modern **Méridien Montparnasse**, a 25-story high-rise with write-home-about panoramas of the city.

**Taking care of business...** There's no central financial district in Paris; business travelers should choose a hotel near their clients or near the center of town. The big, modern hotels are the best for getting business done, but the decor is generally bland. The **Méridien Montparnasse** has modular conference and exhibition spaces with a capacity of up to 2,000 and a variety of services. The modern **Paris Hilton** has 10 meeting rooms, conference rooms with views over Paris, and two executive floors with a private lounge. The **Holiday Inn** on the place de la République is a classified historical monument, but the cookie-cutter rooms could be in Kansas. Those with hefty expense accounts can afford the rich atmosphere at the 8th-arrondissement *palaces*, though the business facilities may not be as extensive. The discreet Belle Epoque **Royal Monceau** in the same arrondissement is a fair runner-up for meetings. Near the place Vendôme, the **Ritz** goes only for smaller meetings (no riffraff, you know)—it can host up to 80 in its lavish meeting rooms. Businesspeople looking for a more intimate meeting venue can stay on the lovely Ile Saint-Louis; the quaint **Jeu de Paume**, constructed as a 17th-century tennis court by Louis XIII, has three small conference rooms.

**Where the fashion crowd can be found...** The famed weeklong Paris shows—twice-a-year events for haute couture, women's ready-to-wear, and men's ready-to-wear—pretty much take over Paris. If you hit town then, almost no decent hotel will be free of fashion victims. Supermodels, celebrities, and the few remaining socialite haute couture buyers deposit their Louis Vuittons at one of the palace hotels like the new **Four Seasons George V**, but the quintessential place to be see-and-be-seen now is Paris's equivalent of New York City's Royalton: the too-too-trendy **Hôtel Costes** (located around the corner from the snooty place Vendôme), with its Napoléon III decor by Jacques Garcia. Lesser establishments will be full of lesser models, journalists, photographers, fashion students, and other hangers-on. The fashion crowd particularly favors the Left Bank's trendy **Montalembert**, which ditched its staid, old look for a trendy designer decor; the **Prince de**

**Conti**, an intimate Left Bank hotel near the Seine with an interior courtyard and warm, comfy, English-style decor; and the **Lenox Saint-Germain**, also on the Left Bank, where you should definitely ask to be shown your room before signing the register—some are on the small side, but others have dramatic little mezzanines or balconies. Book far in advance if you have to come when the shows are in full swing (in January, March, July, and October) or you may not get a room at all.

**Love in the afternoon...** In the film *Love in the Afternoon*, a young Audrey Hepburn and an aging Gary Cooper had a steamy affair at the storied **Ritz**, and you can too if you can afford it. The romantic and luxurious **Stendhal**, just around the corner, is not much cheaper, but possibly more alluring to those with a literary bent. And what better place for an illicit affair than the staid **Raphaël**, the princely *palace* near the Arc de Triomphe, where you can make love on a horse-hair sofa? The **Istria** has a well-deserved reputation for discretion, having often harbored the illicit trysts of the rich and famous: heiress Nancy Cunard had her secret affairs at this rather out-of-the-way little Montparnasse hotel and Raymond Radiguet cheated on Jean Cocteau here—with a woman, no less. For those with Merchant-Ivory syndrome, there may be no greater turn-on than a four-poster bed (*lit à baldaquin*), which can be found at certain smaller hotels: the elegant **Pavillon de la Reine**, right on the Marais's splendid place des Vosges; the lovely **Angleterre**, near Saint-Germain-des-Prés, where Hemingway once stayed; the Left Bank's **Hôtel de l'Odéon**, a 16th-century building decked out in tapestries, paintings, skylights, and flower boxes; or the Restoration-style **Elysées** (near the Champs d'), where some rooms have views of Europe's greatest phallic symbol, the Eiffel Tower.

**Best courtyard gardens...** In the high-end 8th arrondissement, land is at a premium, so it's a distinct perk to have a garden big enough to stroll in, as guests do at the **Hôtel le Bristol**, a palace on the rue du Faubourg Saint-Honoré. The **Prince de Galles**, a luxury 8th-arrondissement hotel now owned by Starwood, has a large flower-filled courtyard garden, too. Then there are the gardens meant to dine in—near the Tuileries, dinner is served in the flower-filled courtyard of the lavish **Inter-Continental**, where horse-drawn carriages once deposited visitors, while the handsome exterior of the **Holiday Inn**, on the otherwise undistinguished place de la République, hides a large interior garden where guests dine when the weather's fine. The gourmet restaurant Le Jardin is cradled under a glass bubble in the center of the lush courtyard garden of the **Royal Monceau**, off the Champs-Elysées. Gardens are even more of a find over on the Left Bank. Most of the rooms in the refined 17th-century **Saints-Pères** overlook courtyard greenery. The individually decorated rooms of the **Relais Christine**, located in a former 16th-century convent on a quiet side street, look onto either a flower-strewn courtyard or a garden (breakfast here is served in one of the vaulted rooms of the cloister). The tiny courtyard of the delightful little **Hotel de la Tulipe** near the first-rate rue Clerc market in the 7th arrondissement is also a great place to get a breath of fresh air over breakfast al fresco or a coffee in the afternoon.

**Family values...** Most hotels in Paris have rooms that can accommodate three people (sometimes with a proper bed, sometimes with a cot), for hardly more than the cost of a double. But if you've got too many kids to squeeze into that configuration, or if you want a wall between you and other family members, you'll have to search for rare American-style connecting rooms. You will find a few connecting rooms at the friendly **Hotel des Grandes Ecoles** on a quiet cobbled side street; they also have good value triples and quads if you want to keep everyone under one roof and plan on a completely celibate vacation. **Relais du Louvre** also offers connecting rooms, as well as an apartment-sized suite on the top floor, complete with kitchen and washer and dryer. An even better deal might be the nearby **Hôtel de l'Abbaye**, which has four duplex suites with terraces, or, one notch further up the price scale, the duplex suite at the **Relais Christine** (also on the Left Bank), with its warm, wood-paneled lobby and attractive rooms. As for kids' programs, kids' menus, game rooms, room service milk 'n' cookies, and all those other family-friendly perks that chain hotels lay on in America...forget about it.

**For joggers...** The **Paris Hilton**, located right next to the Eiffel Tower, has a jogging path, if running around the Champs de Mars in the 15th arrondissement is your idea of exercise. Those staying at the **Quai Voltaire** have the entire length of the Seine to run along, where you can suck up exhaust fumes to your heart's content. The **Pergolèse** is near the vast Bois de Boulogne, where you can amuse yourself while running by watching customers solicit the transvestite Brazilian prostitutes in the park. To be near the hottest jogging spot in Paris, the Luxembourg Garden, stay at the inexpensive **Cluny Sorbonne**.

**Totally Left Bank...** Does the term "Left Bank" still conjure up for you images of bohemians, the Jazz Generation, philosophers, and intellectuals? If so, don't let the area's currently chic, monied look get you down; this is still the hangout for the *gauche caviar* (limousine lefties). Baron Haussmann never got around to modernizing this side of the river, so there are many more old, rustic buildings here than on the Right Bank. If exposed beams spell charm for you, you'll love the Left Bank. The **Académie**, on the fashionable rue des Saints-Pères has been renovated to let its wooden beams and stone walls show through; bright fabrics, Oriental rugs, and 18th-century-style furniture carry through the decor. The **Odéon Hôtel**, on a side street off the boulevard Saint-Germain, not only has the exposed-beam thing going for it, it even has some romantic little rooms tucked up under the eaves. **Bersoly's Saint-Germain**, a gem of a hotel in a renovated townhouse, has small but pretty rooms, a vaulted basement breakfast room, and exposed beams. The **Angleterre** on the rue Jacob, with its individually decorated rooms, also has exposed beams, some four-poster beds, and a private garden. The lobby of the **Left Bank Saint-Germain**, with its 18th-century Aubusson tapestry, wood paneling, antique baby carriage, porcelain lamps, and Oriental carpets, sets the tone for the rest of the hotel. All hotels in this *très chic* area should be booked way, way, way ahead. Over in the upscale residential areas near the Musée d'Orsay and the Seine, the **Bellechasse** is refreshingly down-to-earth, with bright, liveable rooms and an upbeat staff (for Paris, they're downright chummy). Near the Jardin des Plantes, the **Libertel Maxim**'s rooms are overdecorated in Toile de Jouy fabric (walls, beds, drapes—*everything*), printed with scenes of life in old France. It hardly fits the Latin Quarter image, but has its own bizarre kind of charm.

**Totally Right Bank...** The Right Bank has none of the Left Bank's intellectual, arty tinge: Here we're talking money, bourgeoisie, and staid turn-of-the-century buildings. A good place to start is the exclusive place Vendôme, where the likes of Cartier sell their baubles. First and foremost is the stratospheric **Ritz** and other high-end places like the **Castille**, a fantasia on Venice that seems out of place until you realize that its sense of elegance is pure Paris. The **Astor** is an oasis of 30s-style elegance and has the added advantage of having a restaurant whose chef, Eric Lecerf, is supervised by the supposedly retired master of French cuisine, Joël Robuchon. Around the corner on the rue des Capucines lies the modestly-priced **Mansart**, its tasteful, modern decor an homage to Louis XIV's architect Mansart, who laid out the place Vendôme. Glitzy *palaces* may dominate the 8th arrondissement, but off the Champs-Elysées are the more affordable **Galileo**, a small, well-run hotel whose lounge boasts an 18th-century mantelpiece and an Aubusson tapestry, and the **Majestic**, near the Arc de Triomphe, where the ample rooms have Oriental rugs and period furniture. Near the ultra-posh avenue Montaigne is the **Marignan**, somewhat pricier digs with an uncluttered modern look; a collection of original paintings by contemporary artists decorates its walls. The **Gaillon Opéra** is a small, moderately priced hotel near the Opéra Garnier, the Louvre, and the Palais Royal, with the kind of character you'd expect on the Left Bank— exposed beams, individually decorated rooms, and some antique furnishings. Also near the opera house and the major department stores is the midsized, midpriced **Lafayette**, with a wood-paneled lobby that resembles a gentlemen's club. Across the street from the Louvre and Saint-Germain-l'Auxerrois, the church of the kings of France, the tiny **Place du Louvre** is a real budget-saving find: The attractive guest rooms are modern, but breakfast is served in a vaulted stone basement dating from the 14th century. Another find is the nearby **Ducs de Bourgogne**, where little touches like a hat rack with three antique *chapeaux* hanging on it show that attention is paid to detail.

# The Index

| | |
|---|---|
| $$$$$ | more than 275 euros |
| $$$$ | 180 to 275 euros |
| $$$ | 120 to 180 euros |
| $$ | 60 to 120 euros |
| $ | less than 60 euros |

*Price ratings are based on the lowest price quoted for a standard double room, including taxes and charges.*

*Hotels accept all major credit cards unless otherwise stated. The word "Hôtel" is generally omitted here if it's the first word in the name of the hotel.*

**Académie.** Wooden beams, stone walls, bright fabrics, Oriental rugs, and 18th-century-style furniture in a 17th-century building.... *Tel 01 45 48 36 22, fax 01 45 49 80 10, toll-free fax from U.S.: 800/246–0041; 32, rue des Saints-Pères, 75007, Métro Saint-Germain-des-Prés. 34 rms.* $$$ **(see p. 24)**

**Angleterre.** Each room in this Left Bank hotel has its own charm, whether it be a four-poster bed, exposed beams, or a view of the garden.... *Tel 01 42 60 34 72, fax 01 42 60 16 93; 44, rue Jacob, 75006, Métro Saint-Germain-des-Prés. 27 rms.* $$$–$$$$ **(see pp. 19, 22, 24)**

**Astor.** In the heart of Proust country and near the high-fashion shopping drag, the Rue du Faubourg-Saint-Honoré, this is a discreet hideaway.... *Tel 01 53 05 05 05, fax 01 53 05 05 30; 11, rue d'Astorg, 75008, Métro Champs-Elysées Clemenceau. 134 rms.* $$$$$ **(see p. 25)**

**Bellechasse.** Comfortable, cheerfully decorated rooms. Great location near the Musée d'Orsay and the Seine.... *Tel 01 45 50 22 31, fax 01 45 51 52 36; 8, rue Bellechasse, 75007, Métro Assemblée-Nationale. 41 rms.* $$$ **(see p. 24)**

**Bersoly's Saint-Germain.** A tiny, quiet hotel in a wonderful renovated Left Bank townhouse.... *Tel 01 42 60 73 79, fax 01 49 27 05 55; 28, rue de Lille, 75007, Métro Saint-Germain-des-Prés. 16 rms. Closed second half of Aug. $$*
**(see p. 24)**

**Castille.** An elegant Venetian-style hotel near the exclusive place Vendôme.... *Tel 01 44 58 44 58, fax 01 44 58 44 00; 37, rue Cambon, 75001, Métro Concorde. 111 rms and duplex suites. $$$$$* **(see p. 25)**

**Cluny Sorbonne.** Across the street from the Sorbonne and a short walk (or jog) to the Jardin de Luxembourg. The rooms are small and the bathrooms cramped, but the price is right.... *Tel 01 43 54 66 66, fax 01 43 29 68 07; 8, rue Victor Cousin, 75005, Métro Luxembourg. 23 rms. $$* **(see p. 24)**

**Crillon.** Palace hotel overlooking the place de la Concorde. Home of the acclaimed restaurant Les Ambassadeurs, another restaurant called the Obelisk, and a courtyard garden.... *Tel 01 44 71 15 00, fax 01 44 71 15 03; 10, place de la concorde, 75008, Métro Concorde. 120 rms and 43 suites. $$$$$* **(see pp. 14, 15)**

**Ducs de Bourgogne.** The price is right at this hotel, located between the Louvre and Châtelet and directly across the river from the Left Bank via the Pont Neuf.... *Tel 01 42 33 95 64, fax 01 40 39 01 25; 19, rue du Pont-Neuf, 75001, Métro Louvre or Châtelet. 50 rms. $$$* **(see p. 25)**

**Elysées.** This Restoration-style hotel has some top-floor Eiffel Tower views.... *Tel 01 42 65 29 25, fax 01 42 65 64 28; 12, rue des Saussaies, 75008, Métro Champs-Elysées-Clemenceau. 32 rms. $$* **(see p. 22)**

**Four Seasons George V.** This legendary pile has been totally overhauled to make it into the first high-tech palace hotel in Paris. Great health club with pool.... *Tel 01 49 52 70 00, fax 01 49 52 70 10; 31, ave George V, 75008, Métro George V. 245 rooms, including 61 suites, 30 with private terraces. $$$$$* **(see pp. 15, 20, 21)**

**Gaillon Opéra.** A small hotel near the Opéra Garnier, the Louvre, and the Palais Royal with rustic touches to its

ACCOMMODATIONS | THE INDEX

decor.... *Tel 01 47 42 47 74, fax 01 47 42 01 23; 9, rue Gaillon, 75002, Métro Opéra. 26 rms. $$$* **(see p. 25)**

**Galileo.** Small hotel near the Champs-Elysées, with handsome lounge and small, well-equipped rooms.... *Tel 01 47 20 66 06, fax 01 47 20 67 17; 54, rue Galiliée, 75008, Métro George-V. 27 rms. $$$* **(see p. 25)**

**Grand Hôtel du Loiret.** Small, basic Marais hotel.... *Tel 01 48 87 77 00, fax 01 48 04 96 56; 8, rue des Mauvais-Garçons, 75004, Métro Hôtel-de-Ville. 30 rms. $–$$* **(see p. 18)**

**Grand Hôtel Inter-Continental.** After some ups and downs, this hotel has been restored to its grand old self, though rooms are modernized. Fitness center, the famous Café de la Paix, and two restaurants.... *Tel 01 40 07 32 32, fax 01 42 66 12 51; 2, rue Scribe, 75009, Métro Opéra. 514 rms, including 35 suites. $$$$* **(see p. 16)**

**Grand Hôtel Jeanne d'Arc.** An attractive hotel on a quiet street in the Marais not far from Bastille. A very good deal. Reserve in advance.... *Tel 01 48 87 62 11, fax 01 48 87 37 31; 3, rue de Jarente, 75004, Métro Saint-Paul. 36 rms. $$* **(see p. 18)**

**Grands Hommes.** The "great men" referred to in the name of this comfortable and newly renovated hotel are buried in the Panthéon across the road.... *Tel 01 46 34 19 60, fax 01 43 26 67 32; 17, place du Panthéon, 75005, Métro Luxembourg. 32 rms. $$$* **(see p. 20)**

**Henri IV.** Very inexpensive hotel on the Ile-de-la-Cité. Rooms are small and very basic, with the shower and toilet down the hall for most, but the place is clean. Book far in advance.... *Tel 01 43 54 44 53; 25, place Dauphine, 75001, Métro Pont-Neuf or Cité. 22 rms. $* **(see p. 18)**

**Holiday Inn.** Typical Holiday Inn–style rooms on the place de la République. Restaurant, bar, garden.... *Tel 01 43 55 44 34, fax 01 47 00 32 34; 10, place de la République, 75011, Métro République. 318 rms. $$$$* **(see pp. 17, 21, 23)**

**Hotel d'Aubusson.** This classy boutique hotel just a few steps from the Odeon has a lot of seigneurial medieval charm with parquet floors, beamed ceilings, and antiques. Ask for one of the rooms with a canopied bed to really get in the mood....

*Tel 01 43 29 43 43, fax 01 43 29 12 62; 33, rue Dauphine, 75006, Métro Odeon. 49 rms. $$$$* **(see p. 17)**

**Hôtel Costes.** Fashion victims fill the lobby of what is now the trendiest hotel in town, around the corner from the place Vendôme. The elaborate Neoclassical decor is rich and comfy.... *Tel 01 42 44 50 00, fax 01 42 44 50 01; 239, rue Saint-Honoré, 75001, Métro Tuileries. 85 rms. $$$$$*
**(see pp. 14, 21)**

**Hôtel de l'Abbaye.** Lovely 18th-century hotel on a quiet Left Bank side street, with 4 duplex suites.... *Tel 01 45 44 38 11, fax 01 45 48 07 86; 10, rue Cassette, 75006, Métro Saint-Sulpice. 46 rms and suites. $$$*
**(see p. 23)**

**Hotel de la Tulipe.** A real gem tucked away in a pleasant neighborhood with a great market and surprisingly cheap cafes to hang out in about a 10-minute walk from the Eiffel Tower. The friendly owners are great sources of local information.... *Tel 01 45 51 67 21, fax 01 47 53 96 37; 33, rue Malar, 75007, Metro Latour-Maubourg or Invalides, RER Pont de l'Alma or Aerogare des Invalides. 22 rms. $$$* **(see p. 23)**

**Hotel de Lille.** This is a serious budget address, so don't expect phones, minibars, or even a shower in your room unless you ask for one. On the other hand, this place is clean, friendly, well-located. Book well in advance.... *Tel 01 42 33 33 42, no fax. 8; rue du Pelican, 75001, Métro Odéon. 13 rms. $–$$* **(see p. 18)**

**Hôtel de l'Odéon.** Beautifully furnished, this 16th-century building has the added advantage of a Saint-Germain-des-Prés location. Small garden.... *Tel 01 43 25 70 11, fax 01 43 29 97 34; 13, rue Saint-Sulpice, 75006, Métro Odéon. 29 rms. $$$* **(see p. 22)**

**Hôtel de Nesle.** A low-priced Left Bank hotel with plenty of character. No reservations accepted; call around 9am the day of arrival.... *Tel 01 43 54 62 41, no fax; 7, rue de Nesle, 75006, Métro Odéon. 20 rms. No credit cards. $–$$* **(see p. 18)**

**Hotel des Grandes Ecoles.** There's something winsomely winning about this rather rustic hotel in the middle of the Latin Quarter—which is actually a complex of 3 old buildings

*ACCOMMODATIONS | THE INDEX*

joined together around a pretty shaded garden.... *Tel 01 43 26 79 23, fax 01 43 25 28 15; 75, rue du Cardinal Lemoine, 75005, Métro Cardinal Lemoine. 51 rms. $$* (see p. 23)

**Hôtel du Louvre.** Lavish 19th-century hotel; Impressionist painter Camille Pissarro immortalized the view from his room here. In-house restaurant and cafe.... *Tel 01 44 58 38 38, fax 01 44 58 38 01; 1, place André Malraux, 75001, Métro Palais-Royal. 197 rms and suites. $$$$$* (see p. 19)

**Hotel Lancaster.** Now that the Champs-Elysées on the up and up, this venerable vestpocket luxury hotel is a truly fine address if you want a calm, elegant, clubby luxury pad in a good location.... *Tel 01 40 76 40 76, fax 01 40 76 40 00; 7, rue de Berri, 75008 Métro George V. 50 rms and 10 suites. $$$$$* (see p. 16)

**Hôtel le Bristol.** A *palace* hotel on a famed designer shopping street, with spacious ornate rooms, swimming pool, enormous garden, fitness center, and sauna.... *Tel 01 53 43 43 00, fax 01 53 43 43 26; 112, rue du Faubourg-Saint-Honoré, 75008, Métro Saint-Philippe-du-Roule. 134 rms and 46 suites. $$$$$* (see pp. 14, 22)

**Ibis.** They are about 20 of these functional, cheap, clean hotels for low-budget business travelers scattered around Paris.... *Tel 01 43 22 00 09, fax 01 43 20 21 78, toll-free reservations from U.S.: 800/221–4542; 160, rue du Chateau, 75014 Métro Pernety. 50 rms. $$* (see p. 17)

**Inter-Continental.** More than a century old, this hotel now attracts many business travelers and has been completely renovated.... *Tel 01 44 77 11 11, fax 01 44 77 10 77; 3, rue Castiglione, 75001, Métro Tuileries. 450 rms and suites. $$$$$* (see pp. 15, 22)

**Istria.** This comfortable small hotel has hosted Nancy Cunard, Rainer Maria Rilke, Marcel Duchamp, and Man Ray, among others.... *Tel 01 43 20 91 82, fax 01 43 22 48 45; 29, rue Campagne-Première, 75014, Métro Raspail. 26 rms. $$* (see p. 22)

**Jeu de Paume.** Louis XIII's tennis court is now a hotel with a handsomely decorated, rustic interior. Private garden.... *Tel*

*01 43 26 14 18, fax 01 40 46 02 76; 54, rue St-Louis-en-l'Ile, 75004, Métro Pont-Marie. 32 rms. $$$$* **(see p. 21)**

**Lafayette.** A bit off the beaten track, but within walking distance of the Opéra Garnier and the major department stores.... *Tel 01 42 85 05 44, fax 01 49 95 06 60; 49, rue Lafayette, 75009, Métro Le Pelletier. 103 rms. $$$* **(see p. 25)**

**Left Bank Saint-Germain.** Rooms have exposed beams, antiques, marble bathrooms, air-conditioning, and sound-proofing. In the heart of the Left Bank.... *Tel 01 43 54 01 70, fax 01 43 26 17 14; 9, rue de l'Ancienne Comédie, 75006, Métro Odéon. 31 rms. $$$* **(see pp. 20, 24)**

**Lenox Saint-Germain.** This Left Bank hotel has been attracting a literary clientele for decades, but now guests are more likely to be in the fashion business.... *Tel 01 42 96 10 95, fax 01 42 61 52 83; 9, rue de l'Université, 75007, Métro rue-du-Bac. 34 rms. $$* **(see pp. 19, 22)**

**L'Hôtel.** This eccentric baroque Left Banker is much-coveted as a place to stay.... *Tel 01 44 41 99 00, fax 01 43 25 64 81; 13, rue des Beaux-Arts, 75006, Métro Saint-Germain-des-Prés. 27 rms. $$$$* **(see p. 18)**

**Libertel Maxim.** Little Latin Quarter hotel near the Jardin des Plantes.... *Tel 01 43 31 16 15, fax 01 43 31 93 87; 28, rue Censier, 75005, Métro Censier-Daubenton. 32 rms. $$$* **(see p. 24)**

**Lutèce.** One of few hotels on pretty little Ile Saint-Louis, this one is cozy and attractive; some rooms have views.... *Tel 01 43 26 23 52, fax 01 43 29 60 25; 65, rue Saint-Louis-en-l'Ile, 75004, Métro Pont-Marie. 23 rms. No credit cards. $$$* **(see p. 20)**

**Lutétia.** A large Art Deco hotel near Montparnasse with many great names in the guest books.... *Tel 01 49 54 46 46, fax 01 49 54 46 00; 45, blvd Raspail, 75006, Métro Sèvres-Babylone. 250 rms and suites. $$$$$* **(see pp. 19, 20)**

**Majestic.** Solid comfort near the Arc de Triomphe and the Champs-Elysées, good-sized rooms.... *Tel 01 45 00 83 70, fax 01 45 00 29 48; 29, rue Dumont d'Urville, 75116, Métro Etoile. 30 rms, including 3 apartments. $$$$* **(see p. 25)**

ACCOMMODATIONS | THE INDEX

**Mansart.** An attractive modern decor designed as an homage to Louis XIV's architect Mansart.... *Tel 01 42 61 50 28, fax 01 49 27 97 44; 5, rue des Capucines, 75001, Métro Opéra. 57 rms. $$$* **(see p. 25)**

**Marignan.** A clean, modern decor and a collection of original paintings by contemporary artists. In-house restaurant and tea room.... *Tel 01 40 76 34 56, fax 01 40 76 34 34; 12, rue Marignan, 75008, Métro Franklin-D-Roosevelt. 57 rms and 16 duplex suites. $$$$* **(see p. 25)**

**Méridien Etoile.** A 1972 chain hotel with live jazz nightly in the Lionel Hampton Jazz Club in the lobby and 3 restaurants.... *Tel 01 40 68 34 34, fax 01 40 55 67 88; 81, blvd Gouvion-St.-Cyr, 75017, Métro Porte-Maillot. 1,025 rms. $$$$* **(see p. 17)**

**Méridien Montparnasse.** The modern, business high-rise par excellence. Near Montparnasse train station. 2 restaurants.... *Tel 01 44 36 44 36, fax 01 40 55 67 88; 19, rue de Commandant Mouchotte, 75014, Métro Montparnasse-Bienvenue. 953 rms and suites. $$$$* **(see pp. 17, 21)**

**Montalembert.** A once-staid hotel that has gone trendy. All rooms have marble bathrooms. Portable phones available to guests (no rental fee, charged by the call).... *Tel 01 45 49 68 68, fax 01 45 49 69 49; 3, rue Montalembert, 75007, Métro rue-du-Bac. 51 rms and 5 suites. $$$$* **(see pp. 17, 21)**

**Odéon Hôtel.** A small Left Bank hotel with modern amenities (air-conditioning, hair dryers, etc.) and the charm of individually decorated rooms and exposed beams.... *Tel 01 43 25 90 67, fax 01 43 25 55 98; 3, rue de l'Odéon, 75006, Métro Odéon. 33 rms. $$$* **(see p. 24)**

**Parc Saint-Séverin.** This Latin Quarter find has simple, attractive modern decor with scattered period furniture. Some rooms have large terraces with views.... *Tel 01 43 54 32 17, fax 01 43 54 70 71; 22, rue de la Parcheminerie, 75005, Métro Saint-Michel or Cluny. 27 rms. $$* **(see p. 20)**

**Paris Hilton.** Next to the Eiffel Tower, the Hilton is 1960s modern; the rooms are spacious, comfortable, and well-equipped.... *Tel 01 44 38 56 00, fax 01 44 38 56 60; 18,*

*ave Suffren, 75015, Métro Bir-Hakeim. 462 rms and suites.*
*$$$$* **(see pp. 17, 20, 21, 23)**

**Pavillon Bastille.** Designer decor in bright yellow and deep blue. For opera lovers, the hotel has special arrangements for obtaining tickets (often hard to get) for the Opéra Bastille; ask when you reserve.... *Tel 01 43 43 65 65, fax 01 43 43 96 52; 65, rue de Lyon, 75012, Métro Bastille. 24 rms and 1 suite. $$$* **(see p. 17)**

**Pavillon de la Reine.** This hotel on the beautiful place des Vosges has lovely gardens. It looks old, but only part of it dates from the 17th century.... *Tel 01 40 29 19 19, fax 01 40 29 19 20; 28, place des Vosges, 75003, Métro Saint-Paul. 55 rms and suites. $$$$$* **(see p. 22)**

**Pergolèse.** Spacious and modern, with splashes of warm color. One beautiful room under the eaves has a view of the neighboring rooftops.... *Tel 01 40 67 96 77, fax 01 45 00 12 11; 3, rue Pergolèse, 75016, Métro Argentine. 40 rms. $$$$* **(see p. 24)**

**Place du Louvre.** A tiny hotel near the Louvre with attractively furnished modern rooms and a breakfast room in a 14th-century vaulted stone basement.... *Tel 01 42 33 78 68, fax 01 42 33 09 95; 21, rue des Prêtres-Saint-Germain-l'Auxerrois, 75001, Métro Louvre or Pont-Neuf. 20 rms. $$*
**(see p. 25)**

**Plaza Athénée.** Elegant *palace* hotel off the Champs-Elysées. Rooms and suites are decorated in Louis XV, Louis XVI, and Regency styles. Home of the gourmet restaurant Le Régence, the more casual Le Relais, and an English-style bar.... *Tel 01 53 67 66 65, fax 01 53 67 66 66; 25, ave Montaigne, 75008, Métro Franklin-D-Roosevelt. 205 rms and suites. $$$$$* **(see pp. 15, 20)**

**Prince de Conti.** English-style comfort in a small, handsome, 18th-century building near the Seine, surrounded by Saint-Germain-des-Prés art galleries, antique shops, and boutiques. All rooms air-conditioned and soundproofed.... *Tel 01 44 07 30 40, fax 44 07 36 34; 8, rue Guénégaud, 75006, Métro Odéon. 26 rms, plus 19 in annex. $$$*
**(see p. 21)**

ACCOMMODATIONS | THE INDEX

**Prince de Galles.** Art Deco *palace* with flower-filled courtyard garden and rooms decorated in yellow or blue Toile de Jouy fabric. Some rooms have balconies. In-house restaurant, Le Jardin des Cygnes.... *Tel 01 53 23 77 77, fax 01 53 23 78 78; 33, ave George-V, 75008, Métro Odéon. 168 rms and suites.* $$$$$ **(see pp. 15, 22)**

**Quai Voltaire.** Left Bank hotel with great views over the Seine toward the Louvre and the Tuileries Garden; insist on one of the 29 rooms in the front of the hotel.... *Tel 01 42 61 50 91, fax 01 42 61 62 26; 19, quai Voltaire, 75007, Métro rue-du-Bac. 33 rms.* $$ **(see pp. 19, 20, 22)**

**Raphaël.** Old World opulence at one of the *palace* hotels. The wood-paneled, English-style bar is a popular celebrity meeting place.... *Tel 01 44 28 00 28, fax 01 45 01 21 50; 17, ave Kléber, 75116, Métro Etoile. 90 rms and suites.* $$$$$ **(see pp. 15, 22)**

**Relais Christine.** A former 16th-century convent located on a quiet Left Bank side street.... *Tel 01 40 51 60 80, fax 01 40 51 60 81; 3, rue Christine, 75006, Métro Odéon. 51 rms.* $$$$ **(see pp. 23)**

**Relais du Louvre.** A small hotel near the Louvre that inspired the setting for Puccini's opera *La Bohème*. An apartment-sized room on the 6th floor can accomodate 6.... *Tel 01 40 41 96 42, fax 01 40 41 96 44; 19, rue des Prêtres-Saint-Germain-l'Auxerrois, 75001, Métro Louvre or Pont-Neuf. 20 rms.* $$$ **(see pp. 19, 23)**

**Ritz.** Nothing beats the fabled Ritz for overdone luxury and snobbery. Houses the gourmet restaurant Espadon as well as a swimming pool and health spa.... *Tel 01 43 16 30 30, fax 01 43 16 31 78; 15, place Vendôme, 75001, Métro Concorde. 178 rms and suites.* $$$$$ **(see pp. 16, 21, 22, 25)**

**Rive Gauche.** A good deal, especially considering its location in the heart of Saint-Germain-des-Prés. The rooms are small but serviceable.... *Tel 01 42 60 34 68, fax 01 42 61 29 78; 25, rue des Saints-Pères, 75006, Métro Saint-Germain-des-Prés. 21 rms.* $$ **(see p. 18)**

**Royal Monceau.** Spacious rooms in a *palace* hotel; the

Michelin 1-star restaurant Le Jardin is located in the courtyard garden, and there's also an Italian restaurant,
Carpaccio. Fully equipped beauty spa, fitness center, and
swimming pool.... *Tel 01 42 99 88 00, fax 01 42 99 89
90; 37, ave Hoche, 75008, Métro Etoile. 212 rms and
suites. $$$$$* **(see pp. 21, 23)**

**Saints-Pères.** Most rooms in this 17th-century hotel overlook
the courtyard garden. The good-sized rooms are tastefully
decorated.... *Tel 01 45 44 50 00, fax 01 45 44 90 83; 65,
rue des Saints-Pères, 75006, Métro Saint-Germain-des-
Prés. 39 rms. $$* **(see p. 23)**

**Stendhal.** Small, luxurious hotel that was once home to the
French author. Cozy bar with fireplace.... *Tel 01 44 58 52 52,
fax 01 44 58 52 00; 22, rue Danielle Casanova, 75002,
Métro Pyramides. 20 rms. $$$$* **(see pp. 19, 22)**

**Style Hôtel.** Clean, attractive, inexpensive Montmartre hotel
with a small courtyard garden. Rooms in 2nd building share
bathrooms.... *Tel 01 45 22 37 59, fax 01 45 22 81 03; 8,
rue Ganneron, 75018, Métro place de Clichy. 80 rms. $*
**(see p. 18)**

**TimHôtel Montmartre.** Exceptional for its quiet location on a
little square in picturesque Montmartre, its panoramic views
from the upper floors, and reasonable prices.... *Tel 01 42
55 74 79, fax 01 42 55 71 01; 11, rue Ravignan (place
Emile-Goudeau), 75018, Métro Abbesses. 60 rms. $$–$$$*
**(see p. 20)**

**Vauvilliers.** A simple, cheap hotel near Les Halles and the
Louvre. Not all rooms have showers. Reserve ahead.... *Tel
01 42 36 89 08, no fax; 6, rue Vauvilliers, 75001, Métro
Les Halles. 14 rms. No credit cards. $* **(see p. 18)**

**Vendôme.** Ultra-luxury on the place Vendôme.... *Tel 01 42 60
32 84, fax 01 49 27 97 89; 1, place de Vendome, 75001,
Métro Concorde. 314 rms. $$$$$* **(see p. 16)**

ACCOMMODATIONS | THE INDEX

# Left Bank Accommodations

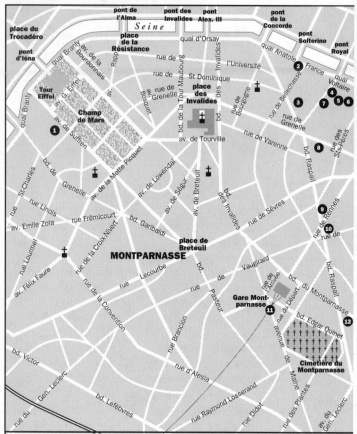

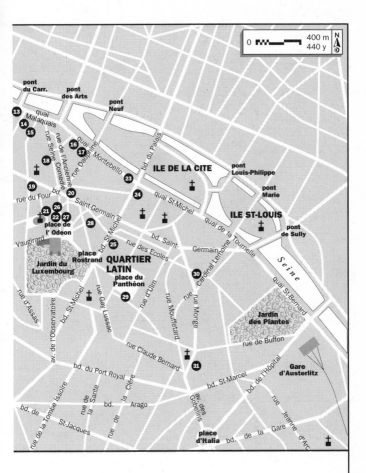

Lutétia **10**

Méridien Montparnasse **13**

Montalembert **7**

Odéon Hôtel **27**

Parc Saint-Séverin **25**

Paris Hilton **1**

Prince de Conti **18**

Quai Voltaire **4**

Relais Christine **24**

Rive Gauche **15**

Saints-Pères **16**

# Right Bank Accommodations

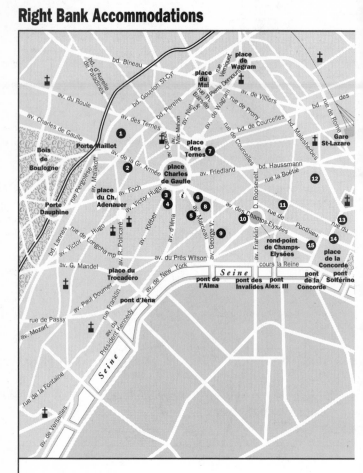

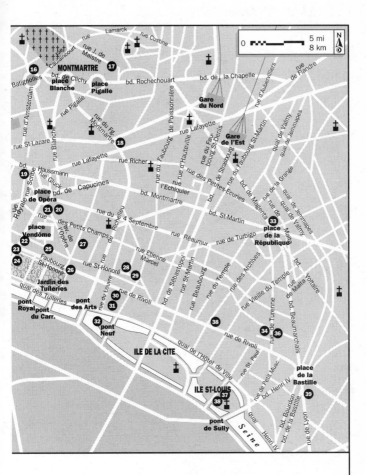

| | |
|---|---|
| Lafayette **18** | Plaza Athénée **9** |
| Lutèce **37** | Prince de Galles **6** |
| Majestic **4** | Raphaël **3** |
| Mansart **21** | Relais du Louvre **30** |
| Marignan **10** | Ritz **24** |
| Méridien Etoile **1** | Royal Monceau **7** |
| Pavillon Bastille **39** | Stendhal **15** |
| Pavillon de la Reine **36** | Style Hôtel **16** |
| Pergolèse **2** | TimHôtel Montmartre **17** |
| Place du Louvre **31** | Vauvilliers **28** |

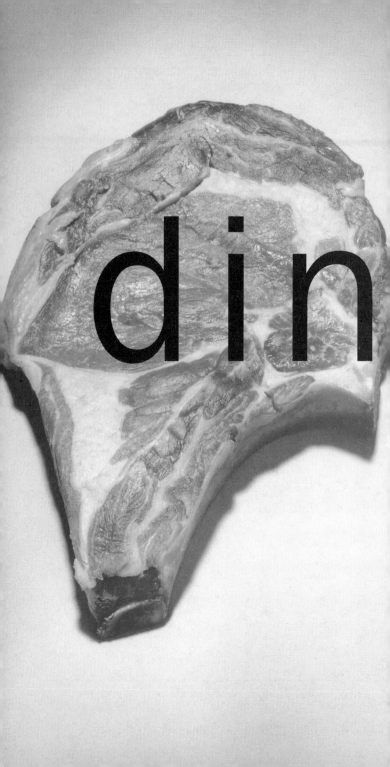

ing 2

The cherished
idea that it's
impossible to have
a bad meal in
Paris is just plain
wrong. If you're
looking for a

cutting-edge dining scene, you'll do just as well in New York, San Francisco, Sydney, or London as you will in Paris, where "fusion" cooking has only recently arrived, and then only because foreigners or expatriate chefs like Jean-Georges Vongerichten, who's new restaurant **Market** is a hit, have set up shop.

Further, if Paris still remains the ultimate global culinary reference, the capital's restaurants are besieged by the introduction of an obligatory 35-hour work week, a make-work-scheme gone wrong that's causing many to pare down their menus and cut back opening hours, as well as such steeply rising costs and taxes, so that most operate on a razor's edge of profitability. Not surprisingly, this has caused many to resort to short-cut industrial ingredients and microwave ovens, so that most of the restaurants and cafes on the city's most heavily traveled streets are awful.

In fact, to eat well in Paris requires as much research and planning as it does in any other city. Many restaurants that survived the most recent recession did so either by catering to an expense-account clientele or throwing in the towel and becoming tourist traps. Most of the restaurants near the city's main sights have become completely mediocre by catering to a never-to-be-seen again and don't-speak-French-so-can't-really-complain foreign clientele, many of whom may not know that gristly steaks, frozen frites, and industrial salads aren't typical French food.

Beyond skidding culinary standards, anyone visiting Paris today should be grateful for the last long French recession. It tolled the end of an era on the city's gastronomic landscape, with the result that Paris has once again become a brilliant destination for anyone who likes to eat not only well, but also inexpensively. These days there are only 15 or so restaurants where it's worth shelling out more than 60 euros per person for a three-course meal.

With the arrival of lean times, restaurant owners suddenly found themselves confronted with a newly price-resistant public, and they reacted by opening annex restaurants, lower-priced offshoots of their big-ticket dining rooms. Chef Michel Rostang led the way with **Le Bistrot d'à Côté** in 1987 and was soon followed by many other chefs, most notably Guy Savoy, who now has four satellites—**Les Bookinistes, La Butte Chaillot, Cap Vernet,** and **Le Bistro de l'Etoile**—around town.

The most important thing that happened during the last recession, though, was that the classic idiom of a culinary career was completely turned upside down. If the big boys were opening annexes, the younger generation, led by chef Yves Camdeborde of the still-fabulous **La Regalade,** decided that the best way to launch yourself after the requisite years of pirouetting through various famous kitchens was by opening a bistro. Yup, a bistro, not a fancy place with fresh flowers and silver candelabra on linen table-cloths—classic bait for Michelin inspectors—but good value bistros offering market menus (menus that change regularly to follow not only the best prices in produce, but the best of the season) where luxury produce, haute cuisine techniques and foreign seasonings were used to create intriguingly and very appetizingly modern versions of old-fashioned bistro dishes and regional specialties. Best of all, this young crowd, including Thierry Breton of **Chez Michel,** Christophe Beaufront of **L'Avant Gout,** and Nicholas Vagnon of **La Table du Lucullus** remain committed to offering a truly memorable feed for around 30 euros.

Higher up the food chain, there's been a spectacular renaissance of regional cooking with the arrival in Paris of chefs from the provinces like southwesterner **Helene Darroze** of the eponymous one-star restaurant on the Left Bank, or Auvergnant Jean-Yves Bath of one-star **Bath's,** and provencale maestro Alain Soliveres at the two-star **Les Elysées du Vernet.** All of these chefs have brilliantly updated one of the many regional kitchens that together form the true glory of French cooking. And up on the Mount Olympus of gastronomy that is the rarified world of three-star dining, chef Alain Passard created a stir last year when he converted his eminent restaurant **Arpège** to an almost all-vegetarian menu. Mad cow disease didn't scare him into to it, either—he says he just wanted a new challenge, which he thinks will be creating healthy but luxurious dishes for the new millenium.

> **You are what you drink**
>
> *In France, un café is like an Italian espresso (but not quite as good). If you prefer it more diluted, ask for a café allongé. A coffee with a splash of milk is a noisette, while café au lait or café crème are about half coffee and half steamed milk (the French usually drink coffee with milk only at breakfasttime). When you order water with your meal, the waiter may assume you want bottled mineral water, which you have to pay for. But however much Gallic attitude he pulls, don't let the waiter pressure you into getting mineral water if you don't want it— restaurants are required to give you a pitcher of tap water with your meal if you want it. Ask clearly for une carafe d'eau, which is understood to be tap water (eau du robinet). It's perfectly drinkable.*

DINING | INTRODUCTION

Finally, with the muscular recovery of the French economy, free-spending Bobo (bohemian bourgeois) couples have—to the scorn and dismay of many locals who care about good food—fueled a fashion-restaurant boom. If you live in New York, L.A., Miami, London, or any other glamor-puss major city, you know these places. They're all about seeing and being seen, ditzy wannabe-model waiters and waitresses, furtive and usually futile star-spotting, a sexy "major-statement" decor where it's always hard to find the toilets, attitude so bad it warrants Alcatraz, and somewhere way out past Pluto, oh yeah, food. For most people a trip to Paris remains a precious chance to get at some mind-blowingly good food, so only a couple of these spots makes the grade here—**Georges,** for its fabulous view from the top of the Centre Pompidou, great terrace during the good weather, decent snacky little meals for a lunch in a museum, and, well, 'cuz even if the food's forgettable there's no doubt it's a happening spot. And the **Buddha Bar** and **Man Ray** for their decor. Anyone who'd chose a meal at any of these three, over say, **Les Elysées du Vernet** or even **Le Train Bleu,** should be shot, however—you've been warned.

**DINING | INTRODUCTION**

## Only in Paris

A few tips to help you negotiate your way through a meal: Every restaurant is required to post its menu outside, so you should not have any surprises when the bill (*l'addition*) arrives. In cafes, the lowest prices are at the bar, where customers stand for a quick coffee or drink; if you sit at a table, you pay more, and if you sit on the terrace, you pay more still. This is all legal, as is charging higher prices after 10pm or if there is live music. Check the board headed *tariffs des consommations* carefully. It lists all the different prices.

Vegetarianism is a concept that is not likely ever to take France by storm. The French are too proud of their traditional cuisine, with all its meats and innards. Even salads commonly contain ham or chicken livers or sliced duck breast. If asked politely, most restaurants will make an effort to put together some sort of meat-free platter for you, but be careful—their idea of meat-free may not be the same as yours.

Eating places are classified as cafes, which serve drinks, snacks, and sometimes meals; bistros, small, simple restaurants, usually with a limited menu; brasseries, which generally offer Alsatian specialties like *choucroute* and beer, oysters and other shellfish (usually banked on ice on the sidewalk), fish, and grilled meats; and proper restaurants with full menus, which usually serve only at traditional mealtimes.

## When to Eat

French people like to do things at specific times, and they flock to lunch spots at precisely 1pm. This means that every decent restaurant in Paris will be jam-packed from 1 to 2pm. The clever visitor will have lunch at noon or even 12:30 (that way you can get a table and still enjoy the uproar of the lunch rush) or at 2. Be careful, though: Many restaurants will not serve lunch after 2:30. If you miss the lunch hour, you might have to settle for a *sandwich jambon-beurre* (sliced ham on a buttered baguette, which can be sublime when made with quality ingredients), a *croque-monsieur* (open-face ham and cheese sandwich with *béchamel* sauce—try it on *pain Poilâne* if it's available), or an omelette. These snacks are usually served at all times in cafes.

Most restaurants are empty at 8pm and only begin to fill up at around 9. It can be difficult to get served after 10:30, however (see "When the play's the thing" and "All-nighters," below, for suggestions).

## Getting the Right Table

Reservations are imperative in Paris, and if you have your heart set on a table with a view or you want to sit outside, make this firmly known when you book. Walk-in customers are given what is available, but if the restaurant is not full, don't be afraid to ask to move if you don't like your table. In chic or expensive restaurants, the best tables are given to the

**Plugged-in cafes**

*The word for "hip" in French is* branché, *which literally means plugged in—the perfect description for* **Café Orbital** *(Tel 40 20 05 14; 4, rue du 4-Septembre, 75002, Métro 4-Septembre), where customers can surf the Internet while eating a panini (pseudo-Italian sandwich) purchased at the snack bar. You have to buy a cinema ticket to get into the* **cybernetic café** *in the Cité-Ciné UGC in the Nouveau Forum des Halles.* **Cyberia** *(Tel 44 54 53 49; Centre Georges Pompidou, 75004, Métro Rambuteau) is set in a wire cage overlooking the central hall of the Centre Pompidou, with appropriately high-tech decor, PCs, a T1 line for fast transmission, and a cafe. The somewhat cheaper* **High-Tech Café** *(Tel 45 38 67 61; 66, blvd de Montparnasse, 75014, Métro Montparnasse) stays open till 7am; it has Macs and X Terminals as well as PCs. The handsomest may be the* **Web Bar** *(Tel 42 74 66 55; 32, rue de Picardie, 75003 Métro République), a glass-roofed three-story cafe-restaurant with a zinc bar, stone tables and stools, overstuffed leather chairs—and PCs on the mezzanine. A cool place to hang, even if you're Internet-impaired.*

rich and famous and regular customers. The best way to assure that you will not be sent to Siberia is to ask the concierge at your hotel to reserve for you.

French restaurants are supposed to have designated smoking and non-smoking areas unless they have a sophisticated ventilation system (very few do). In practice, however, the smoking regulations are generally ignored.

## Where the Chefs Are

The top seven restaurants in Paris—according to the secretive cult/publisher Michelin—are **Alain Ducasse, Taillevent, L'Ambroisie, Lucas-Carton, Arpège , Pierre Gagnaire,** and **Le Grand Véfour**.

If you want a high-altitude meal, the best food and service that Paris can offer, the ones you should consider are Taillevent, L'Amroisie, and Alain Ducasse. The exalted opinion of Michelin notwithstanding, many people are disappointed by the ho-hum decor of Arpége and find Alain Passard's food at once rather too minimalist and intellectual, and while Lucas-Carton is a beautiful restaurant, chef Bernard Pacaud's cooking has its ups and downs and the service is imperious , especially to foreigners. Le Grand Vefour is one of the most romantic restaurants in Paris, with a jewel-box setting in the Palais Royal and a stunning decor of painted glass ceilings, but while chef Guy Martin is indisputably a talent, many Parisian food critics consider that his third star has been awarded rather prematurely, especially when a really marvelous chef like Guy Savoy has been awaiting this ultimate accolade for years.

So assuming that you're unlikely to take in all seven—a meal for two at any of them will run at least $400, depending upon which wine you chose and the exchange rate—which one of them is right for you? Overall, Alain Ducasse is a sublime experience. Located in the plush but edgy—it's a mix of the usual Louis stuff and post-modern cool—dining room of the Hotel Plaza Athenée, this restaurant gets everything right. Service is as graceful and perfectly timed as any ballet, and Ducasse is a genuis at inventing new dishes that tempt, even taunt, the palette without overwhelming it. Come here if you're a serious gourmet who wants to visit the Olympus of Parisian gastronomy without venturing into the realm of the truly experimental or weird.

Taillevant, long the great-aunt of the three-star club, is suddenly the talk of the town for having hired gifted young chef Michel del Burgo away from the Bristol, which he single-handedly put back on the gourmet map of Paris. Del Burgo's cooking is hearty, even lusty, and this has added real interest to a menu that was previously dominated by perfectly executed traditional luxury dishes. Taillevant also has one of the world's great wine lists, and service is nothing less than gallant.

Perhaps the most romantic of the top three is L'Ambroisie, with its exquisite setting in the Place des Vosges and Flemish still-life-like decor by F. Josef Graf. Try sea bass with duxelles (finely hashed mushrooms) and *foie gras* with quince jam.

For a really wonderful, sometimes weird experience of the real cutting-edge of French gastronomy, though, the place to go is **Pierre Gagnaire.** Gagnaire previously had three stars at his restaurant in Saint-Etienne (nondescript south-central industrial city), but went bankrupt and reopened in Paris. The capital has been intrigued by his astonishingly delicious and nuanced cooking, such as a starter of *foie gras* cooked two ways—au natural and then wrapped in bacon and lacquered like a chinese duck.

Tradition takes visitors to **La Tour d'Argent**. The view is gorgeous but the food beyond the signature roast duck is forgettable, the service borders on pomposity, and the overall effect is time-warp zone 1958. Ditto **Maxim's**, still legendary despite its ludicrously high prices, cagey waiters, and frequently morbid ambience, although a new chef means that the food here is improving by leaps and bounds, but not enough to justify its shudderingly high prices.

Though they're a rung down from the three stars, you'll still eat splendidly well at the other best-of-the-best chefs in Paris, including **Le Pré Catalan**, where Robuchon-trained chef Frederic Anton just gets better and better, **Les Elysees** (Alain Soliveres), **Guy Savoy**, Philippe Conticini's **Petrossian, Ledoyen** (Christophe Le Squer), and **Le Bristol**, which pulled off a real coup by hiring young turk Eric Frechon to take over its kitchens when Michel del Burgo decamped to **Taillevant.** Frechon's one of the best of the new generation and previously ran a hugely popular bistro with a prix-fixe menu in the remote reaches of the 19th arrondissement.

The great middle ground of Paris restaurants—tables that run from 50 to 100 euros a head—is dangerous territory these days. A lot of these places, like Chez Pauline, for example, are living off their reputations, so you're far better off assiduously seeking out some of the brilliant new wave of young chefs. Six of the best junior tables are **Yves Camdeborde**'s La Regalade, **Stephane Mole**'s Les Drues, **Thierry Breton**'s Chez Michel, **Pascal Barbot**'s L'Astrance, **Christophe Beaufort**'s L'Avant Gout, and **Rodolphe Paquin**'s La Repaire de Cartouche.

# The Lowdown

**Book before you fly...** Most Paris three-stars should be booked a solid month ahead of time to avoid disappointment. In the case of particularly modish chefs like **Alain Ducasse** or **Pierre Gagnaire,** a two-month lead time is often necessary. If you're staying somewhere swanky, you can, of course, try to get your concierge to shake down a table for you; otherwise lunch is usually much less busy at the haute cuisine places than is dinner, especially since many French execs have had their expense accounts slashed as the previously terrarium-like world of French business has opened up to global competition.

**Overrated...** A diminishing culinary reputation doesn't seem to have hurt the popularity of **La Tour d'Argent**. Customers come despite decent but hardly awesome food, high prices, and a sense that you're lucky to be allowed in.

Long the favorite haunt of politicians, philosophers, and writers, **Brasserie Lipp** ain't what it used to be. It still has the fabulous decor, but the food's only so-so, and the service can be awful. **Maxim's** is also way past its prime, but tourists still flock there. Chez Pauline and L'Ami Louis, a pair of stunningly expensive luxury bistros aren't putting out what they should these days either, and L'Ami Louis is the worst offender, since it lives off a mostly American Hollywood celebrity clientele that has culinary acumen in inverse relationship to the size of the expense accounts they wield.

Although Michelin ranks **Lucas-Carton** as one of Paris's top five restaurants, it loses points with us for its scattered service and dull menu.

Other well-known tables with inflated reputations include the brasseries **Julien** and **La Coupole**—part of the same chain and suffering from the same really mediocre cooking—and the ghastly **Buddha Bar**, where you should drink but definitely not eat.

**The rest of the best...** Now that he has access to one of the most luxurious pantries in the world, Eric Frechon is thriving at **Le Bristol**, where he does original and elegant dishes like veal sweetbreads seasoned with stick cinnamon and served on a bed of spinach and tiny mushrooms, plus killer desserts, including a wild-thyme parfait with choco-

late ice cream and a sauce of salted caramel. At **Ledoyen**
Christian Le Squer keeps the bliss meter beeping with
herbed risotto topped with lobster, langoustines, scallops,
and a thin slice of Spanish Jabugo ham. Shy and intensely
dedicated young chef Alain Soliveres serves exquisite food
at **Les Elysées du Vernet**, the restaurant of the Hôtel
Vernet, and is considered by Parisian gourmets to be the
most prodigious talent of the new generation of chefs. He
tantalizes with dishes like *epeautre* (Provençal wheat
grains) cooked like black risotto with tender baby squid in
its own ink. After being seemingly doomed to senility,
**L'Espadon,** the restaurant at the Hotel Ritz, is back and,
under the aegis of chef Michel Roth, who trained here, it's
once again one of the ritziest spots in the town for a blow-
out feast; dress to the nines before you try superb dishes
like lobster salad, veal chop with a crust of polenta, and the
best millefeuille in town, and be forewarned of its stunningly expensive wine list.

**Baby bistros...** The "baby bistro" phenomenon that was
born of the last French recession and the ongoing cost
squeeze on Paris restaurants has leveled off a bit. It all
began when Michel Rostang launched the trend with his
**Bistrot d'à Côté,** still going strong, which has good traditional French food (try the terrine and the roast
shoulder of lamb), a winsome old-fashioned bistro
decor, and friendly service. Rostang's latest is **Rue
Balzac,** which seems to be his attempt to respond to the
fusion cooking trend with a modish decor that recalls the
Cirque 2000 in New York and a menu that offers his
famous truffle sandwich, risotto with ham and a superb
millefeuille. The other major player in the baby game
has been **Guy Savoy,** who's Left Bank bistro Les
Bookinistes has long been a big hit, maybe too big a hit,
since it's always full of tourists (tip: William Ledeuil, the
wonderful chef here, has just opened his own place, **Ze
Kitchen Galerie,** right next door); for a more Parisian
experience of Savoy's way with a bistro, try **Le Cap
Vernet,** which serves excellent shellfish and fish; another
baby worth any fish fiend's attention is the **Bistrot du
Dôme,** the popular annex of the famous Montparnasse
fish house nearby that serves an impeccably fresh catch-of-
the-day menu at much gentler prices. The only chef still
putting a lot of energy into the bistro concept these days,
though, is Alain Ducasse, with his growing chain of **Spoon**

restaurants (the first one opened in Paris, and they now exist in London, Tokyo, Mauritius, Monaco, and soon Tunisia).

**Cutting-edge bistros...** If the last wave of change on the Paris restaurant scene was the bistro-annexes of famous chefs, the latest is the brilliant crop of easygoing, comfortably priced new bistros that are being opened by a new generation of ambitious, passionate young chefs.

The latest hit in this category is **L'Astrance,** which was opened by brilliant young Pascal Barbot, former second chef to Alain Passard at Arpege and private chef to the head of the French Pacific fleet, a little over a year ago and has since become one of the toughest reservations to snag in Paris. Typical of Barbot's style are his soup of milk and toasted bread crumbs (sounds like hospital food, but really is fabulous) and avocado ravioli stuffed with crab meat. And another rising star is Nicholas Vagnon, whose **La Table de Lucullus,** in a rather charmless storefront space in a remote corner of the 17th arrondissement, is packing them in for really excellent eats, including langoustine carpaccio as a starter and a delicious north African–inspired casserole of shredded lamb, cracked wheat, fresh mint, and dried fruit as a main course.

Though it's way of the beaten track and, like most of this genre, horribly noisy, Christophe Beaufort's **L'Avant Gout** in the 13th arrondissement is worth traveling for. The menu changes daily but might include shellfish bisque as a starter, followed by tomatoes stuffed with oxtail. Over near the Bastille, **Le Repaire de Cartouche** is a fabulous bistro as long as you don't get stuck in the chilly, lost-in-right-field front room. Rodolphe Paquin does hearty, earthy dishes like veal chop in Madeira sauce or a thick steak of grilled bacon. And desserts like carmelized pineapple are moaningly good.

It's worth braving a slightly dreary part of town for the offerings at Thierry Breton's **Chez Michel**. The sophisticated menu is spiked with several old-fashioned and rarely encountered Breton dishes. French food critics have showered **Les Ormes** with deserved acclaim ever since it opened; chef Stephane Mole trained with retired super-star Joel Robuchon and it shows. Another small place gone big is **La Regalade**; make a reservation here before you even unpack so you'll be able to try dishes such as gratin of potatoes and lobster.

**When the play's the thing...** Because many restaurants

stop serving at about 10:30pm or even earlier, it can be difficult to find a good après-movie or -theater meal. The **Bistrot Beaubourg** is an inexpensive, upbeat, little restaurant in the center of town with good, simple French food. In the Marais, the **Coude de Fou,** a popular, laid-back restaurant, offers a special two-course menu between midnight and 12:45am. **Le Boeuf sur le Toit** is an enormous brasserie near the Champs-Elysées with good shellfish and meats. It's part of the Flo Tradition chain, as are the **Terminus Nord** and **Le Vaudeville.** Each has high-quality food; different, old-fashioned brasserie decor that has been carefully restored; a lively atmosphere; good service; and a special, low-priced fixed menu after 11pm (including oysters). The Terminus Nord is especially fun late at night, full of satisfied diners and friendly waiters running from table to table. **Bofinger,** a famous Belle-Epoque brasserie at Bastille, has a similar ambience and menu. Actors come to **La Cloche d'Or**, near Pigalle, when their working nights are done. For something hipper, there's the Costes brothers' desperately cool restaurant **Georges** on the 6th floor of the Centre Pompidou. The views are fabulous, as is the decor, with three huge brushed aluminum pods occupying an airy loft space with lit-from-within brushed glass tables. The food's decent, but not cheap, although you can always just order a club sandwich for 10 euros or an omelette for 9 euros. Make sure to book ahead. In the hot new party precincts off the Champs Elysees in the 8th, you can also catch tasty late eats at the new Paris branch of **Nobu,** the Nippo-Peruvian sushi place that originated in New York and is backed by Robert DeNiro, or get into a perfect pre-club funk at **Market,** New York star Jean-Georges Vongerichten's slick new place in the Christie's headquarters building; with a disco-goes-ethnic decor by Christian Liagre, who did Jean-George's hip Mercer Kitchen in New York, this place is packing major star power for the type of fusion food that tastes best against an aural backdrop of acid-jazz and lounge music. Also see **Le Petit Marseillais.**

**All-nighters...** Most nightclubs in Paris don't open until 11pm or midnight, so by 3 or 4am you may have worked up an appetite. There are several all-night restaurants in the Les Halles area, vestiges of the days when Paris's major wholesale food market was located there. Try **Au Pied de Cochon,** the place to go if you like pig parts, especially at 3am. They actually serve the snout here, cut in two, the tail on the plate along with the trotter. For the squeamish, enormous platters of shellfish, as well as more ordinary fare, are also available 24 hours a day.

Smoky and bawdy, **La Tour de Montlhery** dates back to the days when Les Halles was "the belly of Paris" rather than an ugly mall, and it serves up massive mutton chops and steaks with real *frites*.

**Decor to die for, but skip the food... Chartier** is a Paris experience that's not to be missed despite all the tourists. This is an enormous "bouillon" (originally, a cheap workers' restaurant that served *pot-au-feu*) that hasn't changed much since the 19th century (some of the waiters look as if they've been there since then as well). The food is cheap and acceptable, the service brusque, and the ambience lively. **Brasserie Lipp** no longer stands out for its food or service, but its enormous mirrors, ceramic panels, and frescoes are as memorable as its ghosts. Since the 1920s, nearly all the political nabobs of France have been regulars here, along with an equally long list of writers and other celebrities. Owner Pierre Cardin, the king of commercialization, has thankfully not messed around with **Maxim's** incredible Art Nouveau decor, though the restaurant's pretty much been ruined.

The Flo Tradition chain has also carefully restored the original decor of its brasseries, although food and service often leave much to be desired; if you're an interiors freak and want to clock some of these places, come late, when they're quieter, and order very, very simply. The famous Art Deco **La Coupole** has paintings on the columns by 32 artists who were paid with unlimited free drinks. Saved from destruction in the 1980s when it was declared a national monument, this is one of those places in Paris where the past really seems present. Art Nouveau **Julien** is a work of art in itself. Its carved mahogany bar, glass ceiling with floral motifs, huge mirrors, molded glass panels painted with female allegories of the four seasons, and extravagant moldings are a delight; unfortunately, the same cannot be said for its food and frantic service.

On the more modern side of things, **Man Ray**, a slick *Chinatown*—as in the movie—style mega-seater off the Champs-Elysées is a gorgeous setting in which to tipple. Ditto the slightly past prime **Buddha Bar**, where a gigantic gold-painted polystyrene Buddha remains mum on the mediocre Asian food, or **Barrio Latino**, the latest hipster joint near the Bastille, where the Latino food is feeble but the decor around an open atrium in what was once a furniture showroom is as luxuriant as a honeymoon in Havana.

**Decor to die for, and don't miss the food...** Opened in 1864, **Bofinger** is perhaps the quintessential Paris brasserie, with its stained-glass dome, sweeping staircase, wood paneling, large mirrors, black banquettes, potted palms, and brass coat racks. Waiters bustle about as customers indulge in oysters, *choucroute*, or wild duck. For over-the-top Belle-Epoque decor, **Le Train Bleu** wins hands down. It's also classified as a historic monument, and its sumptuous decorations cover every inch of the walls, while the 11-meter-high ceilings with gilded moldings and paintings by turn-of-the-century artists provide a voyage around France. A similar atmosphere reigns at **Les Elysées du Vernet** under a superb glass *verriere*, or domed ceiling, that was designed by none other than Gustave Eiffel himself. Potted palms, silver candelabras, and waiters in tuexedos complete the counts-traveling-with-steamer-trunks atmosphere here. With its lavish Art Nouveau decor, **Lucas-Carton** is where you should demand that your lover take you if you've just become his frisky mistress or her energetic boy toy. The ceiling squirms with 17th-century plaster cherubim at **Les Ambassadeurs**, the stunning restaurant in the Hotel Crillon, with its black-and-white marble floors, crystal chandeliers, and drop-dead view of the Place de la Concorde, and chef Dominique Bouchet's cuisine is a suave study in discreet luxury against this operatic background. Recently and sensitively renovated, **Le Relais Plaza**, the terribly fashionable brasserie at the Hotel Plaza Athénée, serves up an Art Deco feast reminiscent of the public rooms in the great oceanliners like *La Normandie*, and the straightforward and simple food is actually pretty good.

**Best circus decor...** Two cafes located near Paris's Cirque d'Hiver (Winter Circus) have slapped up a few circus posters and named themselves Rendezvous des Clowns and Circus Bar, but there is only one **Clown Bar**, with hand-painted ceramic tiles that date to the 1920s; wood-framed Art Nouveau windows, door, and mirrors; an S-curved zinc bar; and antique clown memorabilia. Add to all this good food, wine, and atmosphere and you've got just about the perfect little bistro.

**Historic surroundings...** Originally the Café de Chartres in the 18th century, **Le Grand Véfour** was a hangout for plotters of the French Revolution and later of Royalists during the Terror. Famous customers over the decades have included Victor Hugo, Colette, Jean Cocteau, and Greta Garbo. Cocteau designed the menu and the ashtrays.

**Peckish near the Centre Pompidou...** The **Bistrot Beaubourg** is a small, informal, and inexpensive restaurant with tasty food. **Dame Tartine** has a terrace overlooking the wacky and wonderful Stravinksy fountain and serves creative open-face sandwiches that make for a cheap meal. **Georges**, on the sixth floor of the slickly renovated museum, has a striking modern decor and serves nonstop from 11am to 2am; reservations are essential.

**If it's mealtime in the Marais...** As popular as it is for hanging out and having a good time, the Marais is not a great restaurant neighborhood. Aside from the excellent falafel stands along the rue de Rosiers, one of the best deals in this neck of the woods is **La Baracane**, which won't ever show up in a decorating magazine with its worn red carpet, framed posters, and plain vanilla walls but is a crowd-pleaser with its inexpensive and delicious southwestern French cooking. The *confit de canard*, grilled preserved duck, is splendid, and the wines by the glass are cheap and good drinking. Though it's on the very northern fringes of the neighborhood, **Le Reconfort** is worth some shoe leather. This attractive amber-walled bistro draws the shave-heads and unisex pony-tail crowd and, quite surprisingly, the food's very good. As the southern part of the nabe becomes increasingly expensive and tourist-infested, the natives have been migrating north into the 3rd arrondissement (the Marais traditionally has only meant the 4th, but it's a state of mind, dude). A good example of this colonization process is **Le Petit Marseillais,** packed ever since it opened with a hip, friendy, mixed young crowd that chats easily between tables in this small room with dark red walls, black wood tables and chairs, and vintage Murano glass chandeliers. The vaguely provencale food is reasonably tasty, not too expensive, and the mood's perfect, whether this is the end or beginning of your night out.

**Chow time on the Champs-Elysées...** Once a near wasteland of fast-food outlets and dreary, tourist-trap cafes, the Champs-Elysées has been slowly reemerging as a destination for Parisians themselves ever since its makeover four years ago, and one of the reasons the locals are back is that a variety of good—and trendy but less good—restaurants have opened on and off the avenue. Though it may puzzle North Americans, six-star chef Alain Ducasse's doppily named **Spoon, Food and Wine** is a knock-down hit with the locals. What's on offer here is Ducasse's take on world food, which means a menu that includes everything from a very high-tech BLT, to all kinds of pasta, Asian stir-fries, and even cheesecake and donuts (served as a dessert). The food's actually pretty good, it's an ultra-chic scene, and there's a fascinating if pricey wine list, half of which is, to the utter astonishment of the French, from the USA. The other hit in this nabe is the new Paris branch of **Nobu,** the fabulous Nippo-Peruvian place that began in New York. For a quick feed during a stomp down the avenue or before or after a movie, **Lo Sushi**, a conveyor-belt sushi place with video screens and a decor by star interior designer Andree Putmann, is convenient and popular with local trendies.

**Montmartre on an empty stomach...** This is not a great part of town for restaurants, but **Le Moulin à Vin** is a friendly wine bar that provides a taste of old Montmartre. The vivacious patronne, a former banker, serenades diners with old French songs to the accompaniment of an accordion while they eat good, unpretentious French food.

**Other places to eat on the tourist beat...** Tourists seem intimidated by the crowds and the chic of **Le Fumoir**, the wonderful new cafe that Parisians instantly went wild for. Don't let those pretty faces and I'm-so-cool expressions keep you away. The fact is, the people who work here are very friendly and the food is pretty good. It's something of a miracle to find a decent, inexpensive restaurant in the Saint-Germain-des-Prés area, but **Le Petit Saint-Benoît**, a simple bistro, is a safe bet. Don't let the waitress pressure you into ordering from the long menu until you've had the time to digest it; it includes French classics like beef stew with carrots and *blanquette de veau*. **Polidor**, an old restaurant near Odéon, is looking a bit shabby, but the food is still very good. You may be dubious as you walk in, but you'll be won over by the charming female service, classic French food, and low prices.

**Best brunch...** This American habit has now become

established in Paris. The **Café Beaubourg** is a designer cafe in the heart of Paris, inevitably full of too-too-trendy types. Somewhat overpriced, it's still a pleasant cafe to hang out in for an hour or two, and the American-style brunch is available all day, every day for 110 francs. At **Coffee Parisien**, which does a version of American food, there is no set brunch formula, but all the elements are there on the menu: pancakes and bacon, fried eggs, etc. Reservations are a must in this tiny restaurant full of aspiring models. The tea salon in the gift shop **Marais Plus** is a popular brunch spot on Saturday and Sunday, but for a change of pace, try the Moroccan restaurant **404**, or head out to **Quai Ouest**. Though located in the suburb of St. Cloud, it's accessible by Métro, and the riverside location, loft-chic decor, and lively young crowd make it a good destination when you want to take it easy on a sunny weekend.

**Where the media types go...** Alain Ducasse's **Spoon, Food and Wine** is very popular with French television stars, which may explain why the couple at the table next to you look like a game-show host and a weather girl. On the Left Bank, you'll find book editors and writers at **Helene Darroze**, the superb new southwestern restaurant with a sassy contemporary decor, and **La Table d'Aude**, where the lure is first-rate *cassoulet* and as much wine as you can guzzle or dare to request as part of a prix-fixe menu. Movie people favor the lush decor at **Man Ray**, Mick Hucknell (you know, of Simply Red) and Johnny Depp's mega-seater off the Champs-Elysées; **Paul Minchelli**, for superb fish and soft lighting on cosmetically altered bodies; and **La Maison Blanche**, when you're pretending that you're having a casual, discreet night out on the town, but know that photographers from *Paris Match* are regularly lurking. **La Ferme Saint-Simon** on the *très chic* rue de Saint-Simon attracts media and fashion people, as well as deputies from the nearby Assemblée Nationale, for its classic French cuisine. The modern decor of wood, steel, and glass at the high-priced **Arpège** sets the stage for the cuisine of young chef Alain Passard, whose creations include vegetable couscous and sweet-and-sour lobster. If you're a television-video-film-advertising type (and even if you're the manager of a Wendy's, this is a place to put on your list), impress everyone by booking at **Ghislaine Arabian,** which is a superb restaurant that's relatively easy to get to for anyone working in these industries, which are heavily concentrated in the inner-suburbs of western Paris. Arabian, a feisty blonde from Lille and one of the rare well-known female chefs in France, was formerly chef at Ledoyen; now she's back, and better than ever.

**Best brasseries...** When you're in the mood for a good meal (not haute cuisine, but solid food) in a jumping atmosphere, try a Parisian brasserie. **Bofinger**, near the place de la Bastille, is one of the best examples, with its hustle and bustle and Belle-Epoque decor. Unfortunately, most of Paris's brasseries have become part of one of the two local chains, Groupe Flo and Les Freres Blanc, and while these groups are to be grudgingly credited with restoring the authentic decors in some of the city's prettiest and most famous brasseries, the food's often mediocre. The best of the Flo brasseries are **Le Boeuf sur le Toit** (off the Champs-Elysées), **Terminus Nord** (handily across the street from the Gare du Nord), **Le Vaudeville** (next to the Paris Bourse), and **Le Balzar** (right next door to La Sorbonne), which is arguably the chicest brasserie in town, pulling an intriguing crowd of fashion folk, academics, and foreigners. **Au Pied de Cochon** is the star of Les Freres Blanc's stable. The latest brasserie to be submitted to a major renovation is also one of the best in town—**Garnier**, the quiet man in front of the Gare Saint Lazare. Though many local design snobs regret its former decor—seventies ghastly that had just tipped into being fabulous, the new look—dark wood, wicker chairs, original Art Deco light fixtures—is comfortable, and the fish, oysters, and other shellfish here are excellent. Note, too, that they run a tiny belly-up-to-the-counter oyster bar that's a brilliant spot for a quick bivalve snack in you're shopping at Printemps and Galeries Lafayette, the big department stores just down the road.

**Classiest cafes...** The two top cafes are **Café de Flore** for its Art Deco decor, high-quality food, good people - watching terrace, and star-studded clientele, and the **Café Marly**, for its location in the Louvre and its two handsome dining rooms with their completely different ambiences. One manages to be classic and modern at the same time, while the second is brighter and airier. Then there's the **Café Beaubourg**, with Christian de Portzamparc's original interior design, which includes a bridge that connects the two parts of the mezzanine and comfortable wicker armchairs on the terrace facing the Centre Pompidou.

**You can really eat in the hotel?...** The leering-waiter-and-fish-with-white-sauce image of hotel dining in Paris has been banished. In fact today, some of the best restaurants in town are in hotels, which compete fiercely for star chefs. Even before it opened its doors, the new Four Seasons George V had hired chef Philippe Legendre away from Taillevant to bang the pots and pans at its sumptuous new luxury restaurant, **Le Cinq**. Not too surprisingly, Legendre does sublime and very classic luxury cooking rather like what he did at, well, Taillevant, with luscious dishes like a tartare of scallops and oysters with caviar and lobster with chestnuts. Over at the Crillon, chef Dominique Bouchet is keeping the lavish dining room at **Les Ambassadeurs** on course as one of the best tables in Paris, as seen in dishes like a crispy potato pancake topped with smoked salmon, *créme fraiche*, and caviar. Dining under delicate Belle Epoque a *verrière*, or leaded glass ceiling, at **Les Elysées du Vernet** only adds to the pleasure of some really brilliant food from young chef Alain Soliveres. The service here is impeccable, too, and the cheeky young sommelier loves to tease you to venture beyond the usual Burgundies and Bordeaux with little-known and very reasonably priced regional vintages. With a glassed-in dining room overlooking the magnolia-planted inner courtyard for summer and an oval-shaped oak-panelled sanctuary with crystal chandeliers for winter, **Le Bristol** is extremely popular since the arrival of new chef Eric Frechon, who won his reputation with a shrewd prix-fixe bistro in the remote 19th arrondissement. He replaced chef Michel del Burgo, who's gone to Taillevant, and does sumptuous aristo food like *foie gras*–stuffed ravioli in chicken broth with truffle shavings. And the latest haute cuisine act to go hotel is Alain Ducasse, who moved to the swanky Plaza Athenée Hotel two years ago.

**Al fresco...** The French take to the terrace the moment there's a ray of sunshine. Terraces come in all varieties, from lush, peaceful gardens, to a few tables on the sidewalk with exhaust-spouting Citroëns rushing by. **Le Pré Catalan**, one of the city's better restaurants, is in the first category. On a summer evening, its jazzy modern French cuisine can bring you near to paradise. **La Grande Cascade**, also surrounded by lovely gardens in the Bois de Boulogne, serves classic French cuisine. Between these two wonders and the Citroën exhaust, there are the terraces of the top-notch fish restaurant **La Cagouille**; the *très chic* **Café Marly**, housed in the Louvre itself, with a view of Pei's pyramid and an international menu; and the **Café Very** for inexpensive meal-sized *tartines* (open-face sandwiches) under the trees of the Tuileries. The **Restaurant du Palais-Royal**, isolated from the noise of passing traffic in the tranquil confines of the Palais-Royal, where Colette and Jean Cocteau once lived, serves fine French food at moderate prices. Trendy **La Maison Blanche** has a rooftop terrace with a view of Paris, and the food's on par with the view since the three-star Pourcel brothers from Montpelier took over a year ago.

**Great wine bars...** The old-style wine bars in Paris serve nothing but wine and *tartines* (open-face sandwiches). They usually close at around 9:30pm and are often located near food markets. **La Tartine** is a classic example; nothing much has changed since Trotsky drank here. The walls are stained with decades of tobacco smoke, and it would be easy to believe that the eagle-eyed patron, who's pushing 90 but continues to terrify both customers (everyone from yuppies to artsy and intellectual types) and staff, was around when Leon was. It's a great, though intimidating, place for a pre-dinner *kir* or a glass of wine and a *tartine* topped with pâté, *rillettes*, or *cantal*. A friendlier ambience reigns at **Le Baron Rouge**, the place to go after Sunday-morning shopping at the Marché d'Aligre. Even if you're not hungry, you must taste the *délice de canard*, a fantastic duck pâté served with fresh bread and excellent cornichons. An accompanying glass of red wine is *de rigueur*. Bring an empty bottle if you want to buy wine from the barrel.

The newer version of the wine bar is a bistro that serves simple meals to complement an extensive wine list. The atmosphere is usually relaxed and informal in these little restaurants. One of the best examples is the **Clown Bar**, an historic monument. It is located next to the Cirque d'Hiver (Winter Circus)—hence the name (pronounced "kloon") and the colorful tiles behind the bar depicting clowns. The owner of **Le Moulin à Vin** has managed to re-create the atmosphere of old Montmartre in her little wine bar, one of the liveliest in Paris.

Two of the city's better wine bars, more chic than those listed above, are actually owned by Englishmen. **Willi's Wine Bar** has become a fashionable institution here, appreciated both for its excellent selection of wines and its creative, nouvelle-ish cuisine. The owner is known in Paris as a connoisseur of wines from the Rhône region. Its baby brother, **Juveniles**, has lower prices, but the food and wine are in the same excellent vein. The atmosphere is informal, and it is worth chatting about wine with the very knowledgeable owner, Tim Johnston.

***La vie en rose...*** There are still a few places where the old-time, working-man's Paris can be found. For an authentic, old-fashioned Paris bistro, a genus that's almost extinct, try **Chez La Vieille,** one of the worthiest old-fashioned bistros in the city, with superb food, charming service, and taunting wisps of nostalgia—come here if you want to experience how generous Paris bistros once were (this place has never heard of "portion management") or if you've never heard a rotary phone ring before. When you're tired out from shopping at the flea market at Porte de Clignancourt, go to **Chez Louisette**—not for the great food, but for the high-camp atmosphere. The accordion plays, the Edith Piaf imitator sings, the Gypsy lady reads palms, and a good time is had by all. The patronne of **Le Moulin à Vin** wine bar in Montmartre leads the singing of old French songs, accompanied by an accordion player, while diners enjoy simple, well-prepared French food.

**Where to go when you're sick of French cooking...** **Fogon St-Julien**, a side trip to Spain, serves superb paella with great Spanish wines and a lively atmosphere. **Il Baccello**, one of the most authentic Italian restaurants in Paris, is tucked away in the remote reaches of the 17th arrondissement, but is worth the trip and is also a great spot for vegetarians, since it does wonderful pastas and risottos. **Coffee Parisien** serves credible versions of American favorites, including hamburgers and salads. For good couscous try **Chez Omar,** and for something really delicious and different, head for **Djakarta Bali** for a sublime encounter with the Indonesian kitchen. In Europe, Indonesian food is generally associated with Holland, the former colonial ruler, but this link notwithstanding, you'd be hard pressed to find such delicately prepared and seasoned Indonesian eats there (the problem is that Indonesian food is to Holland what Indian food is to England—to wit, so common that it's usually denatured and mediocre when you're lucky). The brother-sister team who run the restaurant are delightful, too, and there are occasional live performances of Indonesian music and dance.

**Cheap eats...** Okay, don't expect miracles, but decent, basic French food is served with flourish at the historic **Chartier**, with its perfectly preserved, 19th-century decor. And now that you've prepared you for the dog-food level of most budget restaurants in Paris, here's one that's so good it'd be worth traveling across town for even if money wasn't an issue. **La Boulangerie,** in so-cool-it's-almost-over Ménilmontant (a nabe that spreads across the 11th and 20th arrondissements and is young, cheap, trendy, and sort of artistic—most of the local arty types like to play with paint but won't be world class anytime soon), offers really good food, and house wine, for about $20 a head—what your cheeseburger, fries, and beer feast now costs at home—depending on the exchange rate, and when you see what you can get for this dough, you'll probably want to eat here more than once. Yo, bro, how's about pears roasted with goat cheese, chicken with spices and grapefruit, and homemade shortbread with apples flamed in Calvados, plus an 8-euro carafe of Chinon? Near the Centre Pompidou **Bistrot Beaubourg** is a spot that serves good, French classics at very low prices, so come and relax with surf and turf at this unpretentious neighborhood hangout. Parisian and tourist alike love sitting at the outdoor tables. **Le Petit Saint-Benoît** in Saint-Germaindes-Prés serves French classics like beef stew with carrots and *blanquette de veau* to a crowd that's largely slumming. **Le Petit Keller**, with a fabulous Fifties decor, is a great spot for dinner if you're planning to do the lively bar scene in and around the Bastille. Delicious homecooking—the *daube de boeuf*'s better here than at many much pricier places—and low tabs will leave you with more francs for after-dinner guzzling.

**Lunching out cheaply...** In terms of the quality and sophistication of food, **L'Ebauchoir** near Bastille rates as the best in this category. In addition to now hard-to-find onion soup, the menu includes escargots, raw sardines stuffed with minced vegetables, and tuna steak with orange sauce. Three restaurants with the same owner have made a success out of converting what has traditionally been a wine-bar snack, the *tartine*, into something more substantial and inventive. Two of them are called **Dame Tartine** (one is located across from the Bastille opera house and the other has a terrace next to the Stravinsky fountain near the Centre Pompidou). The other, the **Café Very**, is located in the Tuileries and is a pleasant spot for an outdoor lunch or dinner on a nice day. The cute little bistro **Chez Nénesse** in the Marais is frequented by neighborhood people, both artsy and working-class. Red-and-white tablecloths, a wood stove, and plants and flowers provide the backdrop at lunchtime for inexpensive French dishes. **Au Babylone**, open for lunch only, is great for a cheap, solid meal in a quintessentially Parisian setting if you're doing a long trek around the Left Bank. This place is almost a Parisian equivalent of a good New York coffee shop.

**Luxury lunches at bargain prices...** Le Reminet, a tiny and friendly bistro on the Left Bank just across from Notre-Dame, offers a fine 20-euro feed from a menu that changes daily but might include such treats as lentil salad with *foie gras,* smoked duck breast, and a poached egg in a balsamic vinaigrette. **Chantairelle**, a pleasant little Latin Quarter bistro specializing in the hearty food of the central Auvergne region, and **Les Ormes**, a stylish spot with a talented young chef in the 16th arrondissement, both do your wallet a favor with lunch menus at 15 euros and 25 euros, respectively. Best midday buys at top-flight tables include **Lucas-Carton** (60 euros), **Arpège** (105 euros), **Pierre Gagnaire** (79 euros), and, the best of the bunch, the 54-euro menu at **Ledoyen**.

**Where to seal a deal...** The trendy, designer-decorated restaurant at **Le Montalembert** serves market-fresh dishes with French, Italian, and Chinese influences. **Café Marly** in the Louvre is another hot spot at lunchtime and also serves good international cuisine. **Le Relais Plaza** in the Plaza Athénée hotel specializes in grilled meats and has its original Art Deco interior. In the old days, Maurice Chevalier, Josephine Baker, and Marlene Dietrich dined here; today, the person sitting next to you might be Jack

Nicholson, a Kuwaiti oilman, or a rich, old French lady with her two miniature poodles. Another Left Bank choice is **Le Voltaire**, a Paris classic with its sober wood paneling, reliable French food, and excellent service, but if you want to be grand, book at **L'Espadon** or **Ghislaine Arabian**.

**Vegging out...** Until chef Alain Passard went veggie at his three-star Arpege, vegetarian restaurants in Paris were stuck in a 1968 vintage time warp complete with straggly spider plants hanging in macrame holders and dreary tofu and grain concoctions. Now many trendy tables offer good veg options, including **La Maison Blanche, Nobu,** and **Ghislaine Arabian.** One of the best bets in town is **La Ville de Jagannath**, an excellent Indian vegetarian restaurant in switched-on Menilmontant. It serves delicious Thali-style meals with dishes like potato in fresh lemon and ginger sauce, and zucchini and spiced pea curry. The **Piccolo Teatro**, also in the Marais, specializes in delicious vegetarian gratins in a friendly *baba-cool* (hippie) atmosphere. The nearby **Aquarius** offers steamed vegetable plates and vegetable tarts. There's not much in the way of decor, but the food is satisfying and cheap. The 14th arrondissement has another, unrelated, restaurant named **Aquarius**; this one boasts a pleasant blond-wood decor and more sophisticated dishes like soybean *quenelles* and tarragon *cannelloni*. In Montmartre, the laid-back **Au Grain de Folie**, serving salads, tarts, and vegetable and rice dishes, seems like another throwback to the Sixties. Though it's not strictly vegetarian, **Il Baccello**, a stylish Italian restaurant in the 17th arrondissement, serves a lot of first-rate veggie dishes since the chef trained at Joia, the brilliant luxury vegetarian restaurant in Milan.

**Isn't it romantic?...** Romantic settings in Paris are not limited to candlelit tables—lovers here are not shy about staring deeply into each other's eyes and kissing in any public place. For those who are looking for the appropriate romantic ambience, though, there are intimate restaurants like **Prunier**, with its cozy Art Deco dining room and sexy food with a twist of originality—think caviar, smoked salmon, oysters, and chilled vodka or Champagne. If you can afford it, the rosy glow of candlelight at **Les Elysées du Vernet** in the evening can inspire much more than one's appetite. On a balmy night, fill your beloved's eyes with stars by dining under them—book a terrace table at **Le Pré Catalan**. The

Palais-Royal at night is one of the most romantic places in the world. A terrace table at the **Restaurant du Palais-Royal** is spellbinding on a summer night.

**Victuals with a view...** Unlike most restaurants with a view in major cities, **Le Jules Verne** is as famous for what you can eat there as it is for what you can see. Located on the second floor of the Eiffel Tower, its understated gray-and-black interior is designed to not distract attention from the wide-ranging view of Paris, nor from the cuisine of Alain Reix, considered one of Paris's better chefs. **La Maison Blanche** has an unbeatable view of the Eiffel Tower, the Seine, and the Hôtel des Invalides that is especially spectacular at night. The large terrace is an added advantage in summer. Located on the sixth floor of the Théâtre des Champs-Elysées, this lively restaurant serves modern French cuisine to a hip clientele. The super-expensive **La Tour d'Argent** is famous of course, for its view of the flying buttresses of Notre-Dame, but you also get a pretty spectacular view of Paris from the tip of the Ile de la Cité, where you can picnic in almost the same place that Leslie Caron danced with Fred Astaire in *An American in Paris*. And less expensive but much sassier, **Georges,** on the top floor of the Centre Pompidou, also has killer views of gay Paris.

**Something fishy...** Paris may be landlocked, but fresh seafood is shipped in every day from Normandy and Brittany, and there are many excellent restaurants serving the fruits of the sea. Drop-dead chic, the new **Paul Minchelli** has instantly become one of the very best fish houses in the city. **La Cagouille** is airy and modern with a pleasant terrace for summer dining. The seafood is extremely fresh, the desserts sublime, and the service congenial. The second floor diningroom and oyster bar at **Garnier** are considered by sophisticated Parisians to be the ideal back-drop to a swanky seafood feast. Run by chef Michel Rostang's daughter, **Bistrot...Cote Mer** is an excellent and reasonably priced fish house on the Left Bank. Try the roasted mussels with mushroom salad and tartare sauce and scallops cooked in their shells with baby vegetables. Cost-conscious diners should try the chain called **Le Bar à Huîtres**, which guarantees the freshness of its oysters, lobsters, and other seafood.

**Satisfying your sweet tooth...** For the best hot chocolate in Paris, **Angélina** wins hands down for its thick, rich, dark, and creamy "African chocolate." Or sip *chocolat à l'ancien* in the palm-lined gallery of the Plaza Athénée hotel. The truly degenerate have a *Mont Blanc* (supersweet confection of meringue, chestnut puree, and whipped cream) with their chocolate. **Laduree**, an elegant tearoom with two branches, the original of the rue Royale and the newer one on the Champs-Elysées, has created a particularly harmless local species of fetishist: people who would do anything for their macaroons, fragile, sugary cookies that have nothing to do with the heap o' coconut jobs by the same name in North America and which come in a variety of sublime flavors, including chocolate, coffee, raspberry, and lemon. All of their pastries are bliss, and these two addresses make irresistably happy pit stops during any day on the town. The best indigenous ice cream is universally considered to be that of **Berthillon**, which must be the only ice-cream shop in the world that allows itself the luxury of shutting down during the summer. The pear sorbet tastes like a frozen pear (and even has the right texture), and the chocolate and coffee ice creams are sublime. Luckily, other outlets on the Ile Saint-Louis and selected shops around Paris sell Berthillon ice cream year-round.

# The Index

| | |
|---|---|
| $$$$$ | more than 150 euros |
| $$$$ | 100–150 euros |
| $$$ | 50–100 euros |
| $$ | 30–50 euros |
| $ | under less than 30 euros |

**Alain Ducasse.** Ducasse moved from his former townhouse setting in the 16th 2 years ago, and this slickly hotel dining room—think crystal chandeliers hidden inside of giant gray moiree shades, a mix of modern art and Louis something, and unctuous waiters—suits him to a T. The maestro's rarely in the kitchen—he's more of an exec than a chef these days—but the team he trains turns out smashingly good food like langoustines topped with caviar and cream, plus seasonal specials like an earthy, elegant tart of cepes with crayfish or a perfect duckling roasted in fig leaves with a sauce of aged vinegar and pan drippings.... *Tel 01 53 67 65 00; Hotel Athenee, 25, ave Montaigne, 8th, Métro Trocadero. Closed Sat–Sun, open for lunch only on Fri.* $$$$$ **(see p. 48)**

**Angélina.** A chic, Viennese-style, Belle Epoque tea room that serves fabulously rich hot chocolate, refined lunches, and decadent desserts.... *Tel 01 42 60 82 00; 226, rue de Rivoli, 75001, Métro Tuileries. Open until 7pm. Closed Tue in Aug.* $ **(see p. 65)**

**Aquarius.** A satisfying, cheap, and basic vegetarian restaurant.... *Tel 01 48 87 48 71; 54, rue Sainte-Croix-de-la-Bretonnerie, 75004, Métro Hôtel de Ville. Closed Sun and 2 weeks in Aug. No credit cards.* $ **(see p. 63)**

**Aquarius.** This vegetarian restaurant serves generous helpings of inventive, flavorful dishes, including tofu croquettes, soybean *quenelles*, mushroom tarts, and mushroom lasagna. Organic wines available.... *Tel 01 45 41 36 88;*

*40, rue de Gergovie, 75014, Métro Pernety. Closed Sun.* $

**(see p. 63)**

**Arpège.** Modern, elegant, "designer" decor sets the stage for the cuisine of young chef Alain Passard, who recently stunned the food world by converting his 3-star to an almost entirely vegetarian menu. Try the vegetable couscous and sweet-and-sour lobster. Reserve.... *Tel 01 45 51 47 33; 84, rue de Varenne, 75007, Métro Varenne. Closed Sat–Sun lunch.* $$$$

**(see pp. 56, 62)**

**Au Babylone.** Ideal for a cheap atmospheric lunch on the Left Bank. The amiable waitresses fly through the room with plates of grated carrot salad, lamb stew, and runny wedges of Camembert, and most of the crowd drinks the house red by the carafe.... *Tel 01 45 48 72 13; 13, rue de Babylone, 75007, Métro Sevres-Babylone. Lunch only. Closed Sun and Aug. AE not accepted.* $

**(see p. 62)**

**Au Grain de Folie.** A vegetarian restaurant with a *baba-cool* atmosphere. Serves salads, tarts, and vegetable and rice dishes.... *Tel 01 42 58 15 57; 24, rue La Vieuville, 75018, Métro Abbesses. Open daily.* $

**(see p. 63)**

**Au Pied de Cochon.** Open 24 hours. Specializes in body parts of the pig, from the foot to the snout, as well as shellfish platters and more ordinary fare. Lively atmosphere. Reservations taken only until 8:30pm.... *Tel 01 42 36 11 75; 6, rue Coquillière, 75001, Métro Louvre or Les Halles. Open 24 hours daily.* $$

**(see pp. 51, 57)**

**Barrio Latino.** The plush decor here, with a central atrium and a Moorish style back bar, is more clearly aimed at gilded suburban youth than would-be revolutionaries. The menu runs to fashion food like salmon tartare and carpaccio more than any of the earthy grub you find in Latin America.... *Tel 01 55 78 84 75; 46/48, rue du Faubourg Saint Antoine, 750012, Métro Bastille. Open daily.* $$

**(see p. 52)**

**Berthillon.** The best ice cream in Paris is made on the Ile Saint-Louis and sold almost exclusively in the shop itself, in cafes, and from take-out windows. Expect to wait in line.... *Tel 01 43 54 31 61; 31, rue Saint-Louis-en-l'Ile, 75004, Métro Pont-Marie. Take-out window open Wed–Sun 10am–8pm; cafe open Wed–Fri 1pm–8pm and Sat–Sun 2pm–8pm.*

68

*Closed during school vacations except Christmas.* $
**(see p. 65)**

**Bistrot Beaubourg.** An unpretentious, non-touristy, inexpensive, little restaurant near the Centre Pompidou. Neighborhood residents enjoy simple dishes like beef with carrots or perch with shrimp sauce. Outdoor dining in the summertime.... *Tel 01 42 77 48 02; 25, rue Quincampoix, 75004, Métro Rambuteau. Open daily. AE not accepted.* $ **(see pp. 51, 54, 61)**

**Bistrot d'à Côté.** One of the 3 baby bistros created by big-time chef Michel Rostang; it has a very reasonable, fixed-priced lunch menu, but even in the evening you won't break the bank.... *Tel 01 42 67 05 81; 10, rue Gustave-Flaubert, 75017, Métro Courcelles. Closed Sat lunch and Sun in summer only. Also tel 01 47 63 25 61; 16, ave. Villiers, 75017, Métro Villiers. Closed Sat lunch and Sun.* $$ **(see p. 49)**

**Bistrot...Cote Mer.** Chef Michel Rostang's daughter Caroline runs this popular and reasonably priced fish house with a trendy Breton atmosphere. Start with oysters, followed by the catch of the day, and a killer cocoa souffle for dessert.... *Tel 01 43 54 59 10; 16, blvd Saint Germain, 75005, Métro Maubert-Mutualite. Open daily.* $$ **(see p. 64)**

**Bistrot du Dôme.** The lower-priced bistro of the famous Dôme in Montparnasse also specializes in seafood.... *Tel 01 43 35 32 00; 1, rue Delambre, 75014, Métro Vavin. Open daily.* $$ **(see p. 49)**

**Bofinger.** One of the best Paris brasseries, with its stained-glass dome, sweeping staircase, wood paneling, large mirrors, black banquettes, and potted palms. Specialties include oysters, *choucroute*, and wild duck. Reserve, or arrive before 8pm or after 10pm.... *Tel 01 42 72 87 82; 5–7, rue de la Bastille, 75004, Métro Bastille. Open daily.* $$ **(see pp. 51, 53, 57)**

**Brasserie Lipp.** One of the haunts of former president François Mitterrand and a long list of writers and other celebrities. The classic French food and service, however, are not what they used to be.... *Tel 01 45 48 53 91; 151, blvd Saint-Germain, 75006, Métro Saint-Germain-des-Prés. Open daily except 3 weeks in Aug.* $$ **(see pp. 48, 52)**

DINING | THE INDEX

**Café Beaubourg.** This chic cafe facing the Centre Pompidou serves drinks and slightly upscale cafe fare (*croques-monsieurs*, salads). American-style brunch is served at all times.... *Tel 01 48 87 63 96; 100, rue Saint-Martin, 75004, Métro Rambuteau or Hôtel-de-Ville. Open daily. $* **(see pp. 56, 57)**

**Café de Flore.** A classic cafe with an Art Deco interior, ridiculously high prices, high-quality cafe fare, and great people-watching possibilities.... *Tel 01 45 48 55 26; 172, blvd. Saint-Germain, 75006, Métro Saint-Germain-des-Prés. Open daily. D, DC, MC, V not accepted. $* **(see p. 57)**

**Café Marly.** The "in" place for lunch, dinner, or in-between drinks, located in a wing of the Louvre. The eclectic menu includes gazpacho, Caesar salad, poached haddock, and even a cheeseburger (in the Louvre!).... *Tel 01 49 26 06 60; Cour Napoléon, 93, rue de Rivoli, 75001, Métro Palais-Royal. $$*
**(see pp. 57, 59, 62)**

**Café Very.** A cafe in the Tuileries serving tasty open-face sandwiches and crêpes under the chestnut trees or in the woodsy interior.... *Tel 01 47 03 94 84; Jardin des Tuileries, 75001, Métro Concorde or Tuileries. Open daily. $* **(see pp. 59, 62)**

**Chantairelle.** Relaxed and admirably devoted to its regional calling, which is promoting the food and charms of the Auvergne, this little spot in the Latin Quarter is fine for a tasty filling of dishes like stuffed cabbage and bilberry tart.... *Tel 01 46 33 18 59; 17, rue Laplace, 75005, Métro Maubert-Mutualite. Closed Sun Nov–May. $* **(see p. 62)**

**Chartier.** An enormous *bouillon* (originally, a cheap workers' restaurant that served *pot-au-feu)* that has not changed much since the 19th century. Cheap, acceptable food, brusque service, and tons of atmosphere. No reservations.... *Tel 01 47 70 86 29; 7, rue du Faubourg-Montmartre, 75009, Métro Montmartre. Open daily until 9:30pm. AE not accepted. $* **(see pp. 52, 61)**

**Chez La Vieille.** Come to this preciously fusty old bistro for a deep dose of Paris, the eternal capital of Gaul, which comes from the non-decript cobbled-together decor, the waitresses who continuously baby you, and delicious and abundant old-fashioned French cooking. The assorted hors d'oeuvres alone

are a meal, including help-yourself terrines of duck, head cheese, lentils, veal-stuffed courgettes, avocado and tomato salad with hard-cooked egg wedges, marinated leeks, and a sublime celery remoulade. Follow with a steak, roast chicken, veal braised with green olives, and ewe's-milk-cheese stuffed cannelloni, and wash it down with a bottle of Alzipratu, a fine Corsican red.... *Tel 01 42 60 15 78; 1, rue Bailleul/37, rue de l'Arbre Sec, 75001, Metro Louvre-Rivoli. Open for lunch Mon–Wed, Fri, lunch and dinner on Thursdays. $$*
**(see p. 60)**

**Chez Louisette.** High-camp atmosphere in the Porte de Clignancourt flea market provided by an Edith Piaf imitator and a Gypsy palm reader. Go for a drink, but skip the food.... *Tel 01 40 12 10 14; Marché Vernaison, Métro Porte-de-Clignancourt. Open Sat–Mon noon–8pm. $* **(see p. 60)**

**Chez Michel.** Chef Thierry Breton's scallops in cider and *kouign aman*, a sugared puff pastry served with apple sorbet, make a journey to this slightly dreary part of town worth the effort.... *Tel 01 44 53 06 20; 10, rue de Belzunce, 75010, Métro Gare du Nord. Visa only. Closed Sat lunch and Sun. $$* **(see p. 50)**

**Chez Nénesse.** A little neighborhood bistro that serves inexpensive lunches like roast lamb shoulder with white beans or pork ribs with lentils. In the evening, the menu becomes more sophisticated and the prices somewhat higher.... *Tel 01 42 78 46 49; 17, rue de Saintonge, 75003, Métro Arts-et-Métiers. Closed Sat, Sun, and Aug. AE, D, DC, MC not accepted. $ (lunch), $$ (dinner)* **(see p. 62)**

**Chez Omar.** A trendy north African restaurant with marvelous old bistro decor that needs a coat of paint. The couscous and grilled meats are very good and bargain priced.... *Tel 01 42 72 36 26; 47, rue de Bretagne, 75003, Métro Filles de Calvaire. Closed Sun lunch. No credit cards. $* **(see p. 60)**

**Clown Bar.** One of the best wine bars in the city. Circus decor, excellent, market-fresh French food, and well-chosen wine list. Reserve.... *Tel 01 43 55 87 35; 114, rue Amelot, 75011, Métro Filles-de-Calvaire. Closed Sun and part of Aug. No credit cards. $* **(see pp. 53, 59)**

**Coffee Parisien.** A hip, young crowd heavy on aspiring models comes to this little restaurant to sample the perfectly prepared

American fare, including hamburgers, eggs Benedict, and cheesecake.... *Tel 01 43 54 18 18; 4, rue Princess, 75006, Métro Mabillon. Open daily. $*     **(see pp. 56, 60)**

**Coude de Fou.** A popular restaurant in the Marais. Daily specials might include *salade de boudin frit* (salad with fried blood sausage) or an *entrecôte* steak with blue-cheese sauce. A special 2-course menu is offered between midnight and 12:45am. Reserve.... *Tel 01 42 77 15 16; 12, rue du Bourg-Tibourg, 75004, Métro Hôtel-de-Ville. Closed Sun lunch. $*
**(see p. 51)**

**Dame Tartine.** Two restaurants serving creative *tartines* (open-face sandwiches) with toppings like smoked duck with wilted lettuce, chicken with almonds and cinnamon, or beef with artichoke and hazelnut cream.... *Bastille: Tel 01 44 68 96 95; 59, rue de Lyon, 75012, Métro Bastille. Centre Pompidou: Tel 01 42 77 32 22; 2, rue Brisemiche, 75004, Métro Rambuteau. Open daily. AE not accepted. $*     **(see pp. 54, 62)**

**Djakarta Bali.** Tucked away in a side street near Les Halles, this superb Indonesian restaurant, with its pretty decor and gracious service, is a great opportunity to discover the delicious and relatively little-known cuisine of this island republic. Start with the *soto ayam,* a delicate soup of chicken broth, rice noodles and vegetables, and *lumpia,* fried homemade spring rolls served with a fresh peanut sauce, and then try *rendang daging,* beef in coconut milk seasoned with Indonesian herbs and *ayam jahe,* carmelized chicken in ginger sauce.... *Tel 01 45 08 83 11; 9, rue Vauvilliers, 75001, Métro Louvre or Les Halles. Dinner only. Closed Monday. $–$$*     **(see p. 60)**

**Fogon St-Julien.** This little vest-pocket place with stone walls in the Latin Quarter serves delicious paella in several different variations. Friendly service and a laid-back crowd make it a fun night out.... *Tel 01 43 54 31 33; 10, rue St-Julien-le-Pauvre, 75005, Métro St-Michel. Closed Sun. AE not accepted. $$.*
**(see p. 60)**

**404.** One of the best Moroccan restaurants in town. Ask for a seat on the tiny mezzanine, reached via a treacherous, winding staircase. The *pastilla* (pigeon in a flaky pastry crust dusted with cinnamon) is fantastic, as are the couscous and tajines. Reserve. Brunch on weekends.... *Tel 01 42 74 57 81; 69, rue des Grav-*

DINING | THE INDEX

illiers, 75003, Métro Arts-et-Métiers. Open daily. Closed 3 weeks in Aug. $$ (see p. 56)

**Garnier.** As the city's remaining independent brasseries become an increasingly scarcer breed, Garnier soldiers on, and having recently been renovated with a decor that's slightly flashy mix of modern and Art Deco, it's better than ever. This place specializes in seafood—note the charming little oyster bar just inside the front door.... Tel 01 43 87 50 40; 111, rue Saint Lazare, 75008, Metro St-Lazare. Open daily. $$ (see pp. 57, 64)

**Georges.** One of the hippest restaurants in town, with a gorgeous crowd of posers who come to nibble at dishes like shrimp tempura, monkfish with tandoori spices, and smoked salmon. This place really rocks at night.... Tel 01 44 78 47 99; Centre Pompidou, rue Rambuteau and rue Saint Merri, 75004, Métro Rambuteau or Hotel de Ville. Open daily. $$ (see pp. 51, 54, 64)

**Ghislaine Arabian.** Several years after leaving Ledoyen, Ghislaine Arabian, one of the most talented female chefs in France, has opened a superb new restaurant on a quiet street in a laced-up part of town. Arabian is clearly happy to be back at work, which shows in dishes like bechamel-sauce-and-gray-shrimp croquettes with fried parsley—a true Belgian classic—and a spectacular millefeuille of fresh vegetables.... Tel 01 56 28 16 16; 16, ave Bugeaud, 75116, Métro Victor Hugo. Closed Sat–Sun. $$$$ (see pp. 56, 63)

**Guy Savoy.** Blond wood and modern paintings and sculptures brighten the dining room of Guy Savoy, who some call the best chef in Paris. His desserts, especially the crème brulée with apples, are heavenly. Reserve.... Tel 01 43 80 40 61; 18, rue Troyon, 75017, Métro Etoile. Closed Sat lunch and Sun. MC not accepted. $$$$ (see p. 49)

**Helene Darroze.** As her recently minted Michelin star attests, Helene Darroze is the newest female culinary star in Paris. The short menu changes regularly, but leads off with 3 different preparations of foie gras, and runs to dishes like roasted free-range chicken from Les Landes and red mullet with a tomato risotto in beef juice with black olives. The bistro on the main floor is cheaper and more casual than the pricey, stylish main table upstairs.... Tel 01 42 22 00 11; 4, rue d'Assas, 75006, Métro Sevres-Babylone. Closed Sun. $$$$ (see p. 56)

**Il Baccello.** Young chef Raphael Bembaron is a real talent who trained at Joia, the superb gourmet vegetarian restaurant in Milan. Standout specials like a chick pea soup garnished with pancetta-wrapped langoustines.... *Tel 01 43 80 63 60; 33, rue Cardinet, 75017, Métro Wagram. Closed Sun. AE not accepted.* $$ **(see pp. 60, 63)**

**Julien.** A gorgeous Art-Nouveau restaurant with quality brasserie fare.... *Tel 01 47 70 12 06; 16, rue du Faubourg-Saint-Denis, 75010, Métro Strasbourg-Saint-Denis. Open daily.* $$ **(see pp. 48, 52)**

**Juveniles.** An English-owned wine bar. The sausage and mashed potatoes with chutney is an example of a classic French dish (*saucisson avec purée de pommes de terre*) with a twist. Wines can be purchased to go.... *Tel 01 42 97 46 49; 47, rue de Richelieu, 75001, Métro Palais-Royal. Open Mon–Sat. AE not accepted.* $ **(see p. 60)**

**Laduree.** This elegant 1862 vintage tearoom in the heart of town not only serves weepingly good pastries but is a fine way to skip out on a lousy hotel breakfast, since its coffee and croissants are wonderful, too. The new branch on the Champs-Elysées (*Tel 01 40 75 08 75; 75, ave des Champs-Elysées, 75008, Métro Franklin-D.-Roosevelt*) pulls a trendy crowd, while the original pulls grande dames on a shopping spree.... *Tel 01 42 60 21 79; 16, rue Royale, 75008, Métro Concorde or Madeleine. Open daily.* $$ **(see p. 65)**

**L'Astrance.** Occupying a surprisingly edgy space in a part of town that's anything but, this is one of the better restaurants to open in Paris for a while. Chef Pascal Barbot formerly worked at 3-sparkler Arpege in Paris and Ampersand in Sydney, and this experience shows in shrewd, chic, minimalist, and absolutely delicious dishes like baked mussels with a Moroccan style salad of grated carrots; scallops in peanut cream sauce; red mullet cooked in a banana leaf and served with a superb tamarind sauce and a gratin of bananas. For dessert, try the de-constructed apple crumble and milk ice cream with pain perdu. Book well in advance.... *Tel 01 40 50 84 40; 4, rue Beethoven, 75116, Métro Mo Passy. Closed Sun–Mon.* $$–$$$ **(see p. 50)**

**L'Avant Gout.** Check out this noisy, crowded storefront bistro to sample the excellent cooking of rising star chef Christophe

DINING | THE INDEX

Beaufort. It may be short on atmosphere, but it's a great value for the money, there are good, cheap house wines, and the natives are friendly.... *Tel 01 53 80 24 00; 26, rue Bobillot, 13th, Métro Place d Italie. Closed Sun, Mon. $*   **(see p. 50)**

**L'Ebauchoir.** Simple decor and French cuisine with a touch of creativity: onion soup, escargots, raw sardines stuffed with minced vegetables, and tuna steak with orange sauce. Lively ambience and friendly service. Can get very noisy in the evening. Inexpensive, fixed-price lunch menu.... *Tel 01 43 42 49 31; 43–45, rue de Citeaux, 75012, Métro Faidherbe-Chaligny. Closed Sun. AE, D, DC, MC not accepted. $*   **(see p. 61)**

**L'Espadon.** With the arrival of chef Michel Roth, most recently at Lasserre, one of the most sumptuous dining rooms anywhere in the world is yet again one of the best restaurants in Paris, with service so precise and graceful that it's sort of a cross between a classical ballet and a Prussian artillery troop drill. Most importantly, the food's so good that it obviously warrants a second star. Don't miss the lobster salad, veal chop with a crust of polenta, and the best millefeuille in town. *Tel 01 43 16 30 80; Hotel Ritz, 15, place Vendome, 75001, Metro Madeleine or Concorde. Open daily. $$$$–$$$$$*   **(see pp. 48, 63)**

**La Baracane.** Ignore the drab decor for some really good southwestern French cooking. This place is the bistro annex of Chef Michel Baudis, a talented chef whose main table is lost in space near Bercy. The *prix-fixe* menus here are an excellent buy.... *Tel 01 42 71 43 33; 38, rue des Tournelles, 75004, Métro Bastille. Closed Sun. $*   **(see p. 54)**

**La Boulangerie.** This quiet corner of the trendy Ménilmontant district is the setting for some of the finest cheap bistro food in eastern Paris. The 3-course *prix fixe* is the way to go, too. Typical dishes run to a croustade of wild mushrooms, remoulade of mussels, salmon in sherry-spiked onion cream sauce, and yellow plum and caramel millefeuille. The nothing-over-25 euros wine list offers good drinking, including St- Emilion and other faves.... *Tel. 01 43 58 45 45; 15, rue des Panoyaux, 75020, Métro Ménilmontant. Closed Sun dinner. $*   **(see p. 61)**

**La Cagouille.** Excellent seafood restaurant. The meal starts with a complimentary dish of sublime cockles in melted butter and continues with generous portions of fresh fish, perfectly prepared.... *Tel 01 43 22 09 01; 10, place Constantin Brancusi, 75014, Métro Gaité. Closed Dec 23–Jan 3. MC not accepted.* $$ **(see pp. 59, 64)**

**La Cloche d'Or.** A late-night Pigalle area restaurant frequented by actors. Relaxed atmosphere and simple food like onion soup, sole meunière, and mussels (*moules*).... *Tel 01 48 74 48 88; 3, rue Mansart, 75009, Métro Blanche. Dinner only. Open until 4am. Closed Sun and Aug.* $$ **(see p. 51)**

**La Coupole.** The famous hangout of everyone from Ernest Hemingway to Fernand Léger still merits a visit for its ambience.... *Tel 01 43 20 14 20; 102, blvd Montparnasse, 75014, Métro Montparnasse. Open daily except Christmas Eve.* $$
**(see pp. 48, 52)**

**La Ferme Saint-Simon.** Media types and politicians indulge in such delicacies as warm pigeon salad with *fois gras* vinagrette.... *Tel 01 45 48 35 74; 6, rue Saint-Simon, 75007, Métro rue du Bac. Closed Sat lunch, Sun.* $$$
**(see p. 56)**

**La Grande Cascade.** Restored Belle Epoque restaurant at the foot of a waterfall in the Bois de Boulogne. Classic menu features specialties like duckling with sweet-and-sour sauce and ginger and crab ravioli with chervil. Reserve.... *Tel 01 45 27 33 51; Bois de Boulogne, Allée de Longchamp, 75016, Métro Porte-Maillot, then bus 144 (until 8pm; taxi necessary thereafter). Open daily. Closed Dec 20–Jan 20.* $$$$$
**(see p. 59)**

**La Maison Blanche.** Located on the 6th floor of the Théâtre des Champs-Elysées, this trendy modern restaurant, now run by the Pourcel brothers, the 3-star culinary duo from Montpelier, serves dishes like roast kidneys with macaroni gratin and bass tartare made with olive oil and served with sun-dried tomatoes. Great views of Paris and a large terrace. Reserve.... *Tel 01 47 23 55 99; 15, ave Montaigne, 75008, Métro Alma-Marceau. Closed Sat lunch, Sun, and Aug.* $$$$
**(see pp. 56, 59, 63, 64)**

**La Regalade.** This hugely successful place has evolved from delighting neighborhood locals to attracting an international mink-coat crowd. Chef Yves Camdeborde is a veteran of the Crillon, and his credentials shine in dishes like his gratin of pota-

DINING | THE INDEX

toes and lobster.... *Tel 01 45 45 68 58; 49, ave Jean-Moulin, 75014, Métro Alesia. Closed Sat lunch and Mon. AE, D, DC, MC not accepted. $$* **(see p. 50)**

**La Table d'Aude.** Charming owner Bernard Patou and his wife Veronique take a contagious pleasure in serving up the best of their home turf, the Aude, a long narrow *department* in the Languedoc-Roussillon that includes Carcassonne, Castel-naudry—famed for its *cassoulet* and some of the most rapidly ascending vineyards in France, including Minervois and Cor-bieres.... *Tel 01 43 26 36 36; 8, rue de Vaugirard, 75006, Métro Odeon or RER Luxembourg. Closed Sun. AE not accepted. $* **(see p. 56)**

**La Table de Lucullus.** Though the stucco-slathered walls will seem inauspicious, this vest-pocket bistro is home to one of the most promising young chefs in Paris, Nicholas Vagnon. His style runs to highly original dishes like langoustine carpaccio; *foie gras,* brilliantly garnished with rhubarb compote, radishes, sea salt and asparagus; and haddock with artichoke hearts in a lemon-juice-and-olive-oil emulsion.... *Tel 01 40 25 02 58; 129, rue Legendre, 75017, Métro La Fourche. Closed Sun–Mon. $$*
**(see pp. 43, 50)**

**La Tartine.** An ancient wine bar with an ancient owner. A great place for an aperitif and a tartine topped with pâté, rillettes, or cantal.... *Tel 01 42 72 76 85; 24, rue de Rivoli, Métro Hôtel-de-Ville or Saint-Paul. Open until 10pm. Closed Tue, Wed morning, and 2 weeks in Aug. No credit cards. $* **(see p. 59)**

**La Tour d'Argent.** Everyone knows about the fabulous views of Notre-Dame, the famous duckling, and the charming owner, Claude Terrail. They don't always know about the pretentious atmosphere, the ho-hum food, and the fact that a plate of gussied-up scrambled eggs goes for $70.... *Tel 01 43 54 23 31, fax 01 44 07 12 04; 15, quai Tournelle, 75005, Métro Maubert-Mutualité. Closed Mon. $$$$$* **(see pp. 48, 64)**

**La Tour de Montlhery.** If you agree that feasting on country paté and juicy lambs chops in the dead of night is a particularly Parisian pleasure, this is the place for you. Open 24 hours. This old market bistro has loads of scruffy charm and is just as pleasant during regular dining hours. Reservations essential.... *Tel 01 42 36 21 82; 5, rue des Prouvaires, 75001, Métro*

DINING | THE INDEX

*Chatelet. Closed Sat, Sun and July 14–Aug 15. AE not accepted. $$*  **(see p. 52)**

**La Ville de Jagannath.** Though it's a bit off the beaten track, this Indian vegetarian place is extremely popular for its excellent southern Indian cooking. This place pulls a trendy crowd in what's become one of the last affordable neighborhoods in central Paris for young hipsters, and one of the owners is English if you're fumbling in French…. *Tel 01 43 55 80 81; 101, rue St. Maur, Métro St. Maur. Open Daily. $*  **(see p. 63)**

**Le Bar à Huîtres.** A chain restaurant that serves good, fresh seafood, including oysters and lobster, at reasonable prices…. *Tel 01 48 87 98 92; 33, blvd Beaumarchais, 75003, Métro Bastille. Also tel 01 44 07 27 37; 33, rue Saint-Jacques, 75005, Métro Saint-Michel. Open daily until 2am. $$*  **(see p. 64)**

**Le Balzar.** There's always a great buzz in this vest-pocket Left Bank brasserie, which, in spite of tourist popularity, remains much beloved by a frisky and diverse crowd of Parisians. Everybody from headbound academics to fashion designers loves this place for its friendly, aproned waiters, reliable cooking, and uber Parisian atmosphere. Strategically placed ceiling mirrors allow you to scan the whole room, which gives the place an amusing edge. Great choucroute garni (sauerkraut and pork), onion soup, and roast chicken…. *Tel 01 43 54 13 67; 49, rue des Ecoles, 5th, Métro Cluny-La Sorbonne. Open daily. $$*  **(see p. 57)**

**Le Baron Rouge.** This little wine bar is the place to go after Sunday morning shopping at the Marché d'Aligre. Try the *délice de canard*, a fantastic duck pâté, with a glass of red wine…. *Tel 01 43 43 14 32; 1, rue Théophile-Roussel, 75012, Métro Ledru-Rollin. Open 10am–2pm and 5pm–9:30pm. Closed Mon. AE not accepted. $*  **(see p. 59)**

**Le Boeuf sur le Toit.** This busy Art Deco restaurant serves classic brasserie fare of good quality, as do all the restaurants that are part of the Flo Tradition chain…. *Tel 01 43 59 83 80; 34, rue du Colisée, 75008, Métro Saint-Philippe-du-Roule. Open daily except Christmas Eve. $$*  **(see pp. 51, 57)**

**Le Bristol.** This grande dame is a shrewd player in the local gastro-

nomic sweepstakes, since it promptly hired culinary wunderkind Eric Frechon to replace Michel del Burgo when he went
off to Taillevent. The food's sublime, and it plays a real full house
of luxury by having a summer dining room in its inner courtyard
and a winter one with stunning Hungarian oak panelling and
crystal chandeliers.... *Tel 01 53 43 43 00; Hôtel Bristol, 112,
rue Faubourg-Saint-Honoré, 75008, Métro Miromesnil. Open
daily. $$$$* **(see pp. 48, 58)**

**Le Buddha Bar.** Buddha himself surely never suspected that he'd
be at the heart of a busy singles scene.... Better for drinks than
dinner, but the bar snacks are fine.... *Tel 01 53 05 90 00; 8,
rue Boissy d'Anglas, 75008, Métro Concorde. Open daily. $$*
**(see pp. 48, 52)**

**Le Cap Vernet.** Guy Savoy's lunch menu (32 euros) at this baby
bistro includes wine and coffee. Also available: a variety of
starters and main courses as well as salads, shellfish platters,
and great fish.... *Tel 01 47 20 20 40; 82, ave Marceau,
75008, Métro Etoile. Open daily. $$* **(see p. 49)**

**Le Cinq.** Chef Philippe Legendre, formerly at Taillevent, has
apparently been given carte blanche with luxury ingredients
like caviar, lobster, and foie gras. Typical grub here is a delicious lasagna of langoustines between two gossamer sheets
of pasta accented with Parmesan and lime zest. Service is
friendly and earnest but often slow.... *Tel 01 49 52 70 00;
31, ave George V, 75008, Métro George V. Open daily.
$$$$$* **(see p. 58)**

**Le Fumoir.** An intriguing mix of hip Parisians and Euro-lounger
types comes to linger over coffee or eat relatively good food
in a setting of book-lined walls that recall the great cafes of
Mitteleuropa, French colonial Indochina, and the American
Thirties.... *Tel 01 42 92 00 24; place du Louvre, 6, rue de
l'Amiral-Coligny, 75001, Métro Louvre. Open daily until
2am. $$* **(see p. 54)**

**Le Grand Véfour.** Michelin just jacked this grande dame up to 3
stars, but while chef Guy Martin's cooking is great it's not *that*
great. Gorgeous decor, though.... *Tel 01 42 96 56 27; 17, rue
Beaujolais, 75001, Métro Palais-Royal. Closed Sat, Sun, and
Aug. $$$$$* **(see p. 54)**

**Le Jules Verne.** Stunning views of the city from the second floor of the Eiffel Tower. Chef Alain Reix's dishes include rockfish ravioli with mushrooms and artichokes, and new vegetables in puff pastry with morel butter. Reservations are a must.... *Tel 01 45 55 61 44, fax 01 47 05 29 41; 2nd floor, Eiffel Tower, 75007, Métro Trocadéro. Open daily. Closed last 2 weeks of July and 1st week of Aug. $$$$$*          **(see p. 64)**

**Le Montalembert.** Frequented by businesspeople and Left Bank literary and arty types. The international menu includes dishes like deep-fried shrimp with sesame, ginger, and Hoisin sauce, and gnocchi gratin with basil salad.... *Tel 01 45 48 68 11, fax 01 42 22 58 19; 3, rue Montalembert, 75007, Métro rue du Bac. Open daily. $$*          **(see p. 62)**

**Le Moulin à Vin.** A little Montmartre wine bar with simple, good, reasonably priced food.... *Tel 01 42 52 81 27; 6, rue Burq, 75018, Métro Abbesses. Closed Sun, Mon, lunchtime Wed and Thur, and 3 weeks in Aug. $–$$*          **(see pp. 55, 59, 60)**

**Le Petit Keller.** This vintage '50s Bastille spot with friendly tongue-in-cheek waiters and delicious home-cooked dishes like roast guinea hen and duck breast with honey is constantly packed with locals. An added bonus are the very reasonable prices.... *Tel 01 47 00 12 97; 13, rue Keller, 75011, Métro Ledru-Rollin. Closed Sun. AE not accepted. $*          **(see p. 61)**

**Le Petit Marseillais.** This cozy, happy little place run by two child-hood friends from Marseilles is a trendy word-of-mouth hit with the locals. The menu runs to appealing Marseillais home-cooking like starters of sauteed *pleurottes* (oyster mushrooms) with garlic and parsley followed by main courses like tagliatelle with pistou sauce.... *Tel 01 42 78 91 59; 72, rue Vieille-du-Temple, 75003, Métro Rambuteau. Open daily. $–$$*
          **(see pp. 51, 54)**

**Le Petit Saint-Benoît.** An inexpensive bistro in the Saint-Germain-des-Prés area. The menu includes French classics like beef stew with carrots and *blanquette de veau*. Sidewalk dining in nice weather.... *Tel 01 42 60 27 92; 4, rue Saint-Benoît, 75006, Métro Saint-Germain-des-Prés. Closed Sat, Sun, and 3 weeks in Aug. No credit cards. $*          **(see pp. 55, 61)**

**Le Pré Catalan.** The regulars tend to eat inside, but there is little that can match the pleasure of eating outside here amid the emerald green grass and flowers on a balmy summer evening.

Chef Frederic Anton brings a modern touch to dishes like roast duck with tamarind or black risotto with scampi, flavored with Thai basil and citronella. The service is faultless. Reserve.... *Tel 01 45 24 55 58; route de Suresnes, 75016, Métro Porte-Maillot, then bus 144 (until 8pm; taxi necessary thereafter). Closed Sun evening, Mon, and during Feb school vacation.* $$$$$ **(see pp. 58, 63)**

**Le Reconfort.** An international fashion crowd loves this friendly, attractive place on the northern fringes of the trendy Marais neighborhood.... *Tel 01 42 76 06 36; 37, rue de Poitou, 75003, Métro St. Sebastian-Froissart. Closed Sun and Mon.* $$ **(see p. 54)**

**Le Relais Plaza.** The more casual restaurant in the Plaza Athénée hotel still has its original Art-Deco decor. The menu features everything from salads, omelettes, and pasta to grilled meats and seafood.... *Tel 01 47 23 78 33; Plaza Athénée, 25, ave Montaigne, 75008, Métro Franklin-D.-Roosevelt. Closed in Aug.* $$$ **(see pp. 53, 62)**

**Le Reminet.** Chandeliers and mirrors accent the old stone walls of this cozy bistro with a friendly young staff. The *prix-fixe* menus at both lunch and dinner are very good value and include dishes like a salt-cod fillet on a bed of braised endive in a sauce of honey and lemon.... *Tel 01 44 07 04 24; 3, rue des Grands-Degres, 75005, Métro Maubert-Mutualité. Closed Mon and Tues lunch. AE not accepted.* $$ **(see p. 62)**

**Le Repaire de Cartouche.** Tucked away between the Place de la Republique and the Bastille, this cozy bistro is popular for the sensational cooking of young chef Rodolphe Paquin, and its easy prices and friendly service.... *Tel 01 47 00 25 80; 8, blvd des Filles-du-Calvaire, 75011, Métro St. Sebastien-Froissart. Closed Sun.* $$ **(see p. 50)**

**Le Train Bleu.** Though this landmarked dining room has always been one of the most romantic restaurants in Paris, for years the food was so drab that it was only worth coming for a drink. Now, under new management, they're serving delicious traditional French grub like a veal chop with a cap of melted cheese and lobster salad on a bed of walnut-oil-dressed mixed leaves.... *Tel 01 43 43 09 06; Gare de Lyon, 20, blvd Diderot, 75012, Métro Gare de Lyon.* $$ **(see p. 53)**

**Le Vaudeville.** The wonderful Art-Deco decor, the reflections in the mirrors, the huge bright flower arrangements, the speedy but cheerful waiters, and the general hustle and bustle make eating here a nearly total Paris experience. Reservations are a must.... *Tel 01 40 20 04 62; 29, rue Vivienne, 75002, Métro Bourse. Open daily. $$* **(see pp. 51, 57)**

**Le Voltaire.** This meeting place for Left Bank publishers has a clubby, Old World atmosphere. The food is not out of the ordinary, but good and reliable.... *Tel 01 42 61 17 49; 27, quai Voltaire, 75007, Métro Solferino. Closed Sun–Mon. AE, D, DC, MC not accepted. $$$* **(see p. 63)**

**Ledoyen.** Talented young chef Christophe LeSquer runs this restaurant set among the chestnut trees of the Champs-Elysées. Specialties include grilled wild salmon with red pepper mousse, carmelized roast duck, and, for dessert, passionfruit soufflée.... *Tel 01 47 42 35 98; carré des Champs-Elysées, 75008, Métro Champs-Elysées-Clemenceau. Closed Sat–Sun. $$$$*
**(see pp. 49, 62)**

**Les Ambassadeurs.** The elegant marble-lined restaurant in the Hôtel Crillon offers the acclaimed cuisine of Dominique Bouchet: traditional dishes with a modern touch. Specialties include crispy bass with sesame seeds and mullet roasted in fennel oil served with a tomato-mozzarella tart.... *Tel 01 44 71 16 16; Hôtel Crillon, 10, place de la Concorde, 75008, Métro Concorde. Open daily. $$$$* **(see pp. 53, 58)**

**Les Elysées du Vernet.** In addition to chef Alain Soliveres's splendid cooking, this handsome hotel dining room not only has a restful far-from-the-maddening-crowd feel—even though it's just a few steps off the Champs-Elysées—but superlative service, right down to the parting gift of a long-stemmed rose for ladies and a sachet of carmelized nuts for gents.... *Tel 01 44 31 98 00; Hôtel Vernet, 25, rue Vernet, 75008, Métro George V. Closed weekends and Aug. $$$$* **(see pp. 49, 53, 58, 63)**

**Les Ormes.** It's worth the trip to a re,ote part of the 16th to discover the cooking of talented young chef Stephane Mole, who trained with Joel Robuchon—and it shows. His lusty and refined cooking runs to dishes like John Dory with wild mushrooms and artichokes hearts.... *Tel 01 46 47 83 98, 8 rue Chapu, 75016, Métro Exelmans. Closed Sun–Mon. $$*
**(see pp. 50, 62)**

**Lo Sushi.** This cool elf-service sushi bar is a fast alternative to another boring cafe salad, and the quality of the sushi, sashimi, California rolls, makis, and tekamakis is pretty decent. Prepare to wait in line.... *Tel 01 45 62 01 00; 8, rue de Berri, 75008, Métro George V. Open daily. $–$$* **(see p. 55)**

**Lucas-Carton.** Art Nouveau decor, a helpful staff and some of the finest cuisine in the city. Specialties include wild rice risotto with chanterelles, *homard à la vanille*, and *foie gras* with cabbage, and for dessert, *gâteau au chocolat croustillant*. Reserve at least 3 weeks in advance.... *Tel 01 42 65 22 90, fax 01 42 65 06 23; 9, place de la Madeleine, 75008, Métro Madeleine. Closed July, three weeks in Aug, Sat lunch, and Sun. $$$$$* **(see pp. 48, 53, 62)**

**Man Ray.** The decor here at this vast sunken space is tastier than the food, but that doesn't stop a dressed-in-black crowd from settling in on the low arm chairs and banquettes for dishes like duck with lychees or sushi—the menu is variously Asian.... *Tel 01 56 88 36 36; 34, rue Marbeuf, 75008, Métro Franklin-D.-Roosevelt. Open daily. $$* **(see pp. 52, 56)**

**Marais Plus.** See Shopping. **(see p. 56)**

**Market.** Jean-Georges Vongerichten stars at this furiously popular Euro-Asian fusion spot in the glamorous new Christie's building in the 8th arrondissement just off the Champs-Elysées. If you've been to any of his other restaurants, from Hong Kong to London or Las Vegas, you know the Franco-Asian gig.... *Tel 01 56 43 40 90; 15, ave Matignon, 75008, Metro Champs-Elysées-Clemenceau. Closed Mon. $$.* **(see p. 51)**

**Maxim's.** Mediocre brasserie-style food at extreme prices in an authentic Art-Nouveau setting.... *Tel 01 42 65 27 94; 3, rue Royale, 75008, Métro Concorde. Open Mon–Fri until 10:30. $$$$$* **(see pp. 48, 52)**

**Nobu.** This slick new place has hit the same nerve with self-conscious fashion types as the other branches of Nobu (this is, of course, the fourth major Nobu around the globe. The difference is that in the still rather staid context of Paris, the jazzy flavors and textures of chef Matsuhisa Nobuyuki's stylish hybrid Peruvian-Japanese cooking are wild and hugely welcome. Try the tempura of Florida rock shrimp, sublime sushi and sashimi, and miso-marinated black cod.... *Tel 01 56 89 53 53; 15, rue Marbeuf, 75008, Métro Franklin-D.-Roosevelt. $$$.*

**(see pp. 51, 55, 63)**

**Paul Minchelli.** Chef Paul Minchelli, formerly of once-great Le Duc, demonstrates that good fish cooking is about precision in cooking times and seasoning. Try the baby clams with hot peppers and the sea bass. If you're traveling alone, book to eat at the bar.... *Tel 01 47 05 89 86; 54, blvd de Latour-Maubourg, 75007, Métro Ecole Militaire. Closed Sun–Mon. AE, D, DC, MC not accepted. $$$$*

**(see pp. 56, 64)**

**Piccolo Teatro.** Tasty vegetarian gratins are served in a pleasant, slightly hippie-ish atmosphere.... *Tel 01 42 72 17 79; 6, rue des Ecouffes, 75004, Métro Saint-Paul. Closed Mon, Tue, and Aug. MC not accepted. $*

**(see p. 63)**

**Pierre Gagnaire.** Pierre Gagnaire is an extraordinary cook. Go to his cobalt blue dining room for veal sweetbreads roasted with cardamom and coffee, served with a fondue of endives and cigarette-like rolls of toasted eggplant.... *Tel 01 44 35 18 25; 6, rue Balzac, 75008, Métro George V. Closed Sat, Sun lunch, and Aug. $$$$$*

**(see pp. 48, 62)**

**Polidor.** A shabby, old restaurant with good, cheap food, and charming service. Try the escargots, the duck, the *blanquette de veau*, or the *boeuf bourguignon*.... *Tel 01 43 26 95 34; 41, rue Monsieur-le-Prince, 75006, Métro Odéon. Open daily. No credit cards. $–$$*

**(see p. 55)**

**Prunier.** The lavish Art-Deco mosaics add glamour to a meal at this luxury restaurant near the Arc de Triomphe, where caviar stars. French caviar from the Gironde River near Bordeaux is excellent and less expensive than anything Russian or Iranian. The smoked salmon and baked potato with caviar are heaven, too, and there's a great list of vodkas served iced in carafes.... *Tel 01 44 17 35 85; 16, ave Victor Hugo, 75016, Métro Charles-de-Gaulle-Etoile. Closed Sun, Mon lunch, and August. $$$$–$$$$$*

**(see p. 63)**

**Quai Ouest.** This vast, airy warehouse-type space is industrial chic, with rough plank flooring, aluminium lights, and a fashionable clientele. The Sunday brunch is great for children, and dishes

DINING | THE INDEX

like scrambled eggs with smoked salmon are nicely done.... *Tel 01 46 02 35 54; 1200, Quai Marchel-Dassault, 92210 St-Cloud, Métro Pont de St-Cloud. Open daily. $$* **(see p. 56)**

**Restaurant du Palais-Royal.** This restaurant looks out upon the gardens of the Palais-Royal; some tables are actually in the peaceful gardens. A sampling from the menu: tuna carpaccio and cod with tomatoes and olive oil.... *Tel 01 40 20 00 27; 110, Galerie de Valois, Jardins du Palais-Royal, 75001, Métro Palais-Royal. Closed Sat lunch and Sun. $$* **(see pp. 59, 64)**

**Restaurant Petrossian.** Occupying an elegant dove-gray dining room over the boutique of this famous supplier of caviar and smoked fish, this is the place for anyone looking to encounter some delicious and thrillingly out-there cooking. Chef Philippe Conticini won his 1st Michelin star this year for sublime dishes like smoked salmon with white-salmon sorbet and smoked swordfish with a compote of corn and a ragout of turnips. Desserts are amazing, too, including "Teaser, Five explosions of taste," a colorful mixture of fruit coulis, jellies, and creams garnished with sugared pistachios.... *Tel 01 44 11 32 32; 18, blvd de La Tour Maubourg, 75007, Metro Invalides or La Tour Maubourg. Closed Sat lunch and Sun. $$$–$$$$*

**(see p. 47)**

**Rue Balzac.** Chef Michel Rostang and fading rocker Johnny Hallyday (it's a French thing) have created this stylish new bistro that offers tempting modern French food like a truffle sandwich. The decor's a bit clownish, but the crowd's interesting.... *Tel 01 53 89 90 91; 8, rue Lord-Byron, 75008, Métro George V. Closed Sun. $$$* **(see p. 49)**

**Spoon, Food and Wine.** This extremely popular World Food bistro pulls a lot of models and media people along with a surprising following of middle-aged voyeurs who come for the thrill of eating such unknown delicacies as barbecued spare ribs and charred squid with a curry dipping sauce, washed down with, *Mon Dieu*, a Californian wine. Reserve well in advance.... *Tel 01 40 76 34 44; 14, rue Marignan, 75008, Métro Franklin-D.-Roosevelt. $$–$$$* **(see pp. 49, 55, 56)**

**Terminus Nord.** If you are starving when you arrive at the Gare du Nord from London via the Chunnel, you can't go wrong with the Terminus Nord, a classic brasserie serving shellfish, *choucroute*, grilled meats, and fish in handsome decor dating from

1925.... *Tel 01 42 85 05 15; 23, rue de Dunkerque, 75010, Métro Gare du Nord. Open daily. $$* **(see pp. 51, 57)**

**Willi's Wine Bar.** A British-owned wine bar and restaurant. Willi's has become a fashionable institution, with an excellent selection of wines and nouvelle-ish cuisine.... *Tel 01 42 61 05 09; 13, rue des Petits-Champs, 75001, Métro Bourse. Closed Sun. AE not accepted. $$* **(see p. 60)**

**Ze Kitchen Galerie.** Okay, the name is unfortunate, but this new place next door to tourist-trail pit stop Les Bookinistes is excellent—an attractive modern bistro with a good menu that's organized around four themes: soup, "cru" (raw, as in fish), pasta, and *a la plancha* (grilled).... *Tel 01 44 32 00 32; 4, rue des Grands-Augustins, 75006, Métro Saint-Michel. Closed Sun; Sat dinner only. $.* **(see p. 49)**

# Left Bank Dining

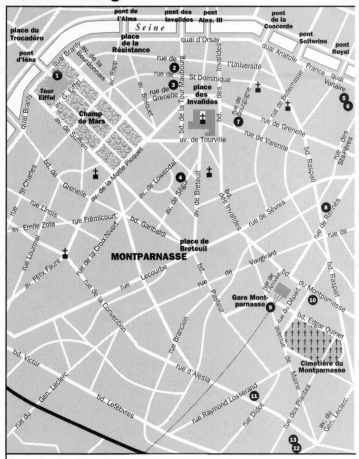

| | |
|---|---|
| Aquarius **11** | Fogon St-Julien **23** |
| Arpège **7** | Helene Darroze **8** |
| Bistrot...Cote Mer **25** | L'Avant Gout **27** |
| Brasserie Lipp **16** | La Cagouille **9** |
| Café de Flore **15** | La Coupole **10** |
| Chantairelle **26** | La Regalade **13** |
| Coffee Parisien **17** | La Table d'Aude **21** |

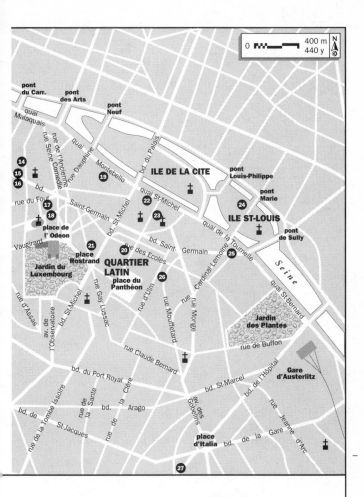

La Tour d'Argent **12**

Le Balzar **20**

Le Bistrot d'à Côte **24**

Le Jules Verne **1**

Le Montalembert **6**

Le Petit Saint Benoit **14**

Le Reminet **22**

Le Voltaire **5**

Les Olivades **4**

Paul Minchelli **2**

Polidor **18**

Restaurant Petrossian **3**

Ze Kitchen Galerie **19**

88

# Right Bank Dining

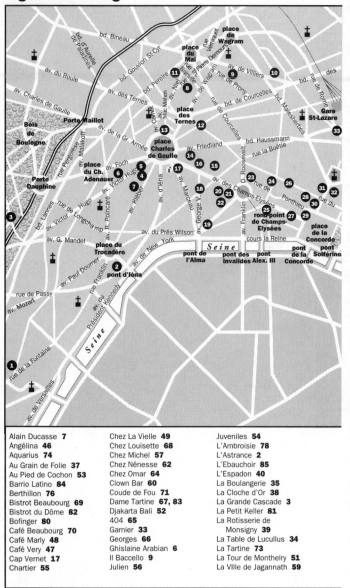

| | | |
|---|---|---|
| Alain Ducasse **7** | Chez La Vielle **49** | Juveniles **54** |
| Angélina **46** | Chez Louisette **68** | L'Ambroisie **78** |
| Aquarius **74** | Chez Michel **57** | L'Astrance **2** |
| Au Grain de Folie **37** | Chez Nénesse **62** | L'Ebauchoir **85** |
| Au Pied de Cochon **53** | Chez Omar **64** | L'Espadon **40** |
| Barrio Latino **84** | Clown Bar **60** | La Boulangerie **35** |
| Berthillon **76** | Coude de Fou **71** | La Cloche d'Or **38** |
| Bistrot Beaubourg **69** | Dame Tartine **67, 83** | La Grande Cascade **3** |
| Bistrot du Dôme **82** | Djakarta Bali **52** | La Petit Keller **81** |
| Bofinger **80** | 404 **65** | La Rotisserie de |
| Café Beaubourg **70** | Garnier **33** | Monsigny **39** |
| Café Marly **48** | Georges **66** | La Table de Lucullus **34** |
| Café Very **47** | Ghislaine Arabian **6** | La Tartine **73** |
| Cap Vernet **17** | Il Baccello **9** | La Tour de Montlhery **51** |
| Chartier **55** | Julien **56** | La Vllle de Jagannath **59** |

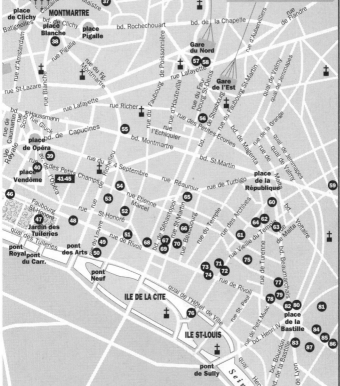

Laduree **32**
Le Baracane **77**
Le Bar à Huîtres **79**
Le Baron Rouge **87**
Le Bistrot d'à Côté **8, 10**
Le Bistrot de
  l'Etoile **4, 11, 13**
Le Boeuf sur le Toit **23**
Le Bristol **26**
Le Buddha Bar **28**
Le Cinq **18**
Le Fumoir **50**
Le Grande Véfour **42**
Le Jardin **12**
Le Moulin à Vin **36**

Les Ormes **1**
Le Petit Marseillais **61**
Le Repair de Cartouche **63**
Le Train Bleu **86**
Le Vaudeville **41**
Ledoyen **27**
Les Ambassadeurs **29**
Les Elysées du Vernet **25**
Lo Sushi **15**
Lucas-Carton **31**
La Maison Blanche **19**
Man Ray **20**
Marais Plus **75**
Market **24**
Maxim's **30**

Nobu **22**
Piccolo Teatro **72**
Pierre Gragnaire **14**
Prunier **5**
Restaurant du Palais
  Royal **43**
Rue Balzac **16**
Spoon, Food and Wine **21**
Terminus Nord **58**
Willi's Wine Bar **45**

3

## sions

Face it: the main
reason you come
to Paris is just to
be in Paris. It's
an incredibly
seductive place—
anyone who visits

is likely to be spellbound by its beauty. The truth is, contrary to its popular image as a boisterous, giddy city, Paris can be a somber and lonesome place sometimes. Despite all the "Paris is for lovers" hype, more than half of the city's residents live alone. The good part about that is that Paris is a great place to visit if you are traveling by yourself—you'll fit right in. Parisians themselves are not even remotely self-conscious about being solitary. Anyone with the price of a cup of coffee can lay claim to a cafe table and watch the people pass by on the sidewalk for hours on end. Paris's glamour gets you going with all sorts of romantic expectations, but don't be offended if they are promptly cold-shouldered by the natives. Parisians tend to be nervous and reserved, unlikely to strike up a conversation with a stranger. In general, they'd rather be spectators than participate in what goes on around them.

Another thing that puts a damper on local spontaneity is that Paris is probably the most bourgeois city in the world; individuality is regarded with skepticism here. In Paris, there is a right way and a wrong way to do absolutely everything. Browse around any of the city's wonderful street markets, for example, and note how every batch of strawberries has been neatly piled into the requisite little pyramid and each pear has been wrapped in tissue paper. This tells you all you need to know about the degree to which Parisians are addicted to form.

Fortunately, their obsession is not with form for its own sake, as is the German penchant for order. It is more precisely a preoccupation with *agréments (de la vie)*, the adornments of life. This fixation with aesthetic minutiae may sometimes be aggravating to foreigners who have made their home here, but at the same time it is exactly what makes Paris such a beautiful city to visit. Some of the most rewarding things to do here are the most ordinary. There's no better movie-going city in the world, for example, and there are few experiences better than strolling the banks of the Seine at night and admiring the city's artfully illuminated bridges.

Oddly, Paris is most beautiful when it's most empty, so rise early and stay up late. Paris is more intimate, mysterious, and relaxed after dark than it is during the day. Wander around and you can catch the city unawares—say, a glimpse into the fluorescent-lit kitchen of a *boulangerie* (bakery) where a pastry chef is spooning preserves into the middle of neat triangles of dough. It may be just a moment, but it can be your window into the soul of Paris.

## Getting Your Bearings

Paris has been cleverly divided by the city fathers into 20 arrondissements, with the 1st arrondissement situated at its heart. The other arrondissements snail around it clockwise, ending with the 20th arrondissement in the northeast. The last two digits of the five-digit postal code indicate the arrondissement. All Paris postal codes begin with 75—75003 is in the 3rd arrondissement, and so on. The Seine river arcs through the city, entering in the southeast and exiting in the southwest, and dividing it in two: the Right Bank (*Rive Droite*) in the north and the Left Bank (*Rive Gauche*) in the south. Métro lines are numbered, with line 1 running east-west across the city. They are also known by the end stations—line 1 is the La Défense-Château de Vincennes line, for example. The RER suburban train network is also handy for getting around more quickly in Paris. (See Hotlines & Other Basics for details on public transportation.)

The **1st arrondissement**, in the heart of the city, contains some of the city's biggest tourist attractions: the Louvre, the Palais-Royal, the Tuileries Gardens, and the *très chic* place Vendôme for shopping (not to mention the ugly underground Forum des Halles shopping mall and the sleazy rue Saint-Denis nearby.) The first's main artery is the traffic-choked rue de Rivoli. North of the 1st is the heavily commercial **2nd arrondissement**, home of the Paris Bourse and the old Bibliothèque Nationale. Moving east, you come to the **3rd arrondissement**, the northern part of the **Marais**, with its ancient buildings and narrow streets. To the south is the **4th arrondissement**, which takes in the rest of the Marais (including the place des Vosges and the Centre Pompidou), part of the Ile-de-la-Cité (where Notre-Dame stands), and picturesque Ile Saint-Louis. The former Jewish quarter centers on the rue des Rosiers (the Marais still has the highest concentration of synagogues in the city), but nowadays the Marais is known as the gay ghetto. At night the area around the rue Vieille du Temple between the rue de Rivoli and the rue des Francs-Bourgeois bustles with restaurant- and bar-goers.

Across the river, you come to the **5th arrondissement**, the famous **Latin Quarter**, home of the Sorbonne, the Panthéon, the Jardin des Plantes, and many small, inexpensive restaurants. From place Saint-Michel, just south of the Seine, Boul' Mich (boulevard Saint-Michel) rolls south, sluggish with traffic; the side streets east of the Boul' Mich are the true Latin Quarter. Go west for the **6th arrondissement**, home of cafes, restaurants, antiques shops, art galleries, and clothing boutiques of **Saint-Germain-des-Prés**. This neighborhood is what most visitors think of as the Left Bank, peopled by the *gauche caviar* (wealthy Leftist intellectuals) as well as the simply rich and lots of artsy types. Its landmark is the graceful steeple of the Eglise Saint-Germain-des-Prés; the Jardin du Luxembourg is here, too. The **7th arrondissement** abuts Saint-Germain-des-Prés to the west and shares some of its characteristics—a wealthy, sedate residential area containing the Assemblée Nationale, the Musée d'Orsay, the Musée Rodin, Hôtel des Invalides, and, most famously, the Eiffel Tower. The ritzy **8th arrondissement** faces the seventh from the Right Bank of the Seine. The avenue des Champs-Elysées bisects the area, littered with overpriced cafes, tourists, and pickpockets. Landmarks here include the Arc de Triomphe, the Grand Palais, and many of the palace hotels. Tree-lined avenue Montaigne is full of designer boutiques, and the rue du Faubourg-Saint-Honoré is Fashion Central for top designers. On the northern edge of the arrondissement is the lovely Parc Monceau, surrounded by the 19th-century homes of the discreet bourgeoisie. To the east, the **9th arrondissement** is primarily residential, with an emphasis on artsy types; along its grand boulevards you'll find the ornate Opéra Garnier and the big department stores, Printemps and Galeries Lafayette. A lively nightlife scene has developed along its northern edge, just below the strip joints of Pigalle.

East of the 9th is the **10th arrondissement**, a lower-middle-class residential area that visitors hardly ever see unless they're coming and going from its train stations, the Gare de l'Est and the Gare du Nord. The **11th arrondissement**, to the southeast, has a similar profile until it reaches the newly hip rue Oberkampf and the **Bastille**, the area around the new opera house, where hectic nightlife around the rue de Lappe draws rowdy suburbanites into town on weekend nights. Further south, sprawling as far east as the Bois de Vincennes is the **12th arrondissement**, the site of Paris's new development at Bercy, with the Palais d'Omnisports de Paris-Bercy and the new Ministry of Finance.

The outer ring of arrondissements is primarily residential. Across the Seine is the **13th arrondissement**—a mix of traditional Paris (on its border with the 5th) and modern high-rises (of very uneven architectural value) at the place d'Italie and beyond. It is also home to Paris's largest Chinese community (and many good Asian restaurants), as well as the low-rise, almost bucolic area around the rue de la Butte aux

Cailles. West of the 13th lies the **14th arrondissement**, **Montparnasse**. Boulevard Montparnasse, with its legendary cafes, lies at its northern edge. The middle-class **15th arrondissement** continues on west to the Seine. Across the river is the aristocratic **16th arrondissement**, which fills in the area between the river and the Bois de Boulogne in the west. Originally the village of Passy, this is the bastion of the French "BCBG" (*bon chic, bon genre*): monied, traditional, culturally and politically conservative folk. North of it lies the **17th arrondissement**, a mixed bag housing the wealthy and the bourgeoisie in the area between the Arc de Triomphe and Villiers, and elsewhere the much less wealthy. To the east, the heterogeneous **18th arrondissement** spans picturesque **Montmartre** (home to the rich and famous), the trendy Abbesses area, the tourist mecca that is the Sacré-Coeur, sleazy-but-trendy **Pigalle**, large African communities around Barbès-Rochechouart, and the Goutte d'Or, a poor neighborhood notorious for its drug dealers. The working-class **19th** and **20th arrondissements** lie to the east; tourists rarely come here except to visit Père Lachaise cemetery, but the area's low rents attract many young people and artists. These neighborhoods are gradually becoming trendy and rents are on the rise.

**Discounts and Passes**

Discounts for children, students, senior citizens, and teachers are offered at many attractions; be sure to ask before buying your ticket. A pass good for multiple visits to 70 museums and monuments over a given period of time (one, three, or five consecutive days, at 13 euros, 26 euros, and 39 euros, respectively), called the **Carte Musées et Monuments**, is available at major Métro stations, participating museums and monuments, tourism offices in the railway stations, and the Paris Tourism Office (tel 08 36 68 31 12 /recorded information in French and English, 127, ave des Champs-Elysées, 75008; open daily 9–8; www.paris-touristoffice.com). The beauty of the pass is that you don't have to wait in line at most attractions, a tremendous advantage at such favorite shrines to art as the Louvre and the Musée d'Orsay.

# The Lowdown

**Must-sees for first-time visitors from Peoria...**
**Centre Pompidou**, the popular museum of modern art in the heart of Paris, reopened in 1999 after a $90 million

renovation. Inaugurated in 1977, the museum, which looks like a refinery turned inside out, was receiving eight million visitors annually before it closed, and this huge crowd had wornout a structure designed to receive half that number. Aside from having its physical plant renewed, the museum was enlarged by fifty thousand square feet, which allows it to put 1,400 works from its permanent collections on display, as opposed to just 800 when it closed. The museum is now home to a new bookstore and boutique, both of which are run by the Printemps department store. Georges (see Dining), the critically acclaimed restaurant on the sixth floor, is run by local trend-makers the Costes Brothers. One much-loved attribute of the Centre was changed during museum's makeover, though: The ride up the escalators for the fantastic view now costs 4.57 euros—it used to be free. The centuries-old **Louvre**, on the other hand, is still standing firm, and ongoing renovations have made it more beautiful than ever. The most recent addition is the Sackler Wing, housing 2,000 works of ancient Iranian and Arabian art. The Louvre can be dazzling, overwhelming, irritating, or exhausting, depending on your point of view. Many visitors to Paris just skip it or go to the new underground shopping mall. What is there to say about the **Eiffel Tower**, known the world over as the symbol of Paris and the ultimate tourist attraction? That its lacy ironwork is lovely to look at; that riding the glass elevator slantwise upwards is exciting and kind of scary; that the views are just a little disappointing, because you're so high up and Paris is so flat. Unless you're going to eat at its first-rate restaurant Le Jules Verne (see Dining), you might want to skip the long lines for the elevator. Tourists also flock to the **Sacré-Coeur**, a Byzantine-style church on a Mont-martre hilltop consecrated in 1919. The second symbol of Paris, it draws more visitors than the Cathedral of Notre-Dame, but many are disappointed by its tacky wedding-cake architecture and boring interior. Visitors to **Notre-Dame**, on its own little island in the Seine, admire the grandeur of the interior, the rose window, the magnificent flying buttresses, and the wonderfully grotesque gargoyles, which can be better appreciated from the cathedral towers, 387 steps up. The **Arc de Triomphe**, with its Empire architecture and colossal high-relief sculptures, is yet another symbol of Paris you probably won't want to miss.

**Only in Paris...** Across the Seine from the Tuileries is the **Musée d'Orsay**, a magnificent conversion of one of Paris's splendid train stations, with a grand collection of those Impressionist paintings most people associate with Paris. Then there's the **Musée National Picasso**, which gives a comprehensive overview of the 20th-century master's work. Even if you aren't a great Picasso fan, come for the setting, a beautiful 17th-century *hôtel particulier* (mansion) in the Marais. Paris's big cemeteries are nothing like those in the United States: Graves stand crowded together, and many of the older ones have tiny chapels—some fallen into eerie ruin, others well-kept and decorated with flowers, photos of the deceased, and/or sacred images. If you have time to see just one, go to **Père Lachaise**, out on the city's eastern fringes. With its little stone chapels on most of the graves, it is truly a city of the dead (Jim Morrison, Marcel Proust, Oscar Wilde, Colette, and Edith Piaf are among its residents). Just as you must have your photo taken feeding the pigeons in the Piazza San Marco in Venice, in Paris you must ride on one of the *bateaux mouches* (literally, fly boats), à la Audrey Hepburn and Cary Grant in the film *Charade*. It's a good way to get off your tired feet for an hour and get an overall impression of the monumental buildings that line the Seine. It's most fun at night, when the boats' high-powered floodlights illuminate the banks of the river, blinding the residents (most of whom, strangely enough, don't seem to mind at all—they're generally fond of the *bateaux mouches*). The disadvantage is that you're accompanied by 300 other tourists and are forced to listen to a superficial multilingual commentary on a scratchy sound system. An alternative way to see Paris from the Seine in the summertime is on the **Bat-O-Bus**, a hop-on-hop-off riverboat service.

**X-rated street scenes...** It's not on most tourist itineraries, but many visitors stumble on it by accident. The **rue Saint-Denis**, in the center-city district of Les Halles, is one of the prime marketplaces for prostitution, which is tolerated—but not legal—in France. Almost all of the doorways are draped with women (of all ages) dressed in costumes ranging from schoolgirl to dominatrix, designed to appeal to the varying tastes of their clients. In Montmartre, on the **rue des Martyrs**, **rue André-Antoine**, and **rue Germain-Pilon**, some very aggressive transvestite prostitutes openly ply their trade. The specialty of the **Bois de Boulogne** is Brazilian transvestites, known for their beauty and style. For something even more lurid and bizarre, take a taxi down the little street right behind the Russian Embassy (40, blvd. Lannes, 75016), known to the French as the **rue des Branleurs** (Jerk-off Street), where exhibitionists live up to the nickname. While puritanical Americans may cluck and stare, Parisians just chuckle.

**Choice churches...** **Notre-Dame**, built on the site of a Gallo-Roman temple, marked the beginnings of the classic Gothic style. Of course, it took nearly two centuries to build this pile, which was finished around 1330, and over the subsequent centuries it suffered many alterations—particularly during the Revolution, when the public, mistaking the facade's statues of kings of Israel for French monarchs, decapitated them. (What's left of the originals—they've been replaced by replicas on the facade—can be seen in the **Musée de Cluny**). Many kings of France were married or crowned in the cathedral, and Napoléon crowned himself Emperor here. These days, the most famous church in Paris is looking rather swell after a multimillion-dollar clean-up of its soot-blasted facades, and for the first time in many generations, you can see how astonishingly delicate much of its stonework actually is. The **Sacré-Coeur** came much later, finally consecrated in 1919. It was built at the instigation of two conservative Catholic businessmen to commemorate Paris's survival of the Franco-Prussian War of 1870 and the Paris Commune, a workers' uprising that took control of Paris for a few weeks in 1871. For more than 100 years, relays of volunteers have continually prayed here to expiate the sins of humanity. But the reason most visitors come here is for the views of Paris from its dome and from the hilltop on which it resides and for walks around the winding streets and steep stairways of picturesque Montmartre. The lovely 11th-century church of **Saint-Germain-des-Prés** is the oldest in Paris; its graceful Romanesque bell tower defines the skyline of its namesake neighborhood. Try to come here for one of its frequent, inexpensive chamber music concerts. Universally referred to as a "jewel," the 13th-century Gothic **Sainte-Chapelle**, hidden inside the Palais de Justice on the Ile-de-la-Cité, should be visited in the daytime to appreciate its incredible stained-glass windows, but evening concerts of classical music here are a treat, too.

**Out-of-the-ordinary religious experiences...** On the Left Bank's rue du Bac, there's a brisk business in "miraculous medals" at the **Chapelle Notre-Dame-de-la-Médaille-Miraculeuse**. Hordes of supplicants pray to the body of a young nun, Catherine Labouré, who is perfectly preserved under glass. In 1830 she had a vision of the Virgin Mary, for which she was later beatified by the Catholic church. The chapel has a glowing statue of the Virgin. For a truly eerie experience, go at midnight to the candlelit **Saint-Gervais-Saint-Protais** church in the Marais, sandwiched between the rue François-Miron and the rue des Barres behind the Hôtel de Ville. This 17th-century church, a flamboyant example of Gothic-style construction with a classical facade, is home base for a devout Catholic sect whose adherents keep up a round-the-clock vigil, kneeling silently in their robes on the cold, hard stones before the altar. At night, enter through the ordinary-looking door at the back of the church on the rue des Barres. "Buddhamania" is sweeping France, and those with Buddhist leanings might want to visit the **Centre Bouddhique** in the Bois de Vincennes, a Tibetan Buddhist temple with a 9-meter-high gilded statue of the Buddha. It's open to the public during Buddhist festivals.

**Most hated architecture...** Parisians are a funny bunch. When something new arrives in their city, they bitch and complain about it, claim to hate it, and then, within a very short period of time, learn to love it. Even the **Eiffel Tower**, now the universally beloved symbol of Paris, was considered a hideous eyesore when it was built more than one hundred years ago. *Plus ça change...*. The late president François Mitterrand got endless flak for his *grands projets* program—people accused him of seeking kinglike immortality in a series of monumental structures that changed the face of Paris. At the height of the controversy over the **Opéra Bastille**, rumors circulated that an error had been made—that the building constructed after Carlos Ott's design was not the one that Mitterrand had selected from an architectural competition. People still complain halfheartedly about it, but they flock to performances (which are nearly always

DIVERSIONS | THE LOWDOWN

sold out). I.M. Pei's glass pyramid in the Cour Napoléon of the **Louvre** also raised an initial storm of protest, but the day that the pyramid was unveiled, curious Parisians came in droves to see it, and they had to admit that the airy structure actually added to the beauty of the refurbished palace surrounding it, offering a focal point in the courtyard and new perspectives through its glass. Likewise the sharp-edged, open cube of the **Grande Arche de la Défense**, which on completion turned out to be a graceful addition to the city's western perspective, looking somehow delicate in spite of its massive size. (It is high enough to tower over Notre-Dame.) Architect Dominique Perrault's design for the **Bibliothèque Nationale de France**, the last of Mitterand's projects, was harshly attacked because its four glass towers—meant to resemble open books—were devoted to storing fragile volumes, while human visitors were relegated to the basement. The design had to be revised, at great cost, to add special wooden paneling that protects the books from light. The final result is impressive, thanks primarily to the natural woods and other materials, but still seems cold and impersonal. Mitterrand can't be blamed for the Forum des Halles (see Shopping), the tacky, cheap-looking shopping center that replaced Victor Baltard's lovely 19th-century, wrought-iron market building in the heart of Paris. No one dares to admit liking it, but at least the newest part of the development, on the western side, has been attractively landscaped and provided with imitation Baltard structures. The **Centre Pompidou** horrified many Parisians when it was completed in 1977. Designed by Renzo Piano and Richard Rogers, it's a textbook example of "high-tech" architecture that exposes a building's innards, a briefly popular style that was already out of vogue by the time the building opened. Now, however, the Centre Pompidou is a fixture in Paris, a lovable oddity that's already been through a major renovation. The architecture of the new **Maison de la Culture du Japon** on the quai Branly is so discreet that it has raised few eyebrows. Architect Masayuki Yamanaka made a successful attempt to blend it into its surroundings with a curved facade of jade-colored glass. The interior, with its warm wood fittings, is spacious and airy. The **American Center** cost so much to build that the organization, strapped for funds, sold off the edifice and went out of business right after the building was finished, but fans of architect Frank Gehry might want to check out the building's wacky, sculptural exterior.

**Museums to get lost in...** It's almost shocking to see the excessive of riches on display at the **Louvre**—shelves and shelves loaded with painted Greek vases, for example, or masterpiece paintings crowded together and hung one above the other. And as if the massive art collections weren't mind-boggling enough, there are also the added distractions of the book and gift shops and the fairly new adjacent underground shopping mall (complete with a horrible, very un-French cafeteria with an "international food court"). Plan your visit carefully: Use a museum map, available at the reception desk in the Hall Napoléon, under I.M. Pei's once-controversial but now well-loved glass pyramid, the museum's main entrance. There's rarely a line at the second entrance through the shopping gallery at 99, rue de Rivoli or via the stairway next to ave du Carrousel. If you're going just to see the "Mona Lisa" ("La Joconde" on museum signs) as many visitors do, you may be disappointed to find the enigmatic smile hidden behind bulletproof glass and your view obstructed by hordes of gawkers. The beautifully renovated Richelieu Wing is a bright, spacious section, where two courtyards under glass roofs have been turned into sculpture gardens complete with trees. If you don't want to tackle the museum on your own, ask about guided tours in English. Most tourists visit the **Musée d'Orsay** to see the works of the Impressionists, and that's a good choice, except for the fact that Renoir and company are housed in anonymous rooms that don't take advantage of this magnificent turn-of-the-century structure, with its vast spaces and lofty glass roof. Italian architect Gae Aulenti's conversion of the Left Bank train station into a museum is obtrusive but can't be termed a complete failure. Be sure to pick up a plan of the museum—the signage here is very confusing. Built for the Universal Exhibition of 1900, the **Grand Palais** (between the Champs-Elysées and the Seine) has a beautiful glass roof that's recently been repaired after several wobbly years. This is one of the most important venues in Paris for important temporary art shows, and it also often holds exhibitions of the charming...not to be missed.

**Museums to find yourself in...** Lovers of medieval art and history will rejoice in the **Musée de Cluny**, full of tapestries (including *The Lady and the Unicorn* series), illuminated manuscripts, jewelry, paintings, and sculptures.

Possibly the most serene museum in Paris, it's housed in a 15th-century Gothic mansion built in the Latin Quarter on the ruins of a third-century Roman bathhouse, the remains of which are visible in the basement. Out in Passy, the **Musée Guimet** houses a major collection of art from Asia, including China, Japan, India, Vietnam, Cambodia, Tibet, Thailand, Laos, and Indonesia. There is also an annex, with a collection of Japanese Buddhas and a Japanese garden. The **Musée des Arts Décoratifs**, near the Tuileries Gardens, traces the history of the decorative arts from the Middle Ages on; the Art Deco and Art Nouveau displays are the real winners. Favorite nooks here include the bedroom of Hector Guimard, the Art Nouveau designer who created the emblematic Métro entrances. (One of the best remaining examples can be seen at Métro Abbesses.) In the same wing of the Louvre is the just-renovated **Musée de la Mode et du Textile**, with a permanent exhibition covering the history of fashion (which changes every six months) and occasional temporary exhibitions. The collection at the **Musée d'Art Moderne de la Ville de Paris** is housed along the Seine to the west, in a building constructed for the Universal Exhibition of 1937. Since the works of the Impressionists were moved across the river to the Musée d'Orsay, their former home, **Jeu de Paume** in the Tuileries Gardens, has been revamped and turned into a gallery for exhibitions of contemporary art. But here's the good news: The huge windows have been uncovered, letting light into the once gloomy space.

**New on the museum scene...** An important new addition is the **Maison Européenne de la Photographie** in the Marais, which holds quality temporary photo exhibitions in a renovated mansion with a modern addition. The **Musée de la Musique** in the La Villette complex traces the history of music from the 17th century to the present with a collection of 900 instruments. The **Fondation Cartier pour l'Art Contemporain** near Montparnasse is notable for its appealing modern architecture by Jean Nouvel and its creative theme exhibitions. Dina Vierny, who owns an important art gallery, met the sculptor Maillol when she was 15 and was his model for the next 10 years. In 1995, she opened the **Musée Maillol** in a beautifully restored 18th-century townhouse on the Left Bank. In addition to Maillols, there are also works by Picasso, Rodin, Gaugin, Bonnard, and Degas, as well as a variety of Russian arts.

**One-man museums...** Housed in a graceful 17th-century mansion in the Marais, the **Musée National Picasso** is a must-visit. In lieu of paying inheritance taxes after the artist's death, the family gave the French government first choice of his works. A later donation by his widow Jacqueline added to this exceptional collection, which spans the artist's entire career. The handsome light fixtures and bronze banquettes, chairs, and tables were designed by Diego Giacometti. An equally marvelous setting is the **Musée Rodin**, which shows off the sculptor's most famous works, including *The Kiss* and *The Thinker,* in the 18th-century mansion where he once lived and worked, near the place des Invalides. If you haven't the time to do the whole collection, or if you're not all that keen on statues, come here anyway to stroll around the lovely rose-filled English garden where some of the statues live; it can be visited for a token fee without entering the museum.

**Sexy stuff...** Where else but in Pigalle would you find the **Musée de l'Erotisme**? This museum—just down the street from the Moulin Rouge—eschews the surrounding sleaze and goes for the arty approach to porn, with a fascinating collection of works from Africa, the Americas, Asia, Europe, and Oceania, many of which will raise a giggle.

**Little-known museums...** In the Latin Quarter, the handsome **Institut du Monde Arabe**, by French architect Jean Nouvel, includes an architectural novelty: One wall (on the courtyard side) has a set of apertures that react to light like a camera lens, opening and closing to let in just the right amount of natural light, creating a beautiful pattern reminiscent of Arab designs. If you happen to be out in the vast Bois de Vincennes park, you may want to drop by the **Musée des Arts d'Afrique et d'Océanie**, housed in a building in the Bois de Vincennes left over from the Colonial Exhibition of 1931, with a striking frieze depicting the history of colonialism on the facade. If you're with kids, skip the African and South Pacific art and head straight for the aquarium of gaudy tropical fish. The **Musée Edith Piaf** houses a collection of memorabilia—letters, photos, clothing—from the life of France's beloved chanteuse, who was born in this same working-class Bastille neighborhood. Cinema critic Henri Langlois nurtured the careers of François Truffaut and Jean-Luc Godard and coined the term "New Wave," and the **Musée du Cinéma Henri Langlois**, out in Passy, displays his exhaustive collection of some 5,000 objects illustrating the history of film around the world. You'll see Edison's kinescope, costumes, magic lanterns, posters, and a set from that enduring 1945 French classic *Les Enfants du Paradis* (*Children of Paradise*).

**Best museum cafe...** The wealthy 19th-century art collector Edouard André married the artist who came to paint his portrait, Nellie Jacquemart. Together they indulged their passion for art, traveling throughout Europe and coming back with such treasures as the fabulous Tiepolo fresco that adorns the ceiling of the cafe in their mansion-turned-museum, the **Musée Jaquemart André** near the Champs-Elysées. Have lunch or afternoon tea after admiring works of the Italian Renaissance and 18th-century French school. On a warm day, get thee to another rich man's home: the **Musée Albert Kahn**, just outside Paris. Modest exhibitions of anthropological interest are held here, but the main draw is the variety of vegetation in the French, English, and Japanese gardens, the rose garden, the fruit orchard, the "blue" forest, the pine forest, and the swamp. The cafe is in the glass "palmarium," where you can take tea indoors under the palm trees or on the terrace with a view over the gardens.

**Literary pilgrimages...** The **Musée de la Vie Romantique** is dedicated to George Sand, the iconoclastic 19th-century writer. This Pigalle villa wasn't Sand's home, but artist Ary Scheffer lived here. Sand, who lived in the neighborhood, was a frequent visitor to Scheffer's salon, along with Chopin, Liszt, Ingres, and Delacroix. Decorated in the style of the period, the house is full of Sand memorabilia, including her jewels, furniture, and family portraits. The French Dickens, Honoré de Balzac, lived for seven years in the house out in the Passy area now called the **Maison de Balzac**. The museum's holdings include Balzac portraits, a collection of books, and the desk at which he wrote. The **Musée Carnavalet**'s permanent collection, covering the history of Paris, is fairly inconsistent in quality, but the reason to visit here is the building itself. This handsome Marais *hôtel particulier,* reconstructed in the 17th century by Mansart (the man primarily responsible for the architectural style of Paris), was once the home of the witty Madame de Sévigné, whose prolific letters to her daughter give us a priceless insider's view of the court of Louis XIV. Don't get the idea that Marcel Proust wrote his epic novel here—his cork-lined bedroom was located on the other side of town.

**Modish museums...** It's only fitting that the fashion capital of the world would have two museums dedicated to the couturier's art. The renovated **Musée de la Mode et du Textile** has a huge collection of haute couture clothing, costumes, and accessories. The **Musée de la Mode et du Costume,** housed in the Palais Galliera, a 19th-century Italian Renaissance–style mansion near the Champs-Elysées, holds temporary exhibitions on the history of fashion, sometimes going back as far as the 18th century. (Yes, there was fashion before Coco Chanel.)

**Where the Impressionists are...** Everybody knows that the most extensive collection of the Impressionist masters is in the **Musée d'Orsay**—and that's the problem. If you can't bear to fight the crowds, try the **Orangerie** in the Tuileries Gardens, a little treasure of a museum that's often overlooked by tourists. Here, in an intimate setting, you can peacefully view Claude Monet's renowned water lily series, as well as works by Cézanne, Renoir, Picasso, Rousseau, and Utrillo. Another often-neglected museum is the **Musée Marmottan**, set in a handsome 19th-century mansion out by the Bois de Boulogne that was the home of French art collector Paul Marmottan. Along with his Empire paintings, furniture, and *objets d'art,* there are plenty of Monet paintings, including some of his water lilies and the exceptional *Impression, Sunrise,* which gave the movement its name. Part of Monet's personal collection is exhibited here, including works by Renoir, Caillebotte, Pissarro, Morisot, and Boudin. The **Petit Palais**—a small-scale version of the Grand Palais across the street—houses the art collection of the City of Paris, including works by Delacroix, Ingres, Courbet, Cézanne, and Impressionists Monet, Pissarro, Sisley, and Morisot.

THE LOWDOWN | DIVERSIONS

**Views for free...** Paris is mostly flat, and most of its buildings are the same height, so you need to scout out a really tall building or one of the few hills to get a panorama of the city. The fun is in picking out landmarks such as the Eiffel Tower, the golden dome of Invalides, the Panthéon, the skyscraping Tour Montparnasse, and Notre-Dame Cathedral. You don't have to visit the boring interior of the **Sacré-Coeur** to enjoy the view of Paris from the Montmartre hill it sits on. The **Samaritaine** department store is right in the heart of the city, and from the top floor of Magasin 2 you get a close-up view of the Seine and the Left Bank, with the Eiffel Tower in the background. The top floor of the **Institut du Monde Arabe** on the Left Bank offers great views of the Seine and the flying buttresses of Notre-Dame. The **Parc de Belleville**, a small neighborhood park in the out-of-the-way 20th arrondissement, offers views of Paris from an unusual angle, with the Eiffel Tower far in the distance.

**Views for euros...** The daytime view from the top of the **Eiffel Tower** can be a bit disappointing because you are so high up that the flat world far below becomes a boring blur. It's better to stop on the second floor for a closer view—or better yet, go at night when the *bateaux mouches* light up the buildings along the Seine with high-powered beams. Just as the top of the **Arc de Triomphe** offers a sweeping perspective on the city's architectural sightlines, straight down the place de la Concorde to the Tuileries and the Louvre, so does the farther-out **Grande Arche de la Défense**, former president François Mitterrand's contribution to the French love of form and symmetry. From the Grande Arche, you will also have a good look at the modern architecture of the office complex La Défense—but the problem is you have to go all the way out west of the city to reach it. And then there's nothing else to do there—unless you want to shop in one of the largest malls in Europe. If your time's precious, stick to the Arc de Triomphe. The ferris wheel at the carnival that springs up next to the Tuileries Gardens (Métro Tuileries) twice a year offers a charming view of Paris, with the added thrill of swinging in the breeze when you're stopped at the top. It's especially fun at night.

**Secret gardens...** You go through a tunnel to reach the Jardin Alpin, a mini-paradise hidden in a little valley in the

**Jardin des Plantes**, along the Seine east of the Latin Quarter. In the alpine garden's moist microclimate, some 2,000 species of mountain plants and flowers from all over the world thrive, and a little stream runs through its artificial miniature mountains to form a pool in the center. Tucked away in a corner of the **Jardin du Luxembourg** is the rarely visited Verger du Luxembourg, or National Conservatory of Apples and Pears (see Getting Outside), founded by Napoléon in 1809, with its bewildering variety of apple and pear trees—come in spring for profusions of blossoms. Out west in the 15th arrondissement, the **Parc André Citroën** has a whole range of hidden miniature gardens, from rock gardens to fields of wildflowers (see Getting Outside). At the **Bagatelle**, a magical English garden within the **Bois de Boulogne**, peacocks strut across the wide lawns while summertime visitors inhale the perfume of the extravagant rose garden and enjoy gazing at the irises and water lilies. Many tourists "discover" the lovely English garden of the **Musée Rodin**, where his famous statue *The Thinker* sits surrounded by roses; if only they'd known ahead of time that they could visit the garden for a token fee and skip the rest of the museum completely.

**The stars at your feet...** Right behind the Sacré-Coeur, on a street frequented by tourists, there is a secret that most tourists never discover. The last block of the **rue du Chevalier-de-la-Barre** (Métro Abbesses) turns into one of those picturesque Montmartre staircases that Utrillo liked to paint, with iron railings and a row of old-fashioned street lamps in the center. This one has an expanse of cobblestones on each side of the stairs, giving sculptor Patrick Rimoux and cinematographer Henri Alekan the wacky idea of implanting constellations in the cobblestones, reflecting the way the sky looks on July 1 and January 1. You have to see it from below at night: The twinkling lights in various shades of blue and white (made of fiber optics and glass) look truly magical, especially on a misty night with the towers of the Sacré-Coeur rising behind it.

**Best hidden courtyard...** If you lived in Paris, you would want to stay in the **cour de Rohan**, a series of three utterly calm, picturesque courtyards accessible from the rue du Jardinet or the medieval cour de Commerce Saint-André (Métro Odéon). Diane de Poitiers once lived here, and the archbishops of Rouen (whence "Rohan") were based here in the 15th century. Look around and you'll spot rare vestiges of old Paris, including a mule-mounting block and a well.

**Mlle. Liberty in Paris...** The small-scale replica of Auguste Bartholdi's Statue of Liberty that stands next to the **pont de Grenelle** (crossing the Seine between the 15th and 16th arrondissements) had its back turned to the United States until 1937, when she was spun around to face the mother country. Another miniature Liberty can be seen in a garden in the northwest corner of the **Jardin du Luxembourg**.

**Where to meet your lover...** The **pont des Arts**, a wooden pedestrian bridge that spans the Seine between the Louvre and the Institut de France, is a magical place in the heart of Paris. Linger as long as you like, soaking in the beauty of the buildings that line the banks and watching the Paris sky, a scene straight out of a 19th-century painting of the city. Bring a bottle of champagne and watch the sun set—if you're lucky, it'll light up the glass roof of the Grand Palais with a rosy glow. Some couples even bring a table, dishes, wine, and a real meal for a candlelit dinner on the bridge.

**How to find the real Latin Quarter...** For the *American in Paris* vision of the city, head straight for the Left Bank's Quartier Latin, which is still lively despite being touristy as all getout. Around the fountain in **place Saint-Michel**, unsavory young *clochards* (street people) accompanied by their German shepherds mingle with folks from Vancouver, Melbourne, and Des Moines, listening to street musicians sing Beatles tunes. Along the tourist-clogged rue Saint-Séverin and rue de la Harpe nearby, mediocre Greek and French restaurants send multilingual touts out into the streets to lure gawking out-of-towners. **Boulevard Saint-Michel** (Boul' Mich, as it's affectionately known to students) is lined with cheap clothing boutiques, record shops, and bookstores. **Shakespeare & Company** (see Shopping), a musty, English-language bookstore whose name was borrowed from Sylvia Beach's renowned establishment, is a big draw for visiting Americans who think they've found a bit of old Paris (no resident would ever be caught dead here). There's still real magic in the quarter, though, in the crooked little streets beyond this touristic triangle—jazz clubs, bookstores, cinemas showing classic films, little restaurants, and bars. After all, the Latin Quarter has been the student part of town from time immemorial; it's home to the Sorbonne and the elite Ecole Normale Supérieure, where legendary philosophers such as Jean-Paul Sartre and Simone de Beauvoir led the intellectual life. In the 12th century, the theologian Abélard (best known for his tragic affair with Héloïse) settled his students here after a scholarly spat with his colleagues on the Ile-de-la-Cité; it's called the Latin Quarter because until the Revolution, students were required to speak Latin because their education was being provided by the church. (Of course, that never stopped students from being rowdy and decadent.) This was the battlefield of the student uprising of 1968, though you can no longer see the paving stones of the Boul' Mich, which were pried up and slung at the police in the great Parisian tradition—the authorities have prudently covered the street with a thick layer of tar, a wise precaution because student riots still regularly occur in the neighborhood. Among the Latin Quarter's sights, one of the few must-sees is the **Musée de Cluny**, with its medieval treasures and remains of Roman baths. Also worth seeing are two churches: the Flamboyant Gothic **Saint-Séverin** (rue des Prêtres) and **Saint-Julien-le-Pauvre** (rue St-Julien-le-Pauvre), one of the oldest churches in Paris, now a Greek Orthodox chapel. (Both are near Métro Saint-Michel.) The landmark dome of the **Panthéon** (RER Luxembourg) rises in this neighborhood, but there's not much to see inside, even though Voltaire, Rousseau, Hugo, Zola, and others major figures are interred here.

**Hanging out in Saint-Germain-des-Prés...** It all began with a Benedictine abbey and a church built to house a fragment of the Cross, but the abbey was mostly destroyed by the Revolution and was finished off in the 19th century. Visitors now make pilgrimages to the boulevard Saint-Gemain's famous cafes, **Deux-Magots** (no. 170) and **Café de Flore** (no. 172), where Jean-Paul Sartre and Simone de Beauvoir used to hang out. (The waiters at the Flore would complain about how long de Beauvoir would sit writing over one cup of coffee.) **Brasserie Lipp** (no. 151) was where François Mitterand and other political honchos hung out. At 27, rue du Fleurus, Gertrude Stein and Alice B. Toklas entertained Picasso, Hemingway, et al. Eugène Delacroix, Albert Camus, Antoine Artaud, and Jacques Prévert were other habitués of this Left Bank neighborhood, and in the 1950s, it was the hot spot for the jazz generation. Many of its tenants are now antiques dealers selling bits of the past, but there are also art galleries, publishing houses, cafes, restaurants, and boutiques of all sorts, from haute couture to mass-market rags. Just to soak up atmosphere, don't miss the lovely and peaceful square on the **rue de Furstemberg**; the **Marché Saint-Germain**, once a fair-ground, now a covered market with an international flavor; or the colorful little marketplace on the **rue de Buci**. Around the Odéon Métro station are several cinemas showing new releases in *V.O.* (*version originale,* or the language they were made in).

**The many faces of the Marais...** During the last 20 years, the Marais, once a poor quarter destined for urban renewal, has become totally chic—for better or for worse. Dozens of ancient buildings have been saved from destruction and beautifully renovated, but gentrification has sent property prices skyrocketing. Boutiques and art galleries open and close in the blink of an eye, pushing out the little bakeries and other food shops that make a neighborhood liveable. The Marais has many different identities. The area around the **rue de Vieille du Temple** has become the city's gay ghetto, but this culture coexists quite happily with straight nightlife and the ancient Jewish quarter around the **rue des Rosiers**, where you can still buy newspapers in Hebrew, not to mention fantastic rye bread and falafels. Check out the strange-looking synagogue on the rue Pavée, designed by Hector Guimard, who also created the famous Art Nouveau Métro entrances. Unfortunately, the trendy clothing boutiques have already invaded rue des Rosiers and its Jewish flavor may soon be lost forever. A mini-Chinatown has grown up around the **rue au Maire** and the **rue de Gravilliers**, where many of the wholesale shops are owned by Chinese immigrants. The **rue Rambuteau** and the **rue de Bretagne** are food-market streets where you can still find great little *boulangeries* (bakeries), cheese shops, wine shops, and restaurants among the incursions of boutiques. Once a swamp (that's what the word *marais* means), the Marais has gone in and out of style many times over the centuries. In the 13th century, the Knights Templar and other religious communities built monasteries here; in the 14th century, Charles V set up housekeeping in the Hôtel

DIVERSIONS | THE LOWDOWN

Saint-Paul. Aristocratic families took over the area in the 17th century, after Henri IV had the lovely **place des Vosges** built; the graceful *hôtels particuliers* (mansions) of that era give the Marais much of its charm. For a look inside one, stop in the **Musée Carnavalet**, where the famous letter-writer Madame de Sévigné once lived. By the time of Louis XVI, the nobles had moved on to the Ile Saint-Louis, the Faubourg Saint-Honoré, and the Faubourg Saint-Germain, and the Marais eventually became a slum—as recently as the early 1970s, a majority of the apartments here still didn't have private toilets or hot running water. All that has changed now, of course, but the Marais is still rakish enough to thumb its nose at Sunday-closing laws, making it the best place in the city to stroll around on a Sunday afternoon.

**Up and away in Montmartre...** Parisians hear it so often that it's become a cliché: "*Montmartre, c'est un village.*" But it is true that Montmartre has somehow remained a little world apart, up on its hill with its steep staircases lit by old-fashioned street lamps and its narrow, winding cobblestone streets. A creeping trendiness is invading the area around the picturesque **place des Abbesses** (come here to check out one of the few remaining and intact Art Nouveau Métro entrances designed by Hector Guimard), but there is still a feeling of Old Paris here, accompanied by the strains of accordion music in the streets and restaurants. Explore the wonderful market streets, the **rue des Abbesses** and the **rue Lepic**, with their dozens of bakeries, cheese shops, butchers, and fishmongers. Visit the **Montmartre Cemetery**, where François Truffaut and the French pop singer Dalida are buried, then follow the winding rue Lepic up the hill (Vincent Van Gogh lived at number 54 with his brother Theo a century ago), past the **Moulin de la Galette** and the **Moulin du Radet**, the sole survivors of Montmartre's 30 windmills. On **avenue Junot**, where the wealthy Montmartois live, take a look at number 15, once the home of Dadaist writer Tristan Tzara. It was designed in 1926 by Austrian architect Adolf Loos. In keeping with his functionalist principles, it gives no ground to frivolous decoration: A white block sits, set back, on a beige stone block, looking like two different buildings, while recesses contain windows of varying sizes. If you continue upward and eastward, you will end up at the **place du Tertre**, overrun with caricature portrait artists and tourists (some six million per year visit this tiny square), and the **Sacré-Coeur**. You have now left the village and entered touristland.

**Tourist-free neighborhoods...** Few tourists venture into **Butte aux Cailles**, a bucolic area in the 13th arrondissement near the place d'Italie, with its trendy music bars and inexpensive restaurants. Rue de Butte aux Cailles translates as Quail Hill Street, although the word *cailles* used to refer to the prostitutes who trolled the streets (the area was considered too dangerous for the police to enter). In 1783, when the world's first hot-air balloon flight set down here in what is now the place Paul-Verlaine, the hilltop was still countryside dotted with windmills. In 1871, however, it was a hotbed of insurrection, with the Communards fighting off government troops. Some restaurants and bars on the street still hark back to those times, with names borrowed from the Communards' anthem "Le Temps des Cerises" (the Merle Moqueur and La Folie en Tête, for example); the Marxist Library is located on the nearby rue Sigaud. For sheer picturesqueness, check out the **rue des Cinq-Diamants**, **Passage Barrault**, **Passage Boiton**, and **rue Daviel**, with their little houses and gardens. Another hilltop village is in the **Belleville** area in the 20th arrondissement, a working-class area where ugly high-rise apartment buildings set a general theme of god-awful modernization. But the **Parc de Belleville** gives a wonderful view of Paris from its summit, and a few pockets of the old neighborhood still survive. Right next to the hideous housing project on the place des Fêtes (Métro place des Fêtes), a peaceful alleyway leading off 11, **rue des Fêtes** is occupied by adorable little houses, each with its own flower garden—if only city life were always like this. For more of the same, try the little passageways off the rue de Bellevue. This area is called **L'Amérique**, and no one really knows why, but legend has it that the products of the former quarry site were exported to the United States. Near Métro Porte-de-Bagnolet, between the boulevard Mortier and the place Octave-Chanute, is an area called **La Campagne à Paris,** which has more little houses and gardens—originally workers' cottages and now coveted real estate among Parisians who'd rather be living in the country. Belleville has only recently been "discovered" by the young and trendy. Come here now before the boutiques invade and take over.

**Where to read a book...** Bring a novel by Colette to the gardens of the **Palais-Royal**, where she lived until her death. Though in the heart of the city (the Palais-Royal lies across the rue de Rivoli from the Louvre), the gardens are sheltered from the noise of traffic—all you'll hear is the soothing sound of water rushing from the fountain. The Medicis Fountain in the **Jardin du Luxembourg** is a peaceful and romantic place to sit and read or just watch the goldfish swimming languidly in the pool. From the hillside **Parc de Belleville**, you will have a panoramic view before you when you lift your eyes from your book. For indoor reading, the **Bibliothèque Mazarine** in the Institut de France will transport you to another time. After mounting a gem of a 19th-century marble staircase, you enter the calm precincts of the library, with its wood paneling and Corinthian columns, green-shaded reading lamps, and busts of famous men. Bring a passport-sized photo and ID and you can get a *carte de lecteur* (reader's card).

**The big sleep...** **Père Lachaise Cemetery** is the premier resting place for the illustrious dead—the roster includes Colette, Honoré de Balzac, Frédéric Chopin, Guillaume Apollinaire, Abélard and Héloïse, Molière, and La Fontaine, along with many other long-gone celebrities. Some of them, however, are not necessarily resting in peace. Jim Morrison's grave is always surrounded by pilgrims (not always of the most savory kind); the bust that used to adorn his grave has long since been stolen, and surrounding gravestones are covered with handwritten messages of love to him. There are even rumors of Satanic rituals taking place around his grave at night. Marcel Proust's grave is touchingly simple and elegant; Edith Piaf's is always heaped with flowers. Sexual scandal surrounds Oscar Wilde even in death—the handsome sculpture of a sphinx on his grave had its testicles chopped off by two scandalized visitors. (The offending parts were thereafter used for years by the cemetery's director as a paperweight.) The statue on the grave of Victor Noir has kept its genitalia, which are so awesome that visitors have rubbed them shiny, in hopes of increasing their own sexual powers. The atmosphere around mystic Allan Kardec's grave is truly spooky, with his followers (his philosophy of spiritism is wildly popular in Brazil) silently waiting their turn to touch his gravestone and commune with his spirit, departed from this world more than 100 years ago. Apart from the departed, the other permanent inhabitants of the cemetery are wild cats, who are regularly fed by kindly old ladies. Since Père Lachaise is a city unto itself, be sure to purchase a map (1.52 euros) from one of the street vendors stationed outside of the cemetery to help find your way around and, more importantly, your way out before the 5:15 closing time. Parklike **Montmartre Cemetery** has its share of celebs too, including Hector Berlioz, Heinrich Heine, Stendhal, Vaslav Nijinsky, Edgar Dégas, Jacques Offenbach, Sacha Guitry, Aldolphe Sax (inventor of the saxophone), and Alphonsine Plessis (the model for the heroine of *La Dame aux Camélias*). François Truffaut, who once sneaked into the cemetery to shoot a scene for a film after the authorities refused him permission, specified that he wanted to be buried here. Left Bank intellectuals who wound up in the **Montparnasse Cemetery** include Jean-Paul Sartre and Simone de Beauvoir, along with Samuel Beckett, Charles Baudelaire, Tristan Tzara, Brancusi, Alfred Dreyfus, Marshall Pétain, Guy de Maupassant, and Americans Man Ray and Jean Seberg (the incandescent Iowa beauty who tramped up and down the Champs-Elysées in Godard's *Breathless*, hawking the *Herald Tribune*).

**Go backstage...** A tour behind the scenes of the **Opéra Bastille** is a fascinating experience: The spaces are unbelievably immense, the huge sets make you feel like a Lilliputian, and the stage machinery is the most sophisticated of any opera house in the world. This "opera of the people" (with sky-high ticket prices) has been plagued with controversy since its inception in 1989. Just about no one admits to liking its exterior; two beloved international musical stars, Daniel Barenboim and Myung Whun-Chung, were fired from their posts with great public uproar; and its super-high-tech stage machinery has been beset with technical problems. If you want "the Phantom's" opera, however, you've got to go to its predecessor, the opulent **Opéra Garnier**. It's your classic, late 19th-century opera house, with a lavish interior rife with gilt, marble, crystal, and sculpting. The auditorium ceiling, painted by Marc Chagall in 1963, is beautiful in itself but clashes with the rest of the look. Mostly dance performances are held here now, and in the daytime you can go inside on your own to peek at the grand staircase, the public rooms, the auditorium, and the exhibition space (guided tours are also available). There's also an opera history museum, located in what was once the emperor's private entrance. Listen closely for the strains of the Phantom's organ drifting up from the underground lake beneath the opera house. For a behind-the-scenes look at how a radio station operates, take a guided tour of the **Maison de Radio France**'s futuristic aluminum-faced circular building—actually three concentric circles, with the middle housing 70 recording studios (the round shape solved the acoustical problem of how to avoid parallel walls in the studios). A museum on site covers the history of recording, with re-creations of early radio and television stations.

**For cinephiles and cineastes...** The favorite topic of conversation at any French dinner party is movies, and not just the latest ones—the French are fans of everything from old Ernst Lubitsch films to *Rambo* or the latest Godard. The number of films made in Paris is mind-boggling, and they can all be seen at the **Vidéothèque de Paris**, in Les Halles, an archive of videos and films related to Paris. For a small fee, you can stay all day, plunked in an armchair beside your own individual video screen, watching anything from *The 400 Blows* to silent footage of street life in Paris at the turn of the century. Out west near Trocadero, the **Cinémathèque Française**, another archive, has an enormous collection of classic and rare films and holds festivals on themes like Charlie Chaplin or film noir. It is also the home of the **Musée du Cinéma Henri Langlois**, with its amazing collection of film memorabilia. The **Cinémathèque de la Danse** has a collection of 400 films and 2,000 videos related to dance, with everything from Nureyev to Fred Astaire (private viewings are possible by appointment). Eccentric **Studio 28** in Montmartre is the most wonderful movie theater in Paris, with camp chandeliers in the auditorium that were supposedly designed by Jean Cocteau.

**Kid-pleasers...** The best overall place to go is the **Jardin d'Acclimatation** on the northern side of the Bois de Boulogne, a combination park, carnival, zoo, and playground. With its bears and bumper cars, donkey rides and boat rides, hall of mirrors and shooting galleries, it has something that every kid and adult can enjoy. Then there's Parc de la Villette's **Cité des Sciences et de l'Industrie**, a museum in a former slaughterhouse, which is full of things that kids love: a full-sized model of a supersonic bomber, rocket and space station exhibits, a planetarium, and educational computer games. The science-oriented kids' section, Cité des Enfants, is so popular that it's sometimes hard to get in—thank goodness there are plenty of other attractions in the park, including a real submarine and eight fascinating theme gardens, including one with a monster slide. And the **Foire du Trône** carnival (out east in the Bois de Vincennes from March to the end of May) is like a wholesome version of an American midway, with Ferris wheels and other rides and shooting galleries. The Bois de Vincennes also has the largest zoo in Paris, the **Parc Zoologique de Paris**, where the wild beasts live in nearly natural habitats. If you'd rather stick to the center of town, there are the tried-and-true favorites: sailing rented boats in the pools of the **Tuileries** and **Jardin du Luxembourg**. The Luxembourg also has a marionette theater and a large, well-equipped playground, and twice a year the Tuileries hosts a carnival with a super Ferris wheel. It's all so Parisian, you almost expect to see Madeleine and her convent school chums filing past. Little monsters (and their parents) adore the colorful monsters in the **Stravinsky Fountain** next to the **Centre Pompidou.** The wacky sculptures by Jean Tinguely and Niki de Saint-Phalle—each named after one of the great composer's works—spin and spout water in all directions (when it's working). Nearby, the **Musée de la Poupée**, a private doll museum, has a collection of some 200 dolls dating from between 1860 and 1960 (yes, Barbie is included). Down on the Left Bank, the **Ménagerie** in the **Jardin des Plantes** is a fascinating little zoo with everything from panthers, monkeys, and bears to wild goats and insects. Want to drop your kids off? Try the **Jardin des Enfants aux Halles**, a high-tech, kid-pleasing playground for ages seven to 11 in the new part of the Forum des Halles, with labyrinths, tunnels, climbing walls, toboggans, and a "mysterious island." Kids can stay one hour at a time, and no adults are allowed (there is adult supervision within). Younger children can visit with adults on Saturdays. Show up early (beginning at 10am) if you don't want a disappointed child on your hands because limited numbers of kids are admitted each hour. In summer, the **Louvre** runs some English-language classes about art history in its **Atelier des Enfants** (call 40 20 52 63 at 9am that morning to reserve). If they insist, take your kids to **Disneyland Paris**, reachable by suburban train (RER A4). You know what to expect: Mickey, Goofy, Main Street U.S.A., Frontierland, Discoveryland, etc. On a nice day, expect to wait in long lines for most attractions.

**Keeping surly teenagers happy...** Nothing will amuse them if they have to do it with adults. For those with macabre tastes, whip up to Montparnasse for the **Catacombs,** old quarries where the city dumped leftover skeletons from Paris's overcrowded cemeteries (at one point, bones were actually jostling up out of the soil). Various skeletal parts have been decoratively arranged into walls and other frightening formations—awesome, if not disturbing. If their minds are in the gutter, haul them over to the Quai d'Orsay to explore the famous **Sewers of Paris** (*égouts*). Not so long ago, having fancy-dress parties in the sewers was the chic thing to do for young upper-class Parisians—talk about slumming!

**Traces of Rome...** The name Paris comes from the Parisii, a Celtic people who were holed up on the Ile-de-la-Cité in 52 B.C., when the Romans hit town. The Romans conquered the Parisiis' settlement, Lutetia (Lutèce), and stuck around for more than five centuries, when invaders from the north finally made the Romans clear out. The Roman influence still lurks in some parts of Paris, especially at the well-preserved **Arènes de Lutèce,** the ruins of an amphitheater that could hold up to 10,000 people to watch gladiators fight off wild beasts or be eaten by them. (There was also a stage to regale the populace with less bloody theatrical performances.) Uncovered in 1869, the ruins today host modern-day gladiators: old men playing *boules.* Under the **Musée de Cluny** have been unearthed the remains of Roman baths, including the frigidarium and bits of the mosaics and frescoes that once decorated it. You don't have to pay the price of a museum ticket to see them, however—just peer through the iron fence from the boulevard Saint-Michel. Further archaeological excavations are now underway here. At the **Crypte Archéologique de Notre-Dame de Paris**, parts of the wall built to defend the Parisians from barbarian invaders in the fourth century can still be seen, along with other Gallo-Roman remains, including two rooms heated by the Romans' early version of a central-heating system. You can see the basements of medieval houses here too, but that's another era.

# The Index

**American Center.** Designed by architect Frank Gehry, housed a gallery, theater, cinema, library, and restaurant, before the controversial building was put up for sale.... *Tel 01 44 73 77 00; 51, rue de Bercy, 75012, Métro Bercy.* **(see p. 100)**

**Arc de Triomphe.** The famous triumphal arch originally ordered by Napoléon provides tourists with a view of the Champs-Elysées from its rooftop.... *Tel 01 44 09 89 94; place Général-de-Gaulle, 75008, Métro Etoile. Open 10–10:30, Sun–Mon 9:30–6:30. Admission charged. Use underground passage from Champs-Elysées sidewalks to enter.* **(see pp. 96, 106)**

**Arènes de Lutèce.** Ruins of a Roman amphitheater.... *Entrances at 49, rue Monge and on rue Navarre, 75005, Métro Jussieu.* **(see p. 117)**

**Bagatelle.** An English garden within the Bois de Boulogne.... *Tel 01 40 67 97 00; route de Sèvres-à-Neuilly and route de la Reine-Marguerite, Métro Pont-de-Neuilly, then take no. 43 bus, or Métro Porte-Maillot, then take no. 244 bus. Open 8:30–8 in summer; hours vary in other seasons. Admission charged.* **(see p. 107)**

***Bateaux mouches.*** Several different companies provide this tour-boat service on the Seine.... *Boats can be boarded at the pont de l'Alma (Métro Alma-Marceau), Port de la Bourdonnais (Métro Trocadéro), Quai de Montobello (Métro Saint-Michel), Port de Suffren (Métro Bir-Hakeim), and the square du Vert-Galant on the Ile-de-la-Cité (Métro Pont-Neuf). Boats run every 30 minutes, 10–10:30; some close at lunchtime.* **(see pp. 97, 106)**

**Bat-O-Bus.** A bus-boat that plies the Seine in the summer.... *Board at the Eiffel Tower (Métro Bir-Hakeim), the Musée* d'Orsay (Métro Solferino), the Louvre (Métro Louvre), Hôtel de Ville (Métro Hôtel-de-Ville), or Notre-Dame (Métro Cité). Boats run every 30 minutes, 10–7, May–Sept. **(see p. 97)**

**Bibliothèque Mazarine.** A lovely 17th-century library in the eastern wing of the Institut de France.... Tel 01 44 41 44 06; 23, quai de Conti, 75006, Métro Pont-Neuf. Open weekdays 10–6. Admission free. **(see p. 113)**

**Bibliothèque Nationale de France.** The new, super-high-tech national library.... Tel 01 53 79 59 59; 11, quai François-Mauriac, 75013, Métro Quai de la Gare. Open Tue–Sat 10–7, Sun 12–6. Admission free. **(see p. 100)**

**Catacombs.** The spooky repository of thousands of skeletons moved from Paris's overcrowded cemeteries to old underground quarries.... Tel 01 43 22 47 63; 1, place Denfert-Rochereau, 75014, Métro Denfert-Rochereau. Open Tues–Fri 2–4, Sat–Sun 9–11 and 2–4. Admission charged. **(see p. 117)**

**Centre Bouddhique.** A Tibetan Buddhist temple, open to the public for meditation sessions. Call first.... Tel 01 40 04 98 06; Bois de Vincennes, Métro Porte Dorée. **(see p. 99)**

**Centre Pompidou.** A newly renovated cultural center with a modern art collection, open-access library, cinema, bookstore, and children's center.... Tel 01 44 78 12 33; rue Rambuteau and rue Saint-Merri, 75004, Métro Rambuteau or Hôtel-de-Ville. Open noon–10, weekends 10–10. Closed Tue. Admission charged for permanent collection and some temporary exhibitions. **(see pp. 95, 100, 116)**

**Chapelle Notre-Dame-de-la-Médaille-Miraculeuse.** Pilgrims come to this chapel to pray to a saint whose body is preserved under glass and to buy "miraculous medals".... Tel 01 49 54 78 88; 140, rue du Bac, 75007, Métro Sèvres-Babylone. Open Wed–Mon 7:45–1 and 2:30–7, Tue 7:45–7. Admission free. **(see p. 99)**

**Cinémathèque de la Danse.** A collection of 400 films and 2,000 videos related to dance. Call to schedule a private viewing on a Friday.... Tel 01 53 65 74 70; 4, rue de Longchamp, 75116, Métro Iéna. By appointment only. **(see p. 115)**

**Cinémathèque Française.** The French film archive shows retrospectives of often-rare films.... *Tel 01 47 04 24 24; Palais de Chaillot, corner of ave Albert-de-Mun and ave du Président Wilson, 75016, Métro Trocadéro. Admission charged.* **(see p. 115)**

**Cité des Sciences et de l'Industrie.** A kid-pleasing science museum with rocket and space station exhibits, a planetarium, and educational computer games. The Cité des Enfants has organized educational activities for children.... *Tel 01 40 05 72 23; 30, ave Corentin-Cariou, 75019, Métro Porte de la Villette. Open Tues–Sat 10–6, Sun 10–7. Admission charged.* **(see p. 115)**

**Crypte Archéologique de Notre-Dame de Paris.** 4th-century defensive walls, Gallo-Roman artifacts, and the basements of medieval houses in the crypt of Notre-Dame.... *Tel 01 43 29 83 51; place du Parvis-Notre-Dame, 75005, Métro Cité. Open daily 10–4:30. Closed public holidays. Admission charged.* **(see p. 117)**

**Disneyland Paris.** A morsel of Americana in the French countryside.... *Tel 01 60 30 60 30; Marne-la-Vallée, RER line A to Marne-la-Vallée. Open 10–6, weekends 9–8. Admission charged.* **(see p. 116)**

**Eiffel Tower.** The symbol of Paris.... *Tel 01 44 11 23 45; Champs de Mars, 75007, Métro Bir-Hakeim, RER Champs-de-Mars. Open 9:30–11. Admission charged.* **(see pp. 96, 99, 106)**

**Foire du Trône.** A carnival held in the Bois de Vincennes from March to June. You pay 1.50 or 3 euros for each ride.... *Métro Château de Vincennes.* **(see p. 116)**

**Fondation Cartier pour l'Art Contemporain.** Modern art museum in a handsome modern building by Jean Nouvel.... *Tel 01 42 18 56 50; 261, blvd Raspail, 75014, Métro Raspail. Open noon-8. Closed Mon. Admission charged.* **(see p. 102)**

**Grande Arche de la Défense.** A monumental arch providing views of Paris and La Défense from its rooftop.... *Tel 01 49 07 27 57; place du Parvis-de-la Défense, Métro/RER La Défense. Open daily 10–7. Admission charged.* **(see pp. 100, 106)**

**Grand Palais.** A glass-roofed structure built for the Universal

Exhibition of 1900 hosts traveling exhibitions and occasional blockbuster shows.... *Tel 01 49 87 54 54; 3, ave du Général-Eisenhower, 75008, Métro Champs-Elysées-Clemenceau. Open 10–8, until 10pm Wed. Closed Tue. Admission charged.* **(see p. 101)**

**Institut du Monde Arabe.** Architect Jean Nouvel's handsome building houses a museum showcasing the arts of the Arab world and a Lebanese restaurant.... *Tel 01 40 51 38 38; 1, rue des Fossés-Saint-Bernard, 75005, Métro Jussieu. Open 10–6. Closed Mon. Admission charged.* **(see pp. 103, 106)**

**Jardin d'Acclimatation.** A park, carnival, zoo, and playground.... *Tel 01 40 67 90 82; in the Bois de Boulogne, Métro Sablon. The Petit Train also leaves from behind the Orée de Bois restaurant at Porte Maillot after 1:30pm every 10 minutes on Wed, Sat, Sun (every day during French school holidays). Open 10–6, 10–7 in summer. Admission charged. Extra charge for some attractions.* **(see p. 115)**

**Jardin des Enfants aux Halles.** A state-of-the-art playground in the western side of Les Halles, for children 7–11. Supervised, 1-hour-long visits; no adults allowed, except on Sat from 10–2, when younger children are also admitted.... *Tel 01 45 08 07 18; 105, rue Rambuteau, 75001, Métro Les Halles. Call for opening times. Closed Sun and when it rains. Admission charged.* **(see p. 116)**

**Jardin des Plantes.** Botanical garden, home of the newly refurbished National Museum of Natural History; the Jardin d'Hiver, a tropical garden in a greenhouse; the Jardin Alpin; a reptile house; a small zoo; and galleries of minerology, paleontology, entomology, and paleobotany.... *Tel 01 40 79 30 00; 57, rue Cuvier, 75005, Métro Gare d'Austerlitz. Galleries open 10–5. Closed Tues. Garden open daily 7:30–8, 7:30–5:30 in winter; hours vary for other attractions. Admission charged for some attractions.* **(see pp. 107, 116)**

**Jardin du Luxembourg.** Classic French formal gardens on the Left Bank.... *Métro Odéon/RER Luxembourg. Admission free.* **(see pp. 107, 108, 113, 116)**

**Jeu de Paume.** A gallery of contemporary art in Napoléon III's former tennis court.... *Tel 01 42 60 69 69; place de la Con-*

DIVERSIONS | THE INDEX

corde, 75001, Métro Concorde. Open Tue noon–9:30, Wed–Fri noon–7, Sat–Sun 10–7. Admission charged.
(see p. 102)

**Louvre.** The fabled museum in a palace. Home of the Mona Lisa.... Tel 01 40 20 51 51 for general information; rue de Rivoli, 75001, Métro Palais-Royal. Open 9–6, until 9:45pm Wed. Richelieu Wing open Mon till 9:45pm. Closed Tue and some public holidays. Admission charged.
(see pp. 96, 100, 101, 116)

**Maison de Balzac.** Balzac's former home is a museum containing many of his belongings.... Tel 01 42 24 56 38; 47, rue Raynouard, 75016, Métro Passy. Open Tues–Sun 10–5:45. Admission charged. (see p. 104)

**Maison de la Culture du Japon.** Japanese cultural center near the Eiffel Tower, with art exhibitions, performances, and a library.... Tel 01 44 37 95 00; 101 bis, quai Branly, 75007, Métro Bir Hakeim. Open Tues–Sat noon–7. Admission charged. (see p. 100)

**Maison de Radio France.** The headquarters of the French national radio stations.... Tel 01 42 30 22 22 or 01 42 30 15 16; 116, ave du Président-Kennedy, 75016, Métro Iéna. Guided tours Mon–Sat at 10:30, 11:30, 2:30, 3:30, and 4:30. Admission charged. (see p. 115)

**Maison Européenne de la Photographie.** This Marais photo museum shows works by everyone from Pierre et Gilles to Helmut Newton.... Tel 01 44 78 75 00; 5–7, rue de Fourcy, 75004, Métro St-Paul. Open 11–8. Closed Mon–Tue and public holidays. Admission charged. (see p. 102)

**Montmartre Cemetery.** A parklike cemetery where François Truffaut and Dalida, among others, have found their final resting place.... Tel 01 43 87 64 24; entrance on ave Rachel, 75018, Métro Place de Clichy or Abbesses. Open Mon–Fri 8–5:30, Sat 8:30–5:30, Sun 9–5:30. Admission free. (see pp. 111, 114)

**Montparnasse Cemetery.** An impressive roster of Left Bank notables, including Jean-Paul Sartre, Simone de Beauvoir, and Samuel Beckett are buried here.... Tel 01 44 10 86 50; 3, blvd Edgar-Quinet, 75014, Métro Edgar-Quinet.

*Open Mon–Fri 8–5:30, Sat 8:30–5:30, Sun 9–5:30. Admission free.* **(see p. 114)**

**Musée Albert Kahn.** Interesting anthropological exhibitions and fantastic gardens, with a tea room in the palmarium.... *Tel 01 46 04 52 80; 14, rue du Port, 92100 Boulogne, Métro Pont-du-St-Cloud. Open 11–6. Closed Mon.* **(see p. 104)**

**Musée Carnavalet.** The museum of the history of Paris is located in the mansion where Madame de Sévigné once lived. Good temporary photography exhibitions, a nice gift shop.... *Tel 01 42 72 21 13; 23, rue de Sévigné, 75003, Métro Saint-Paul. Open 10–5:40. Closed Mon and public holidays. Admission charged.* **(see pp. 105, 111)**

**Musée d'Art Moderne de la Ville de Paris.** The city of Paris's modern art museum often holds good temporary exhibitions.... *Tel 01 53 67 40 00; 11, ave du Président-Wilson, 75016, Métro Iéna. Open Tues–Fri 10–5:30, Sat–Sun 10–6:45. Closed Mon. Admission charged.* **(see p. 102)**

**Musée de Cluny.** A museum of medieval art, with a collection of tapestries, paintings, and sculptures. Housed in a 15th-century Gothic mansion built on the ruins of a 3rd-century Roman bathhouse.... *Tel 01 53 73 78 00; 6, place Paul-Painlevé, 75005, Métro Cluny–La Sorbonne or RER Saint-Michel–Notre Dame. Open 9:15–5:45. Closed Tue. Admission charged.* **(see pp. 98, 101, 109, 117)**

**Musée de l'Erotisme.** Erotic art collection from around the world in the heart of sleazy Pigalle.... *Tel 01 42 58 28 73; 72, blvd de Clichy, 75018, Métro Pigalle. Open 10–2am daily.* **(see p. 103)**

**Musée de la Mode et du Costume.** Temporary exhibitions about the history of fashion.... *Tel 01 47 20 85 23; 10, ave Pierre-1er-de-Serbie, 75008, Métro Alma-Marceau. Open (during exhibitions) 10–5:40. Closed Mon. Admission charged.* **(see p. 105)**

**Musée de la Mode et du Textile.** An extensive collection of haute couture, costumes, and accessories.... *Tel 01 44 55 57 50; 107, rue de Rivoli, 75001, Métro Palais-Royal. Open Tue, Thur, Fri 11am–6pm, Wed until 10pm, Sat–Sun 10am–6pm. Closed Mon. Admission charged.* **(see pp. 102, 105)**

DIVERSIONS | THE INDEX

**Musée de la Musique.** Collection of 900 musical instruments from the 17th century to the present. Research library.... *Tel 01 44 84 44 84; 221, ave Jean-Jaurès, 75019, Métro Porte de Pantin. Open Tues–Thur noon–6, Fri-Sat noon–7:30, Sun 10–6.* **(see p. 102)**

**Musée de la Poupée.** A private collection of some 200 dolls dating from 1860–1960.... *Tel 01 42 72 73 11; Impasse Berthaud (entrance at 22, rue Beaubourg), 75003, Métro Rambuteau. Open Tues–Sun 10–6. Admission charged.* **(see p. 116)**

**Musée de la Vie Romantique.** George Sand memorabilia in a period setting.... *Tel 01 48 74 95 38; 16, rue Chaptal, 75009, Métro Pigalle. Open 10–5:40. Closed Mon and public holidays. Admission charged.* **(see p. 104)**

**Musée des Arts d'Afrique et d'Océanie.** Art from Africa and Oceania and an aquarium with some 300 species of tropical fish.... *Tel 01 43 46 51 61; 293, ave Dausmesnil, 75012, Métro Porte Dorée. Open Mon–Fri 10–11:45 and 1:30–5:20, weekends 10–5:45. Admission charged.* **(see p. 103)**

**Musée des Arts Décoratifs.** A museum tracing the history of the decorative arts from the Middle Ages to the recent past. Also has large collections of dolls and posters.... *Tel 01 44 55 57 50; 107, rue de Rivoli, 75001, Métro Palais-Royal. Open Wed–Sun 12:30–6. Closed major holidays. Admission charged.* **(see p. 102)**

**Musée d'Orsay.** A magnificent collection of art from the 2nd half of the 19th century, housed in a beautiful turn-of-the-century converted train station.... *Tel 01 40 49 48 14; 1, rue de Bellechasse, 75007, Métro Solférino, RER Musée d'Orsay. Open 10–6, until 9:30 Thur. Closed Mon. Admission charged.* **(see pp. 97, 101, 105)**

**Musée du Cinéma Henri Langlois.** A collection of some 5,000 objects illustrating the history of film around the world.... *Tel 45 53 21 86; Palais de Chaillot, place du Trocadéro, 75016, Métro Trocadéro. Open Wed–Sun 10–5, guided tours (available in English) every hour except noon. Closed public holidays. Admission charged.* **(see pp. 104, 115)**

**Musée Edith Piaf.** Letters, photographs, and clothing

belonging to France's beloved *chanteuse*.... *Tel 01 43 55 52 72; 5, rue de Crespin-du-Gast, 75011, Métro Menil-montant. Open by appointment Mon–Thur 1–6pm. Call for appointment. Admission charged.* **(see p. 104)**

**Musée Guimet.** A major Asian art museum with an especially fine Khmer art collection and a bamboo garden in the annex. Annex open Wed–Mon 9:45–6.... *Tel 01 45 05 00 98; 6, place d'Iéna, 75016, Métro Iéna.* **(see p. 102)**

**Musée Jaquemart André.** A private art collection displayed in the restored 19th-century mansion of its owners, who raided Europe for Italian Renaissance art and more.... *Tel 01 42 89 04 91; 158, blvd Haussmann, 75008, Métro St-Philippe-du-Roule. Open 10-6.* **(see p. 104)**

**Musée Maillol.** Interesting and atmospheric museum in a beautifully restored 18th-century townhouse mainly devoted to the works of the sculptor Maillol but also exhibiting works by Degas, Picasso, and others.... *Tel 01 42 22 59 58; 59–61, rue de Grenelle, 75005, Metro Rue du Bac. Mon, Wed–Sun 11–6, closed Tues. Admission charged.* **(see p. 102)**

**Musée Marmottan.** A 19th-century mansion near the Bois de Boulogne, with a large collection of Impressionist paintings and a fine assemblage of illuminated medieval manuscripts.... *Tel 01 42 24 07 02; 2, rue Louis-Boilly, 75016, Métro Muette. Open 10–5:30. Closed Mon. Admission charged.* **(see p. 105)**

**Musée National Picasso.** Works spanning the artist's entire career on display in a 17th-century mansion.... *Tel 01 42 71 25 21; Hôtel Salé, 5, rue de Thorigny, 75003, Métro Saint-Sébastien-Froissart or Saint-Paul. Open 9:30–5:50. Closed Tue. Admission charged.* **(see pp. 97, 103)**

**Musée Rodin.** The sculptor's most famous works, including *The Kiss* and *The Thinker,* in an 18th-century mansion.... *Tel 01 44 18 61 10; 77, rue Varenne, 75007, Métro Varenne. Open 9:30–5:15. Closed Mon. Admission charged.* **(see pp. 103, 107)**

**Notre-Dame.** The 14th-century Gothic cathedral has suffered many indignities over the centuries but still stands in all its glory and has been cleaned up for the new millennium.... *Tel 01 42*

*34 56 10; place du Parvis-Notre-Dame, 75004, Métro Cité. Cathedral open 8–6:45, closed Sat 12:30–2; towers open 10–6 in summer, hours vary slightly throughout the year. Admission charged for tower visits.* **(see pp. 96, 98)**

**Opéra Bastille.** The controversial and technologically sophisticated new opera house. For details about performances, see Entertainment.... *Tel 01 40 01 19 70; 120, rue de Lyon, 75011, Métro Bastille. Guided 75-minute tours begin at 1pm; call for dates. Closed 2 weeks in July and all of Aug. Admission charged.* **(see pp. 99, 114)**

**Opéra Garnier.** This ornate theater is the venue for dance performances and some opera.... *Tel 01 40 01 17 89; 8, rue Scribe, 75009, Métro Opéra. Open 10–5:30, guided tours at 1pm (except during matinees). Closed Jan 1 and May 1. Admission charged.* **(see p. 114)**

**Orangerie.** A small museum that houses a fine collection of Impressionist works.... *Tel 01 42 97 48 16; Jardin des Tuileries (on the Seine side near the place de la Concorde), 75001, Métro Concorde. Open 9:45–5:15. Closed Tue. Admission charged.* **(see p. 105)**

**Parc de Belleville.** An off-the-beaten-track hillside park with views over the city.... *Rue Piat, 75020, Métro Pyrénées.* **(see pp. 106, 112, 113)**

**Parc Zoologique de Paris.** A zoo in the Bois de Vincennes where the animals live in natural habitats.... *Tel 01 44 75 20 10; 53, ave de Saint-Maurice, 75012, Métro Porte Dorée. Open 9–6, until 5 in winter. Admission charged.* **(see p. 116)**

**Père Lachaise Cemetery.** The permanent resting place of everyone from Abélard and Héloise to Jim Morrison.... *Tel 01 43 70 70 33; entrance at corner of rue de la Roquette and blvd Ménilmontant, 75020, Métro Père Lachaise. Open 8–5:15. Admission free.* **(see p. 97, 113)**

**Petit Palais.** Home of the City of Paris's art collection. Often holds good temporary exhibitions.... *Tel 01 42 65 12 73; ave Winston Churchill, 75008, Métro Champs-Elysées-Clemenceau. Open 10–5:40. Closed Mon. Admission charged.* **(see p. 105)**

**Sacré-Coeur.** The famous hilltop church in Montmartre looks like a white wedding cake and has great views of Paris.... *Tel 01 53 41 89 00; 35, rue Chevalier-de-la-Barre, 75018, Métro Anvers. Church open 6–11; dome and crypt open 9–7, until 6 in winter. Admission charged for dome and crypt.* **(see pp. 96, 98, 106, 112)**

**Sainte-Chapelle.** A gorgeous 13th-century Gothic church hidden inside the Palais de Justice, with incredible stained-glass windows.... *Tel 01 53 73 78 51; 4, blvd du Palais, 75001, Métro Cité. Open 10–4:30 Oct–Apr, 9:30–6:30 May–Sept. Admission charged.* **(see p. 98)**

**Saint-Germain-des-Prés.** The oldest church in Paris dates to the 11th century.... *Tel 01 43 25 41 71; 3, place Saint-Germain-des-Prés, 75006, Métro Saint-Germain-des-Prés. Open 7–7:30. Admission free.* **(see p. 98)**

**Saint-Gervais-Saint-Protais.** A 17th-century Flamboyant Gothic church that is open round the clock.... *Place Saint-Gervais, 75004, Métro Hôtel-de-Ville. Admission free.* **(see p. 99)**

**Samaritaine.** Free views of Paris from the top floor of Magasin 2 of this venerable department store.... *Tel 01 40 41 20 20; La Samaritaine, Magasin 2, 2, quai du Louvre, 75001, Métro Louvre-Rivoli. Open 9:30–7, until 10 Thur. Closed Sun. Admission free.* **(see p. 106)**

**Sewers of Paris.** Sophisticated yet stinky sewage system originally constructed under Napoléon III. Don't wear your Sunday best.... *Tel 01 47 05 10 29; entrance at 93, quai d'Orsay, 75007, Métro Alma-Marceau. Open 11–5, until 4 in winter. Closed Thur–Fri. Admission charged.* **(see p. 117)**

**Studio 28.** A charming and eccentric movie theater with a bar and garden.... *Tel 01 46 06 36 07; 10, rue Tholozé, 75018, Métro Blanche or Abbesses. Closed last 2 weeks of July and all Aug. Admission charged.* **(see p. 115)**

**Vidéothèque de Paris.** A video archive with a huge selection of films concerning Paris.... *Tel 01 44 76 62 00; 2, Grande Galerie du Forum des Halles, Porte Saint-Eustache, 75001, Métro Les Halles. Open 1–9, until 10 Thur. Closed Mon. Admission charged.* **(see p. 115)**

THE INDEX

DIVERSIONS |

**128**

# Paris Diversions

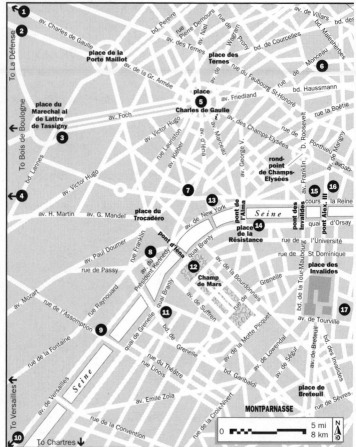

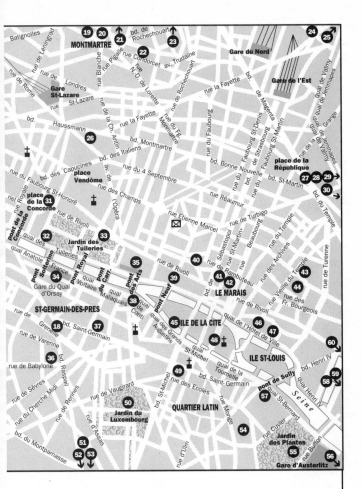

Musée de la Vie
  Romantique **22**
Musée de L'Erotisme **20**
Musée des Arts d'Afrique
  et d'Océanie **58**
Musée des Arts Décoratifs **33**
Musée de la Mode et
  du Textile **33**
Musée d'Orsay **34**
Musée du Cluny **49**
Musée Edith Piaf **29**
Musée Guimet **7**
Musée Jacquemart-
  André **6**
Musée Maillol **18**
Musée Picasso **43**
Musée Rodin **17**

Notre-Dame **47**
Opéra Bastille **60**
Opéra Garnier **26**
L'Orangerie **32**
Parc de Belleville **27**
Parc Zoologique **59**
Père Lachaise Cemetery **30**
Petit Palais **16**
Sacré Coeur **23**
Sainte-Chapelle **45**
Saint-Germain des Prés **37**
Saint-Gervais-Saint-
  Pretais **46**
Samaritaine **39**
Sewers of Paris **14**
Studio 28 **21**
Vidéothèque de Paris **40**

getting

# 4

## outside

The French idea
of a garden dic-
tates that nature
be tortured and
tamed into sym-
metrical shapes
and designs.

Instead of green expanses of lawn, you get dirt. If there is grass, you're usually not allowed to sit on it—it's only to be looked at. This produces beautiful gardens, not places where you go to have fun. Paris does have a few wide-open green spaces, but they're so civilized—and in good weather so crowded with people—that you hardly feel you're outdoors.

And then there's the traffic. There are often pollution alerts in the summer, but the city government seems unwilling to take action to cut down on the number of cars. (The strongest measure so far has been to restrict traffic to odd or even license-plate numbers on the day *after* a pollution alert.)

If you know where to go, however, it is still possible to find a bit of tranquility and greenery in Paris and its environs. Just don't expect to "get in touch" with nature.

# The Lowdown

**Taking the air...** Wandering aimlessly through the vast forest of the **Bois de Boulogne** (main entrance near Métro Porte Dauphine) is not very interesting unless, of course, you are intrigued by public sexual activities, often practiced in broad daylight. Whole books and dissertations have been written on the subject of prostitution in the park, with special interest paid to all the Brazilian transvestites who ply their trade in the Bois. If this sort of stuff isn't your priority, head for less sordid areas of the forest, such as the **Pré Catelan**, a pristine little park within the Bois de Boulogne, where a 200-year-old beech tree provides a huge sprawl of shade, and nannies watch their little charges cavorting over great expanses of green. The gourmet restaurant **Le Pré Catalan** (see Dining) is located here, as is the **Jardin Shakespeare**, which has an outdoor theater surrounded by all sorts of trees and plants mentioned by the Bard. Even lovelier is the **Bagatelle**, an English-style garden with peacocks, a spectacular rose garden, and art exhibitions held in a tiny château. The child-oriented **Jardin d'Acclimatation**, a park in the Bois with zoo animals and carnival rides, is fun for adults as well. Boats can be rented for paddling around on **Lac Supérieur**.

Unlike the wooded Bois de Boulogne, the large **Bois de Vincennes** (Métro Château de Vincennes), at the eastern edge of Paris, sometimes seems too civilized and overbuilt. Take a walk in its **Parc Floral** (admission charged), which has a little train running around its perimeter. Rent a rowboat and go out on one of the two lakes, **Lac des Minimes** (Métro Porte-Dorée) or **Lac Daumesnil** (RER Nogent-sur-Marne). Stroll through the **Parc Zoologique** or visit the **Foire du Trône** (a carnival); the **Centre Bouddhique**, a Tibetan Buddhist temple; the **Château de Vincennes**; or the **Musée des Arts d'Afrique et d'Océanie**. Climb to the top of the **Parc de Belleville**, a recently renovated hillside park, and you have Paris at your feet. A monumental stairway leads down the hill, passing terraced lawns with fountains, waterfalls, and pools.

The **Jardin du Luxembourg** (Métro Odéon or RER Luxembourg), a residential area in Roman times and later a private royal property, was liberated during the Revolution and is now open to everyone. Visitors no longer have to pay to rent one of the pretty, green metal chairs that are traditional in French parks—they're free to all. You'll have to pay for a wooden toy boat if your child wants to sail one in the pool in the center of the park, but it's worth it, both to appease the kid and to see the brightly colored sails zipping around in the water. This park is so kid-friendly, it has chess tables, a large playground, a marionette theater—even a *pelouse* (lawn) that children are allowed to play on. (In some Paris parks a new law allows you to sit on *some* lawns but not in the Luxembourg, which is owned by the Senate rather than the city.) In addition to the lawns and cafe under the chestnut trees near the place du Luxembourg, there are various gardens graced with statues. (Look for George Sand to the left of the Saint-Michel entrance and the queens of France surrounding the large, open space in the center.) The most scenic part of the park is the **Medicis Fountain**, built by Marie de Medicis to improve the view from her bedroom window in the Luxembourg Palace, built in 1612; goldfish swim in the long, rectangular pool flanked by Italian-style vines, as a statue of an amorous couple looks on. Tucked away in the southwest corner of the garden is the rarely visited **Verger du Luxembourg**, or the National Conservatory of Apples and Pears, founded by Napoléon in 1809. Here, 360 species of apple trees and 270 types of pear trees are tortured into those unnatural shapes so beloved by French gardeners. And who gets to eat the fruit? Members of the

Senate, of course, who meet in the palace on the other side of the park. (Leftovers are given to a soup kitchen.) Nearby is an apiary, which sells its honey at the end of September in the garden near the intersection of rue de Vaugirard and rue Guynemer.

Once a place for "elegant rendezvous," **Tuileries Garden** (Métro Tuileries), stretching along the right bank of the Seine between the place de la Concorde and the Louvre, is now a gay cruising ground at night. In the daytime, however, this statue-studded formal garden—created by Catherine de Medicis in the 16th century and revamped by Louis XIV's architect, Le Nôtre, in the 17th—is a reasonable spot for a stroll. Some of the statues here date to the 17th century, and four of them were sculpted by Auguste Rodin. Children love the round pool toward the western end of the garden, where they can sail wooden boats rented from a nearby stand. Twice a year, for a few weeks in summertime and at Christmas, a carnival is set up between the garden and the rue de Rivoli; its main attraction an immense Ferris wheel with stellar views of Paris from the top (well worth risking an attack of vertigo). Two major museums, the **Orangerie** and **Jeu de Paume** (see Diversions), are in the Tuileries, and a renovated garden, the **Jardin du Carrousel** (which contains no carousel at all), has opened here next to the Louvre, with lawns adorned with statues by Aristide Maillol. Its flower beds are a treat for the eye, and its comfortable lawn chairs are a welcome place to take a load off.

Paris's newest park, the **Parc de Bercy** (Métro Bercy) is a good reason to visit this area on the eastern side of Paris, which the city has been unsuccessfully trying to redevelop for years. Located among abandoned wine warehouses along the Seine, the park has inherited hundreds of old trees and has a "jardin romantique," an aromatic garden, a rose garden, a "philosopher's" garden, a vegetable garden, fruit orchards, a small lake, a labyrinth, and the ruins of a small château. The **Parc André Citroën** (tel 01 45 58 35 40; rue Balard and rue Blanc, 75015, Métro Balard) in the southwest corner of the city is an urban park par excellence. It doesn't try to pretend it's not part of a city; instead, architectural elements are used to create hidden corners with varying miniature landscapes, ranging from rock gardens to mini-fields of wildflowers. Fountains and waterways, mazelike walkways, and several beautiful, modern greenhouses (one of which holds changing exhibitions) add more variety to this unusual park. In the center is a large stretch of lawn surrounded by a mock moat. In summer, children have a great time playing in the jets of a fountain between the two large greenhouses.

The ubiquitous Baron Haussmann, who in the late 19th century created the grand boulevards that give Paris its present form, also designed the **Parc des Buttes-Chaumont** (Métro Buttes-Chaumont or Botzaris), set on a former hilltop quarry in the northeastern part of the city. All of the "natural" features you see here—the "mountains" and the lake—are man-made. The temple situated on an outcropping in the lake offers good views of the city, topping off this romantic tableau. The whole scene is straight out of Wordsworth or Keats.

**On the run...** Don't be surprised if people stare at you when you lace up your Nikes and hit the pavement—jogging is still considered pretty odd here along city streets, although it is gradually becoming popular among the stubbornly sedentary French. And while running along the **Seine** is a romantic idea, the health benefits are debatable; with three or four lanes of heavy traffic running alongside you, you'll be breathing lungfuls of exhaust fumes. The same goes for the Right Bank's **Canal Saint-Martin**. Happily, the city now closes the quays of the Seine and the streets along the canal to automobile traffic for a good part of the day on Sundays, leaving a clear, pollution-free path for joggers and bikers.

Much more pleasant for running are the large parks: the **Jardin du Luxembourg**, the **Tuileries**, the **Parc des Buttes-Chaumont**, the **Parc de Montsouris** (RER Cité-Universitaire), the **Bois de Vincennes**, or the **Bois de Boulogne** (see "Taking the air," above). It's also possible to run in the pretty **Parc Monceau** (Métro Monceau), in the 8th arrondissement, but you'll have to circle the park many times to work up a good sweat. Jogging is not allowed in the city's other large green spaces, the cemeteries: You might rouse the dead.

**Two-wheeling in Paris...** Paris is not a city where you long for a bicycle *(vélo)*, although it is how many city dwellers choose to get around. It is mostly flat, but there is just too much (terrifying) traffic and pollution to make cycling seem like a good idea. With proper guidance, though, it can be a wonderful experience. Luckily, Michele Nöe, a clever Belgian and owner of a company called **Paris à Vélo, C'est Sympa!** (tel 01 48 87 60 01, fax 01 48 87 61 01; www.parisvelosympa.com; 9, 37, blvd Bourdon, 75004, Métro Bastille), had the good idea of not only renting bicycles but also conducting three-hour guided tours of Paris neighborhoods that take riders into little-known corners of the city, showing them delightful places that few residents, let alone visitors, know about. Noë knows the traffic-free streets, the tiny passageways, and the few bicycle paths in the city. He and his assistant provide ongoing commentary (in English, even) on the sights and architecture. He runs night tours of the city, too.

Bicycles can also be rented at stands in the **Bois de Boulogne** near the Relais du Rois on the route de Suresnes (Métro Pont de Neuilly, bus 144) and in the **Bois de Vincennes**, either at the Lac des Minimes (Métro Porte-Dorée) or at the entrance to the Parc Floral (Métro Château de Vincennes). Both parks have bicycle paths *(pistes cyclable)*. If you'd rather not tire out your calf muscles, **Scooters** (tel 01 48 70 13 40) rents motorscooters through some Paris hotels. Call for information, but be warned, no English is spoken. No driver's license is required, and insurance, two anti-theft devices, and the obligatory helmet are provided.

**La Bicyclette Verte** (tel 05 49 63 14 99; www.bicyclette-verte.com; boîte postale 03, 79210 Arçais) organizes bicycle trips that last from one to 10 days and cover various parts of France outside Paris. One such trip goes to Ile de Ré, an island off La Rochelle where you can find white flower-covered houses, salt flats, and great Atlantic beaches. The company arranges for hotels and meals and meets you with ready-to-roll bicycles at the train station of your destination.

**Back in the saddle...** For a brisk gallop through the woods of the Bois de Boulogne, on the western edge of Paris, try either of its two riding centers: the **Cercle Hippique du Bois de Vincennes** (tel 01 48 73 91 28; route de Neuilly à la Muette, Métro Pont-de-Neuilly) and the **Société Equestre de l'Etrier** (tel 01 45 01 20 02;

route de Madrid du Lac, Métro Porte-Maillot, bus 244). The sprawling Bois de Vincennes, just to the east of Paris, also has the **Centre Equestre de la Cartoucherie** (tel 01 43 74 61 25; route de Champs-de-Maneuvres, 75012, Métro Château de Vincennes).

**Get all wet...** Sadly, Paris's beautiful 200-year-old floating swimming pool on the Seine, the Piscine Deligny, sank in 1994. Meanwhile, however, the **Piscine d'Auteuil** (tel 01 42 24 07 59; route des Lacs et Passy, 75016, Métro Ranelagh; www.piscine.auteuil.free.fr), an outdoor pool in the Bois de Boulogne, is open Tuesday through Saturday, 7am to 7pm. 2.43 euros per visit, 19.81 euros for ten visits. **Aquaboulevard** (tel 01 40 60 15 15; 4, rue Louis-Armand, 75015; Métro Balard; open daily 9am to 11pm; about 18 euros to use the pool) is a leisure complex on the south-western edge of the city that has a huge swimming pool (a small part of which extends outdoors) equipped with toboggans, waves, and rapids. There is also an outdoor "beach," a well-equipped gymnasium, a climbing wall, tennis and squash courts, table tennis, billiards, restaurants, snack bars, and shops.

   If you don't feel like trekking all the way out to the burbs for your swim, there are some indoor options in town. The **Gymnase Club**, the largest chain of gyms in Paris, has pools at three branches: place de l'Italie (tel 01 45 80 34 16; 16, rue Vandrezanne, 75013, Métro Place de l'Italie; www.gymnaseclub.fr); place de la République (tel 01 47 00 69 98; 10, Place de la République, Métro Place de la République); and Grenelle (tel 01 45 75 34 00; 8, rue Frémicourt, 75015, Métro Émile Zola). All are open daily well into the evenings, though they close at 4pm on Sundays. All charge 22.87 euros per day for use of all their facilities. The Olympic-sized **Piscine Roger-le-Gall** (tel 01 44 73 81 12; 34, blvd Carnot, 75012, Métro Porte-de-Vincennes), also open daily, has a sliding roof that opens to let in the rays when the weather's good. It goes nudist twice a week, thanks to some dogged demonstrating on the part of a group of naturists (mostly men strip down at these two-hour swim sessions, though all are welcome; call 01 47 78 18 78 for more info). Another Olympic-sized pool is the **Piscine Nouveau Forum des Halles** (tel 01 42 36 98 44; 10, place de la Rotonde, entrance at Porte du Louvre, Métro Les Halles),

**PARIS** | GETTING OUTSIDE

in the new part of the underground Forum des Halles shopping mall, right in the heart of the city. The indoor **Piscine de Pontoise** in the Latin Quarter (tel 01 55 42 77 88; 19, rue de Pontoise, 75005, Métro Maubert-Mutualité or Jussieu; 3.81 euros per visit) is the trendy place to take a dip before dancing all night at your favorite disco. It's open daily, and stays open until midnight four nights a week. The **Ritz Club** (tel 01 43 16 30 30; Ritz, place Vendôme, 75001, Métro Concorde; open 7am to 10pm) is the Ritz's luxurious spa with swimming pool and gym. It is sometimes available for day use if the hotel isn't full. Call the day before and be prepared to cough up as much as 90 to 100 euros.

Where not mentioned above, public pools usually charge 3.81 euros for a dip. Swim on weekdays if possible—these pools are extremely crowded on weekends, especially in summer, and French people seem to have a hard time staying in their lanes when they swim (the same problem they have when they drive).

**The tennis racket...** If you must swing a racket while you're in Paris, the municipal courts at **Tennis Luxembourg** (tel 01 43 25 79 18; Jardin du Luxembourg, blvd Saint-Michel, 75006, RER Luxembourg) and **Centre Sportif La Falguere (La Falguere)** (tel 01 43 74 40 93; route de la Pyramide, Bois de Vincennes, Métro Château-de-Vincennes, bus 112) are available on a first-come, first-serve basis. Go in the morning for the best chance of getting a court. The vast **Aquaboulevard** (tel 01 40 60 10 00; 4, rue Louis-Armand, 75015, Métro Balard) has courts for both tennis and squash (pronounced "*skwatch*" by the French). Squash can also be played at the **Squash Club Quartier Latin** (tel 01 43 54 82 45; 19, rue de Pontoise, 75005, Métro Maubert-Mutualité), **Squash Montmartre** (tel 01 42 55 38 30; 14, rue Achille-Martinet, 75018, Métro Lamarck-Caulaincourt), **Squash Rennes-Raspail** (tel 01 44 39 03 30; rue des Rennes, 75006, Métro Saint-Placide or Montparnasse), and **Squash Front de Seine** (tel 01 45 75 35 37; 21, rue Gaston-de-Caillavet, 75015, Métro Bir-Hakeim). Reserve a court in advance if you can. Most facilities cost between 9.14 and 12.19 euros per person for a half-hour; prices are somewhat lower on weekday afternoons.

**Birds of a feather...** Did you bring your binoculars? Got that field notebook handy? Then visit the bird preserve in the **Bois de Boulogne,** the **Réserve Ornithologique** (Allée de Longchamp, Métro Porte-Maillot, bus 244). Guided bird walks take place regularly in the **Bois de Vincennes** (call Christian Galinet at 01 47 70 29 83 for details). The **Ligue pour la Protections des Oiseaux** (tel 05 46 82 12 34) provides information on birds in the Paris regions and organizes bird-watching walks and trips.

**Best places for pickup...** On weekend afternoons, there are usually pick-up Frisbee and soccer games at the **Esplanade des Invalides** (Métro Invalides); soccer on the lawns of **Parc de la Villette** (Métro Porte-de-Pantin or Porte-de-la-Villette); baseball on the **Plaine de Pershing** (RER Joinville-le-Pont); soccer and Frisbee on the fields near the **Château de Vincennes** (Métro Château de Vincennes). Don't bother going in the morning—the players don't show up until their hangovers have worn off.

**Stretching your legs...** Get out your backpack, fill it with pâté, cheese, fruit, a baguette, a bottle of water, and a bottle of wine, and hop on a train for a day's hike. The **Forêt de Fontainebleau,** the largest forest near Paris, is a favorite spot for rock climbers because of its marvelous rock formations, some of them 20 meters (more than 60 feet) high. Even if you're not interested in hanging like a bat from a rock, you'll appreciate these as scenery—they come in fantastic shapes and all sizes, and some look like enormous Swiss cheese riddled with holes. You'll occasionally come across fountains inscribed with poetry, as well. Take a suburban (*banlieue*) train from the Gare de Lyon to Fontainebleau-Avon (the trains leave about every hour and a half during the day, and the ride takes 50 minutes). When you leave the station, turn right, go past the cafe, and take the stairs up to a busy road. You'll see the forest on the other side, behind the outdoor swimming pool (bring your bathing suit in summer and take a dip after your hike). Paths are clearly marked with colored paint on trees and rocks: A double line along the path means there's a change of direction, a curved line should be followed in the direction it points to, and an "x" means you've headed in the wrong direction.

**Good skates...** Indoor ice rinks, open year-round, are the

**Patinoire d'Asniéres-sur-Seine** (tel 01 47 99 96 06; blvd Pierre-de-Coubertin, 75016, Métro Gabriel-Péri), or the **Patinoire de Saint-Ouen** (tel 01 40 11 43 38; 4, rue du Docteur-Bauer, 93400 Saint-Ouen, Métro Mairie de Saint-Ouen), just outside Paris. Skate rental is included in the overall fee (6.09 to 7.62 euros) at rinks, where packs of speeding kids and teenagers churn up the ice, accompanied in the indoor rinks by the incessant racket of disco music. From mid-December through early March there is a small, free open-air ice rink in the square in front of the Hotel de Ville, Paris's city hall, in the 4th arrondissement (Métro Hotel de Ville); they rent skates, too, for about 4.57 euros a pair. Rollerblading has taken Paris by storm, and every Friday night there's a city-run event called Paris Roller, which leaves the Place d'Italie at 10pm and covers 30 kilometers of city streets with a police escort. This popular event attracts an average of 800 bladers a week, and since most of them are experienced, this is not an occasion to try a new sport. You can rent rollerblades at **Bike n'Roller** (tel 01 44 07 35 89; 6, rue St-Julien-le-Pauvre, 75005) and **Parking Bld Roller Station** (tel 01 42 78 33 00; 107–109, blvd Beaumarchais, 75003) for about 7.62 to 12.19 euros a day or 9.14 to 18.29 euros for the weekend.

**A day at the races...** The Bois de Boulogne has two horse-racing tracks, the **Hippodrome de Longchamp** (tel 01 44 30 75 00; Carrefour de Longchamp, Métro Porte-Maillot, bus 244) for flat-track racing and the **Hippodrome d'Auteuil** (tel 01 45 20 15 98; Métro Porte-d'Auteuil) for steeplechase. The **Hippodrome de Vincennes** (tel 01 49 77 17 17; 2, route de la Ferme;,RER Joinville-le-Pont) in the Bois de Vincennes is a trotters' course; it attracts a more working-class crowd than the tonier Longchamp and d'Auteuil tracks.

**Par for the course...** While the kids are shaking hands with Mickey and Goofy and spending your life's savings on Disney memorabilia, you can try to relax on the 27-hole course at **Golf Disneyland Paris** (tel 01 60 45 68 04, RER Métro Marne-la-Vallée-Chessy). Greens fees are 19.82 euros for nine holes (30.49 euros on weekends). Most other golf courses near Paris are for members only; for information on courses that accept nonmembers, contact the **Fédération Française du Golf** (tel 01 45 02 13 55; 69, ave Victor Hugo, 75016). The **Golf Club d'Etoile** (tel 01 43 80 30 79; 10, ave de la Grande-Armée, 75017, Métro Etoile; 15.22 euros/hr.) is a driving range.

**Working up a sweat...** If you didn't bring your personal trainer with you, **Home Gym** (tel 01 45 77 60 62) will send one to your hotel (except in August) for 58 euros an hour, or 50.38 euros per hour for a two-session plan. Other services include massages and hair styling and cutting. For a touch of luxury (at a price), the elegant gymnasium at the Ritz, the **Ritz Club** (tel 01 43 16 30 30; Place Vendôme, 75001, Métro Concorde) sometimes accepts visitors who pay by the day (91.41 euros per day). For a single visits, the best bet in town is **Club Quartier Latin** in the Latin Quarter (tel 01 55 42 77 88; 19, rue de Pontoise, 75005, Métro Maubert-Mutualite), where a day pass runs 13.72 euros and includes access to the Piscine de Pontoise. They offer a complete range of well-maintained machines, plus a full schedule of aerobic, cardio, stretch, and other classes, and this place is frequented by a friendly young crowd. The leisure complex **Aquaboulevard** (tel 01 40 60 10 00; 4, rue Louis-Armand, 75015, Métro Balard; 22.87 euros/day for all facilities) has an enormous, well-equipped gym complete with a climbing wall.

# ping

"Window-licking"
is an *affaire
d'intérêt* with
Parisians, a matter
of money, if not
survival. It takes a
bulging wallet

(and a stack of credit cards) to actually buy anything at the chic department stores and trendy boutiques, so most locals satisfy their consumer fetishism with what Americans more prosaicly describe as "window-shopping."

You can, however, get your hands on a designer original that already has been worn in a fashion show, or pick up reasonably priced designer "seconds" and used designer clothing at specialty stores around town (see "Bargain Hunting," below). Hip, young Parisians, like their American counterparts, put together their ultra-stylish anti-fashion statements with items from used-clothing stores and thrift shops. The bonus here is, even if you can do without the retro polyester seventies jogging suits, recent castoffs from chic Parisian closets are often just coming into style back at home.

And of course you want to get some sort of souvenir that comes with a story you can repeat to all of your friends, especially if you found the little treasure after an hour-long trek to a local flea market (see "Watch out for fleas and fleecers," below). Who knows, you may end up with a Eiffel Tower enshrined in a plastic altar and decorated with Christmas-tree lights.

If splurging on high-fashion (or tacky souvenirs) isn't your *raison d'être*, you can easily rid yourself of spare cash on other delights for which the French are famous: wine and champagne, gourmet kitchenware, sensuous perfumes, and fine sheets and pillowcases that make you understand a bit more clearly why Marcel Proust spent so much of his life in bed. In general, French spending is down, and has been down for some time, so retailers are desperate to get some of your cash. That means clearance racks and flat-out bargaining are common, no matter where you shop.

Gone are the days of trying to master long division with the French franc to get the U.S. dollar equivalency. Since its inception in 1999, the euro has consistently hovered around the United States dollar (at press time, every dollar was worth 1.08 in euros), so conversion is a cinch. If you have francs left over from a previous visit, these will no longer be accepted by any vendor or establishment, but may be exchanged at any bank or change bureau, usually for a small commission.

One final word of warning—watch out for the *vendeuses*, or female shop assistants, who usually come in one of three varieties: frosty, smarmy, or pushy! Many work on commission and will do Oscar-quality performances when it comes to convincing customers they can't live without the latest ludicrously expensive Starck-designed kitchen gadget. They can also be compliment sluts, so if anyone purrs "Madame! That non-dry-cleanable rubberized dress shows off your figure perfectly" leave the store immediately with a curt "*Et ta mere, cheri!*" ("And your mother, too, sweetheart!").

## Target Zones

The buzzword on the Paris shopping scene continues to be diversity, and the city truly does offer something for everyone. Fashion junkies on unlimited budgets should head straight for the **Triangle d'Or**. This classy quartier around **rue du Faubourg Saint-Honoré** and **avenue Montaigne** is the Parisian equivalent of Madison Avenue and boasts couture houses and luxury boutiques galore. Diamonds are rich girls' best friends on the **place Vendôme** while **rue Royale** and **Place de la Madeleine** are target zones for crystal, chic tableware, and the ultimate in gourmet food.

Parisian department stores, known locally as *les grands magasins* (the Big Stores), are basically just that: multistory emporiums that are fun but confusing

### Le drugstore

*The French are famous hypochondriacs—they just don't feel well if they're not dosing themselves with medications. At school exam times, pharmacy windows are crammed with mysterious remedies for fatigue intellectuelle. Pharmacies also do a booming business in crèmes d'amincissements, products supposed to slim down thunder thighs and get rid of cellulite. (Science says these creams don't work, but you might wonder after a day at a French beach, when you can't spot a dimpled thigh on a single woman in sight.) French pharmacies can be pretty damn intimidating, though. All medicinal products are kept behind the counter, where you have to ask a clerk for them—and you may have to describe your symptoms in front of other customers. You could lurk outside until the pharmacy's empty, but someone's sure to walk in just as you reach the most intimate part. Many pharmacists speak English, and they often serve as substitute doctors here, so if you have a minor problem, don't hesitate to ask the pharmacist for a cure. Don't be surprised, however, if the druggist tries to sell you seven different creams, soaps, and pills for your acne. Homeopathy is widely accepted here, so don't think the guy's a quack if the ingredients read like a grocery list. The new "parapharmacies" have somewhat lower prices.*

SHOPPING | INTRODUCTION

to shop in owing to the ongoing French obsession with bureaucracy (which often has distraught shoppers dashing frantically from cash register to cash register waving multiple slips of paper!). If you prefer more personal, why, God forbid, even *friendly* service, try the new breed of ateliers-boutiques that are springing up all over the city. Shopping in these intimate studio/shops is low-key and relaxing, and you often have the added bonus of meeting the designer behind the clothes! Check out the Marais, a lively area crammed full of ateliers-boutiques, Jewish delis, and kitsch design shops or, if clubwear and funky bohemian styles are your thing, spend an afternoon combing the area around trendy **place des Abbesses**.

Once the favored hang-out of Parisian intellectuals and black-clad existentialists, Saint Germain is now famous for fashion boutiques. Bypass the ultra-touristy Deux Magots and join the crowd of modern-day de Beauvoirs sipping lattes in Emporio Armani. Comme des Garcons, Yohji Yamamoto, British knitwear master and minimalist Joseph, and cult second-hand store Kiliwatch can all be found on **rue Etienne-Marcel**, the street that leads to mini fashion-Mecca **Place des Victoires**. **Rue du Jour** is another fab fashion destination, but underground shopping mall **Forum des Halles** (just down the road) is best avoided, apart from a quick trip to mega-music-book-computer store **FNAC**. Home to tramps, pickpockets, and drug addicts, the Forum smells of cheap aftershave and urine on a good day (and, no, don't even ask about the bad!). The Nouveau Forum des Halles on the western side of the mall is far more savory and attractive and, besides offering a wide range of shops, it also houses the huge UGC cinema complex and a branch of the hip sandwich chain Lina's.

For a classier version of the shopping mall wander through the arcades of **Palais-Royal** (Métro Palais Royal), whose gorgeous covered galleries were built by the debt-ridden Duke d'Orléans in the 18th century. Nearby **Galerie Vivienne**, built in 1823, has also been lovingly restored and is now home to such fashion musts as the Gaultier boutique. Alternatively, enjoy the hustle and bustle of the city's vibrant market streets—**rue Montorgeuil** (Métro Sentier or Etienne Marcel) and **rue Mouffetard** (Métro Monge) are two of the most colorful—or pay a visit to the boisterous flea markets (*marchés aux puces*) on the city outskirts.

## Bargain Hunting

The best fashion deals in town are found in *dégriffé* or *dépôt-vente* boutiques, which carry designer seconds and other covetable items with the label ripped out. Among those with the best selections are **Alternatives** in the Marais, which carries many outfits made for the fashion shows and never worn again; **Le Mouton à Cinq Pattes** stores, where you can paw through a vast selection of men's and women's designer seconds; **Passé Devant** (women's only; new and used) in Montmartre; and **L'Habilleur**, also in the Marais (men's and women's; new only). **La Marelle** in the **Galerie Vivienne** has used clothing in fine condition, with top-designer labels. End-of-season sales are held in most boutiques and department stores in January and July.

Chain stores such as **Kookaï**, **Morgan,** and **Hennes & Mauritz** (H&M) are worth checking out for year-round bargains. These shops "translate"—that's fashion speak for *copy*—the latest runway trends and get them out on the rails for about a tenth of designer prices. OK, so the clothes are often manufactured in crappy fabrics—but who cares when you can pick up a dress for around 30 euros and toss it Kleenex style at the end of the season? The Spanish chain **Zara** and the sale-price annex shop of cult French label **APC** are also firm favorites with the fashion pack.

If you don't mind searching through racks of junky used clothes for that one fabulous find, and you're not allergic to musty polyester jogging suits, head for a **Guerrisold** outlet. Once frequented only by the down-and-out, this chain of used-clothing stores is now a regular haunt of stylish young hipsters and trendy designers looking for inspiration. Already-worn clothes and other secondhand treasures can also be found at Paris's many flea markets on the outskirts of town (see "Watch out for fleas and fleecers," below). The **rue de Paradis** (Métro Poissonnière) in the 10th arrondissement is a paradise for bargain hunters who want big-name tableware at discount prices. Try **Tisanière** (tel 01 47 70 22 80; 21, rue de Paradis, 75010) for Limoges porcelain or **Lumicristal** (tel 01 47 70 27 97; 22 bis, rue de Paradis, 75010) for crystal by Baccarat, Daum, and Limoges. **Baccarat** has a shop and museum on the street, but does not offer discounted prices.

## Trading with the Natives

Bargaining is common for used goods and antiques, but not

for new merchandise. If you're buying a high-priced item, however, don't hesitate to ask for *une petite réduction*, especially in small shops where you may be dealing directly with the owner or manager. You've got nothing to lose.

Most stores are willing to mail purchases and will hold goods for a limited period of time (usually 24 hours). Gift-wrapping services are provided almost everywhere; ask for *un paquet cadeau*. Remember: It's considered rude not to say "bonjour" when you enter a shop ("bonsoir" if after 6pm) and "au revoir" when you leave.

### Hours of Business

Most boutiques open at around 10am and close at 7 in the evening. Smaller shops may also close at lunchtime, usually between 1 and 2:30. By law, retail stores, except those that sell food, must close on Sunday, though many boutiques, particularly in the Marais, flout the law and open on Sunday (usually starting at 2pm). Some boutiques close on Monday mornings. Major department stores are open from about 9:30am to 7pm, and most stay open until 10 one night of the week. Many shops close during August.

### Sales Tax

France's TVA (*taxe sur le valeur ajouté* or value-added tax) is 20.6 percent. This tax has been factored into posted prices; the only way to avoid it is to spend more than 182.99 euros in one store, have a form filled out at the *détaxe* office in the place of purchase, and present it (with your bill) to customs at the airport when you leave the European Union. Don't check your bags before doing this—the customs agents will want to eyeball whatever you're claiming. Cash refunds are sometimes possible, but you may have to wait for a check to be sent to you or have the refund applied to your credit card account. There's no refund available for food products, services (such as your hotel stay), tobacco, medicines, firearms, and uncut gems—and you must be at least 15 years old to qualify for the cost break.

# The Lowdown

*Les grands magasins...* Long renowned as a world center for retail therapy, Paris invented the department store in the 19th century. And the good news is that five of the city's original grands *magasins* still exist today. The oldest is **Le Bon Marché**, a temple of Left Bank chic and luxury goods, whose iron structure was designed by Gustave Eiffel (that's Eiffel as in Tower, dah!). Since its 1998 revamp, Le Bon Marché boasts a state-of-the-art beauty department offering everything from make-up lessons to aromatherapy. **Printemps** and the **Galeries Lafayette**, just around the corner from the Opéra Garnier, have also undergone major facelifts to launch them into the 21st century. Printemps now has an excellent men's department (complete with in-house bar designed by Paul Smith) and a divine Young Designer space, while Galeries Lafayette offers an unbeatable selection of perfume, jewelry, and lingerie. **BHV** has traditionally had a dowdier image than its bigger flashier brothers, but do-it-yourself freaks flock here in droves at the weekend, working themselves into near-religious ecstasy over the nuts and bolts in the hardware basement. **Samaritaine** is worth a visit for its rooftop restaurant and its gorgeous Art Deco staircase (Shop 2), but the staff is mind-bogglingly rude and overall the place just don't have no class.

**Feet first...** Paris is absolute heaven for foot fetishists—slip into strappy slingbacks and gravity-defying heels *chez* **Christian Louboutin**, France's answer to Manolo Blahnik, or pay a visit to French shoe guru **Stephane Kélian**. Kélian's famous for doing classics as well as trends, so you'll find everything from hand-woven pumps to kinky over-the-knee boots in his elegant boutiques. **Kabuki**'s a great address for one-stop trend shopping—you'll find the latest shoes from Prada, Miu Miu, and Sergio Rossi downstairs and cutting-edge men's and women's fashion upstairs. **Charles Jourdan** designs seriously high fashion footwear for men and women while **Free Lance** styles are for wilder party girls who like lots of psychedelic colors and ponyskin. Meanwhile, shoppers with cash-flow problems can find this season's hottest looks with purse-friendly price tags at **Shoebizz**. If you're looking for the latest in trendy Pumas or Nikes, stroll down rue Saint Denis in the Les Halles district for discount athletic and shoe stores.

**Designer dressing...** You have to have serious Attitude

SHOPPING | THE LOWDOWN

to shop on Avenue Montaigne, the land of frosty blonde *vendeuses* who'd sooner impale themselves on a stiletto heel than wish you a nice day. If you're really not up to their withering looks, you can always dawdle outside the boutiques and be a window-licker. Begin with a visit to **Christian Dior**'s sumptuous flagship store, filled with the wildly flamboyant (and wildly expensive) collections dreamt up by in-house eccentric John Galliano. Up the road at **Givenchy**, in-house designer Alexander McQueen—aka the inventor of "butt-crack" trousers—tones his style down for ladies-and-filmstars-who-lunch, while another British fashion talent, Stella McCartney, tempts modern vamps at **Chloe**. **Céline**'s windows used to be full of prim little suits for prissy French madames, but since the arrival of hip New Yorker Michael Kors the Céline logo is back in style with a vengeance. Style slaves should also visit the beautifully revamped **Balenciaga** boutique, where Nicolas Ghesquière pulls the crowds with collections inspired by sci-fi heroines from *Alien* and *Star Wars*.

**Chanel** (as in Kaiser Karl reworking the Coco classics), **Jean-Paul Gaultier,** and **Thierry Mugler** (the high priest of hips and bosoms) are still firm French favorites. **Lanvin** is also worth a visit—if only to eat supermodel salads washed down with ludicrously expensive mineral water at "Café Bleu"—but the one to watch now is **Yves Saint Laurent**. With Fashion God Tom Ford in control of the creative reins the YSL logo is about to become a smokin' property! Venezuelan fashion guru **Maria Luisa** stocks a selection of "happening designers" in her intimidatingly smart boutique, but if you're looking for friendlier service try Left Bank style temple **Onward** for shoes, accessories, and clothes from Gaultier, Martine Sitbon, Helmut Lang, and Alexander McQueen. **Victoire** and **L'Eclaireur** are also good multilabel shops, although in the latter you have to put up with male sales assistants stomping around in Comme des Garçons skirts—but hey, this is the wonderful world of fashion. Cashmere fans will think they've died and gone to heaven in **Malo**—that is, until they've seen the price tags. **Eric Bompard** is (slightly) cheaper and stocks an extensive selection for men and women. Don't be put off by the frumpy-looking vitrines! Fashion junkies who really want to splurge should pay a visit to vintage couture king **Didier Ludot**. Secondhand Dior and Chanel doesn't come cheap. But five-figure price tags are only to be expected now that Miuccia Prada's become one of Ludot's best clients! To find the perfect vintage Hermès bag to go with your new (old) Chanel suit, head to **Les 3 Marches.**

**Jeunes créateurs...** If you're looking for originality, it's better to avoid the Montaigne sector. Escape logo-land and check out the new wave of ateliers-boutiques, where if you're lucky you'll find the designer beavering away on a sewing-machine at the back of the store. In the Marais, **Martin Grant** makes Australian couture to die for, while next door at **iRoo** Korean designer Il-Kwon Park runs up innovative dresses in space-age fabrics. **Kyungmee J** puts on an impressive one-woman show in her cute little boutique, acting as designer, saleswoman, model, and cleaning lady, while around the corner Franco-Japanese duo **Blancs-Manteaux** turn out impeccable minimalist fashion with a twist. Montmartre is another hotbed of young design talent. Worth checking out are **Patricia Louisor**—boho chic in a party atmosphere—and **Fanche et Flo**—a charming duo who go in for colorful, graphic prints on cashmere and blanket fabric.

**Mix, match, 'n' accessorize...** Oh do get real, Chanel bags and Hermès scarves are not the be-all and end-all when it comes to Paris accessories anymore. Why not be more adventurous and visit **La Licorne**, a quirky old-fashioned boutique full of fabulous costume jewelry from the '20s to the '60s? Just up the road, **Devana** is a hip and happening jewelry boutique showcasing contemporary unisex designs. **Marie Mercié** and **Tetes en L'Air** make flamboyant hats for all occasions. If you like the personal touch, you'll love **Cerize**, a chic little boudoir of a boutique done out in eye-catching neo-baroque. Hats, handbags, and jewelry by a range of international designers can all be tried on in individual changing rooms. Hot young French jewelry designer **Delphine Charlotte Parmentier**, whose elegant creations have sparkled on the couture catwalk for Chanel, Lacroix, and Ungaro, is also a must. Creative types will prefer to mix and match their own beads and baubles at

**La Droguerie**, and handbag junkies will get their fill at **Séquoia**, a fabulous minimalist boutique that stocks great-looking but reasonably-priced bags in all shapes and sizes. Stop off at **Sisso's** for more hip finds—from Kathy Korvin jewelry to Prada accessories—and **La Maison de la Fausse Fourrure** for fun fake fur bags, hats, and leopard-skin lampshades. And don't despair if you can't afford the new Dior *joaillerie*—**Tati Or** does cut-price karat pieces starting at 8 euros!

**Marvelous markets...** The outdoor food markets of Paris are full of wonders for visitors, especially those who like to cook. The **Marché d'Aligre** (Métro Ledru-Rollin), an indoor/outdoor food and clothing market near Bastille, is reputed to have the lowest prices in town; on Sunday morning, it's more like an Arab souk than a French marketplace, with vendors calling out their prices and offering samples of their wares to the crowds, and huge piles of fresh mint and coriander scenting the air. In the covered part of the market, one stand sells Portuguese and Spanish products, including Serrano ham, *vinho verde* (a delicious, light white wine), and excellent Portuguese bread made with cornmeal—great picnic ingredients. Every morning except Monday, the lower part of **rue Mouffetard** (Métro Censier-Daubenton or Monge), a Latin-Quarter street dating to Roman times, becomes a food market. On Sunday mornings, the entire neighborhood turns out to do shopping and have coffee or a glass of wine at one of the little cafes; an accordion player even passes out song sheets so the crowd can join in.

**The wine list...** The wine-shop chain **Nicolas** has a wonderfully helpful, friendly staff; at the flagship store on the place de la Madeleine, you can buy such rarities as an 1869 Château d'Yquem for only 5,200 euros. **Le Repaire de Bacchus** is another wine chain with excellent selections; the flagship store, in a fancy shopping alley off the rue Royale, has a friendly English manager and a super tasting-room upstairs.

**Kid stuff...** The French tend to go in for dressing their kids up like Little Lord Fauntleroy, bourgeois tots strutting the streets in **Bonpoint** (luxury kids' clothes at luxury prices), **Jacadi** (cute classics at slightly more affordable prices), and **Tartine et Chocolat** (a fairly chi-chi brand that also does its own line of rather nauseating baby perfume). Film stars dress their designer babies at **Evazou**, the home of mini Versace and DKNY. **Marais Plus** is a great address for wacky knick-knacks and unusual toys and also has a tearoom with fabulous chocolate cake for harassed mothers in need of a quick calorie fix.

**Boys to men...** After stocking up on shirts and cult underwear at **Calvin Klein Homme**, fashionable boys can shop the day away at **Madelios**, Paris's first megastore for men where they'll find everything from Dior, YSL, and Givenchy to Helmut Lang jeans, not to mention a sleek in-store bar and massage studio (not for that muscle, darling). Needless to say, all the major department stores have followed Madelios's example, completely revamping their men's sections, and **Printemps Homme** is well worth a visit these days. **Raw Essentials** is good for streetwise urbanwear and ultrahot G-star jeans, but nothing beats **Boy'z Bazaar**, a gay institution in the Marais, for skimpy T-shirts and cute clubby looks.

**Preening and pampering...** The city's best one-stop shop for perfume has to be **Sephora**, a space-age beauty emporium that boasts wall-to-wall lipsticks, cosmetics, and fragrances arranged in neat alphabetical order. For head-to-toe hedonism you can't beat a trip to **Anne Semonin**. Famous for her revolutionary jetlag cure, France's new beauty guru customizes plant-based products, essential oils, and lashings of seaweed to suit all skin types. If you really want to splash out, pay a visit to **By Terry**, a chic little boutique where Yves Saint Laurent's former make-up artist Terry de Gunzberg will mix up your own unique shade of lipstick. Alternatively, join the supermodel crowd at **Shu Uemera** or drop in to **Shiseido**'s divine mirrored and mosaic-ed HQ and treat yourself to a bottle of personalized perfume. Well-groomed boys will love **Nickel**, a hip male beauty salon in the Marais offering everything from Shiatsu massage to body waxing. If high-class beauty salons are not your thing, treat yourself to an authentic hammam at the **Mosquée de Paris**. The entry pass includes steam bath, massage, vigorous scrubbing with a horsehair glove, and a glass of sweet mint tea.

**Lifestyle, gifts and design...** Colette, a hip multi-story boutique showcasing the latest trends in fashion, art, and design, sparked a citywide craze for lifestyle boutiques. Japanese label **Muji** is currently taking Paris by storm, young hipsters on a budget flocking there in droves to snap up ultra-functional kitchenware, furniture, and home accessories plus trendy stationery and clothing. **La Maison de Famille** and **Autour du Monde** are good one-stop shopping stores that carry everything from tasteful tableware to casual men's and women's clothing. **Galerie Gaultier** sells Jean-Paul's quirky furniture line, as well as his younger labels, JPG and Gaultier Maille. But hardcore design fans will prefer the colorful postmodern objets displayed in the sleek new **Castelbajac Concept Store**. Fans of contemporary design can check out the latest in cutting-edge furniture at the **Galerie VIA** or browse through shelves of covetable lamps, vases, and design collectibles at **Sentou Galerie**. If you're more in the market for kitsch, try **Why?**, where you'll find the inflatable furniture and flower-shaped lamps you've been dreaming of. The **Boutiques Paris-Musées** are fabulous for gift-shopping, offering everything from arty jewelry to reproductions of museum pieces, but the hottest address in Paris for groovy furniture and home furnishings has to be the new **Printemps Design** boutique in the revamped Centre Pompidou. If you're looking for classic French design gifts, take home a horn-handled knife from **Laguiole** or a crystal vase from **Baccarat**.

**A good book (in English)...** Paris has no shortage of English-language bookstores, and most news kiosks sell at least a few papers in English. Near the place de la Concorde, **Galignani** has a peaceful old-world look and a good choice of art and travel books—it holds the distinction of being the first English-language bookshop in Europe. But those with literary inclinations should head over to Saint-Germain-des-Prés and the **Village Voice**, whose well-read owner Odile Hellier is always happy to steer her customers to a good read. Many tourists head to **Shakespeare & Co.**, assuming that it's Sylvia Beach's famous shop of the same name that nurtured the Lost Generation back in the 1920s, and end up disappointed to find a disorganized collection of musty books at inflated prices. You'll be better off around the corner at the **Abbey Bookshop**. For massive selection, head to any branch of the **FNAC** chain.

**Watch out for fleas and fleecers...** Since the Middle Ages, people in need of quick cash have sold used goods outside the city walls to avoid paying taxes; the three major *puce marchés* (flea markets) are still located on the edge of the city. Supposedly the largest flea market in the world, the **Puces de Saint-Ouen** (Métro Porte-de-Clignancourt, just follow the crowds) in northern Paris officially opens at 7:30am, though some fanatics show up at 5am. You'll find old magazines, jewelry, antique furniture, and whatever else sellers have emptied from their closets. Along the avenue Porte de Clignancourt between the Métro and the market proper, street vendors sell scads of tacky gewgaws, from leather jackets to used telephone cards. The market itself has been organized into sections according to the goods sold: Marché Vernais, period furniture and curios; Marché Biron, antiques; Marché Cambo, furniture and paintings; Marché Serpette, antique and rustic furniture, curios; Marché Paul Bert, secondhand goods and bronze objects; Marché Jules-Vallès, rustic furniture; Marché Malik, secondhand clothes, eyeglasses, records. Marked prices for antiques are generally not any cheaper than in the stores, but you can sometimes bargain for a great deal. In eastern Paris, serious shoppers arrive at the smaller **Puces de Montreuil** (Métro Porte-de-Monteuil; open Sat–Mon 6:30am–1pm; admission free) at 6:30am sharp. You can pick up anything from a used car to an accordion as barbers shave customers in the street. Monday is the day to go for used clothing. On the southwest edge of the city, the **Puces de Vanves** (aves George Lafenstre and Marc-Sangnier, Métro Port-de-Vanres; open Sat–Sun dawn–7pm; admission free) has 140 legitimate vendors selling antiques and secondhand stuff, but some of the best deals are from unlicensed merchants, who have to keep on the move to avoid the frequent police patrols. A small, manageable, and fun weekend flea market is held once a month in the **Galerie de la Java**, a classified historical monument dating from 1924, up in the 10th arrondissement. There's a cafe on the top floor where live jazz bands play between 5 and 9pm. Tip: Look or posters in the street advertising *brocantes*, traveling flea markets (selling mostly antiques) that set up in the streets for a few days at a time.

# The Index

**Abbey Bookshop.** An English-language bookstore (used and new) with a good literature section and Canadian publications.... *Tel 01 46 33 16 24; 29, rue de la Parcheminerie, 75005, Métro Saint-Michel. Closed Sun.*

**(see p. 155)**

**Anne Semonin.** Luxury plant-based beauty treatments including the revolutionary "anti-jetlag special".... *Tel 01 42 66 24 22; 108, rue du Faubourg-Saint-Honoré, 75008, Métro Saint Philippe-du-Roule.* **(see p. 153)**

**APC.** A big favorite with stylists and fashion editors, this boutique offers last season's APC collection at discount prices.... *Tel 01 45 48 43 71; 32, rue Cassette, 75006, Métro Saint-Sulpice.* **(see p. 147)**

**Autour du Monde.** Get a designer lifestyle in this chic French boutique, which stocks everything from candles, clothes, and ceramics to tasteful soft furnishings.... *Tel 01 42 77 06 08; 8, rue des Francs-Bourgeois, 75003, Métro Saint-Paul.* **(see p. 154)**

**Baccarat.** The famous house of crystal.... *Tel 01 42 65 36 26; 11, place de la Madeleine, 75008, Métro Madeleine. Also tel 01 47 70 64 30; 30 bis, rue du Paradis, 75010, Métro Poissonnière. Both closed Sun.* **(see p. 154)**

**Balenciaga.** Cutting-edge style from new French wunderkind Nicolas Ghesquière.... *Tel 01 47 20 21 11; 10, ave Georges V, 75008, Métro Alma-Marceau.* **(see p. 150)**

**BHV.** Modestly priced department store where you can find anything you could ever need—except shoes. Its famous basement is a paradise for *bricoleurs* (do-it-yourselfers).... *Tel 01 42 74 90 00; 52, rue de Rivoli, 75004, Métro Hôtel-de-Ville. Open till 10pm Wed. Closed Sun.*
**(see p. 149)**

**Blancs-Manteaux.** Meet the men behind the clothes. This charming Franco-Japanese duo work under their shop in a basement studio and nip upstairs for coffee and a chat every now and then!... *Tel 01 42 71 70 00; 42, rue des Blancs-Manteaux, 75004, Métro Hotel de Ville.* **(see p. 151)**

**Bonpoint.** Bourgeois kids—from tiny tots to young teens—dress in these well-cut clothes made from luxury fabrics. Luxury prices to match.... *Tel 01 47 42 52 63; 15, rue Royale, 75008, Métro Concorde.* **(see p. 153)**

**Boutiques Paris-Musées.** Postcards, books, and reproductions of art objects.... *Tel 01 40 26 56 65; Forum des Halles, 1, rue Pierre-Lescot, 75001, Métro Les Halles. Closed Mon am, Sun. Also tel 01 42 74 08 00; Musée Carnavalet, 23, rue de Sévigné, 75003, Métro Saint-Paul. Closed Mon. Also tel 01 42 76 65 79; 29 bis, rue des Francs-Bourgeois, 75004, Métro Saint-Paul. Closed Mon am.* **(see p. 154)**

**Boy'z Bazaar.** A full range of men's clothing for the gay market.... *Tel 01 42 71 94 00; 5, rue Sainte-Croix-de-la-Bretonnerie, 75004, Métro Hôtel-de-Ville. Open noon–midnight, except Sun 2–9pm.* **(see p. 153)**

**By Terry.** YSL make-up artist Terry de Gunzberg mixes up custom-made cosmetics at her exclusive new boutique.... *Tel 01 44 76 00 76; 21, Passage Véro-Dodat, 75001, Métro Palais-Royal.* **(see p. 153)**

SHOPPING | THE INDEX

**Calvin Klein Homme.** CK's totally Zen men's boutique features smart suits, pristine shirts, and cult underwear galore.... *Tel 01 43 59 10 10; 56, ave Montaigne, 75008, Métro Franklin-D.-Roosevelt.* **(see p. 153)**

**Castelbajac Concept Store.** Fashion designer Jean-Charles de Castelbajac assembles an innovative selection of wacky housewares and accessories in his happening new boutique.... *Tel 01 45 48 40 55; 26, rue Madame, 75006, Métro Saint-Sulpice.* **(see p. 154)**

**Céline.** So hip it hurts—collections based around masses of cashmere, fur, and minimalist chic since the arrival of New Yorker Michael Kors.... *Tel 01 49 52 12 01; 36, ave Montaigne, 75008, Métro Franklin-D.-Roosevelt.*
**(see p. 150)**

**Cerize.** Hats, handbags, and jewelry by a range of international designers including French hat queen Marie Mercié and couture embroiderer François Lesage.... *Tel 01 42 60 84 84; 380, rue Saint-Honoré, 75001.*
**(see p. 151)**

**Chanel.** Boutique where the famous interlocked C's reign.... *Tel 01 42 86 28 00; 29, rue Cambon, 75001, Métro Concorde. Closed Sun.* **(see p. 150)**

**Charles Jourdan.** Sleekly fashionable shoes and capsule collection of ready-to-wear for men and women.... *Tel 01 45 62 29 28; 86, ave des Champs-Elysees, 75008, Métro Georges V.* **(see p. 149)**

**Chloe.** Brit star Stella McCartney has revived this boring old French fashion house with tarty frocks for modern-day vamps.... *Tel 01 44 94 33 00; 54, rue du Faubourg Saint Honore, 75008, Métro Concorde.* **(see p. 150)**

**Christian Dior.** The refurbished Dior empire.... *Tel 01 40 73 54 00; 13, rue François 1er, 75008, Métro Franklin-D.-Roosevelt. Closed Sun.* **(see p. 150)**

**Christian Louboutin.** France's answer to Manolo Blahnik, which means super-chic mules and party shoes for clients like Princess Caroline of Monaco and Anna Wintour, editor

of *Vogue.... Tel 01 42 36 05 31; 19, rue Jean-Jacques Rousseau, 75001, Métro Palais-Royal or Louvre.*
**(see p. 149)**

**Colette.** Minimalist temple to art, fashion, and design.... *Tel 01 55 35 33 90; 213, rue Saint-Honoré, 75001, Métro Tuileries. Closed Sun.* **(see p. 154)**

**Delphine Charlotte Parmentier.** Arty little boutique in the Marais where sought-after designer Delphine Charlotte showcases jewelry and accessories alongside handmade ceramics and pretty beaded sandals.... *Tel 01 44 54 51 72; 26, rue du Bourg-Tibourg, 75004, Métro Hotel de Ville.*
**(see p. 151)**

**Devana.** Chunky unisex jewelry by Danish designer Jacob Taga-Jorgensen.... *Tel 01 42 78 69 76; 30, rue de Sévigné, 75004, Métro Saint-Paul.* **(see p. 151)**

**Didier Ludot.** The French king of vintage couture sells everything from secondhand Dior and Balenciaga to snazzy Chanel suits made by Coco herself.... *Tel 01 42 96 06 56; 20/24, Galerie Montpensier 75001, Métro Palais-Royal. New space devoted to the Little Black Dress: Tel 01 40 15 01 04; 125, Galerie de Valois, Metro Palais-Royal.* **(see p. 151)**

**Eric Bompard.** Gorgeous cashmere sweaters and scarves for men and women in every imaginable but unfailingly tasteful color.... *Tel 01 42 84 04 36; 46, rue du Bac, 75007, Métro Rue du Bac.* **(see p. 150)**

**Evazou.** A chic little boutique in the Marais that dresses trend-setting babies and fashion-conscious kids (up to age 12).... *Tel 01 48 87 93 77; 3, rue de Sévigné, 75003, Métro Saint-Paul.* **(see p. 153)**

**Fanche et Flo.** Highly original and fun to wear. This bohemian duo's collections feature graphic prints and African colors.... *Tel 01 42 51 24 18; 19, rue Durantin, 75018, Métro Abbesses.* **(see p. 151)**

**FNAC.** A chain of large record and book stores. Service can be surly, but the selection is impressive.... *Tel 01 40 41 40*

00; *Forum des Halles, 1–7, rue Pierre-Lescot (level 3), 75001, Métro Les Halles. Also tel 01 49 54 30 00; 136, rue de Rennes, 75006, Métro Saint-Placide. Also tel 01 09 18 00; 26–30, ave des Ternes, 75017, Métro Ternes. Also tel 01 48 01 02 03; 24, blvd des Italiens, 75009, Métro Richelieu-Drouot. Also tel 01 43 42 04 04; 4, place de la Bastille, 75012, Métro Bastille. Blvd des Italiens branch open until midnight. All closed Sun.* **(see p. 155)**

**Free Lance.** Outrageous heels for party girls who don't like going home alone.... *Tel 01 45 48 14 78; 30, rue du Four, 75006, Métro Mabillon.* **(see p. 149)**

**Galerie de la Java.** A flea market on 3 levels, with live jazz in the evening.... *105, rue du Faubourg-du-Temple, 75010, Métro République. Open Fri–Sun, first weekend of the month, 10–10. Admission charged.* **(see p. 156)**

**Galerie Gaultier.** Sells the designer's youthful lines JPG and Gaultier Maille (knitwear), as well as his humorous and practical furniture.... *Tel 01 44 68 84 84; 30, rue du Faubourg Saint-Antoine, 75012, Métro Bastille. Closed Sun.* **(see p. 154)**

**Galeries Lafayette.** Famed department store with an astounding variety of merchandise, including the fashions of many big-name designers. A gourmet food shop and several restaurants and snack bars are also under its roof.... *Tel 01 42 82 34 56; 40, blvd Haussmann, 75009, Métro Chaussée-d'Antin or RER Auber. Open Thur until 9. Closed Sun.* **(see p. 149)**

**Galerie VIA.** The place to see the latest in French furniture design.... *Tel 01 46 28 11 11; 29–37, ave Daumesnil, 75012, Métro Gare de Lyon. Closed for lunch.* **(see p. 154)**

**Galignani.** English-language bookstore with fine selection of art books. Expect a mark-up over U.S. prices.... *Tel 01 42 60 76 07; 224, rue de Rivoli, 75001, Métro Tuileries. Closed Sun.* **(see p. 154)**

**Givenchy.** Alexander McQueen's wild couture and impeccably tailored prêt-a-porter has the fashion pack moaning with pleasure.... *Tel 01 44 31 50 23; 3, ave Georges V, 75008, Métro Alma-Marceau.* **(see p. 150)**

**Guerrisold.** Tons of gritty used clothing, with the occasional fab find.... *Tel 01 42 80 66 18; 17 bis, blvd Rochechouart, 75009, Métro Barbès-Rochechouart. Also tel 01 42 52 39 24; 9 & 21 bis, blvd Barbès, 75018, Métro Barbès-Rochechouart. Also tel 01 47 70 46 08; 22, blvd Poissonnière, 75009, Métro Montmartre. Closed Sun.* **(see p. 147)**

**iRoo.** Cutting-edge looks and space-age fabrics from a hot young Korean designer.... *Tel 01 40 27 80 90; 14, rue des Rosiers, 75004, Métro Saint-Paul.* **(see p. 151)**

**Jacadi.** A chain of classic children's clothing stores for kids ages zip to 14. Prices aren't outrageous.... *Main location: Tel 01 42 65 84 98; 17, rue Tronchet, 75008, Métro Madeleine. Closed Sun.* **(see p. 153)**

**Jean-Paul Gaultier.** Fashion's favorite iconoclast has a boutique to match his image, with Roman statues as mannequins and mosaic floors inset with TV screens. The clothes are likable (unlike the staff) and wearable.... *Tel 01 42 86 05 05; 6, rue Vivienne, 75002, Métro Bourse. Closed Sun.* **(see p. 150)**

**Kabuki.** High-style shoes with very high heels (and prices) by Michel Perry, Prada, Dries Van Noten, Dolce & Gabbana, Dirk Bikkembergs, Vivienne Westwood, and others. A few men's styles of a much more sober nature.... *Tel 01 42 36 44 34; 13, rue de Turbigo, 75002, Métro Etienne-Marcel. Closed Sun.* **(see p. 149)**

**Kyungmee J.** Hip, young, and resonably cheap designer looks from rising Korean-American star.... *Tel 01 42 74 33 85; 38, rue du Roi-du-Sicile, 75004, Métro Saint-Paul.* **(see p. 151)**

**L'Eclaireur.** Trendy retailer carrying hip, young fashion designers ranging from Martin Margiela to Hervé Leger and Helmut Lang.... *Tel 01 48 87 10 22; 3 ter, rue de Rosiers, 75004, Métro Saint-Paul. Also tel 01 43 29 58 01; 24, rue de l'Echaudé, 75006, Métro Mabillon. Also*

SHOPPING | THE INDEX

*tel 01 45 62 12 32; 26, ave des Champs-Elysées, 75008, Métro Franklin-D.-Roosevelt. Champs-Elysées closed Sun; others closed Mon am, Sun.* **(see p. 150)**

**L'Habilleur.** Discount prices on great designer labels, like Plien Sud and Martine Sitbon, for both men and women.... *Tel 01 48 87 77 12; 44, rue de Poitou, 75003, Métro Filles-de-Calvaires. Closed Sun.*
**(see p. 147)**

**La Droguerie.** Fine wool yarns, wonderful buttons, and all the beads and baubles needed to make your own jewelry.... *Tel 01 45 08 93 27; 9–11, rue du Jour, 75001, Métro Les Halles. Closed Mon am, Sun.* **(see p. 152)**

**La Licorne.** Secret tresaure trove of costume jewellery in the heart of the Marais.... *Tel 01 48 87 84 43; 38, rue de Sévigné, 75003, Métro Saint-Paul.* **(see p. 151)**

**La Maison de Famille.** Great gifts galore: kitchen stuff, housewares, clothing, accessories, etc.... *Tel 01 40 46 97 47; 29, rue Saint-Sulpice, 75006, Métro Saint-Sulpice. Closed Sun.* **(see p. 154)**

**La Maison de la Fausse Fourrure.** Everything from fun fake fur handbags to leopard-skin lampshades and dalmatian-spotted furniture!... *Tel 01 43 55 24 21; 34, blvd Beaumarchais, 75011, Métro Chemin Vert.* **(see p. 152)**

**Laguiole.** World-famous knives showcased in a cutting-edge boutique designed by Philippe Starck.... *Tel 01 40 28 09 42; 1, place Sainte-Opportune, 75001, Métro Châtelet.* **(see p. 154)**

**Lanvin.** Boutique of the dated Lanvin fashion house with a fashion cafe in the basement.... *Tel 44 71 33 33; 15, rue du Faubourg-Saint-Honoré, 75008, Métro Concorde. Closed Sun.* **(see p. 150)**

**Le Bon Marché.** The oldest department store in Paris, the only one on the Left Bank. Upmarket product lines.... *Tel 01 44 39 80 00; 22, rue de Sèvres, 75007, Métro Sèvres-Babylone. Closed Sun.* **(see p. 149)**

**Le Mouton à Cinq Pattes.** The place to shop for top-name

designer seconds.... *Tel 01 45 48 86 26 (phone for all locations); 8, 10, 18, and 48, rue Saint-Placide, 75006, Métro Saint-Placide. 19, rue Grégoire de Tours, 75006, Métro Odéon. 15, rue Vieille-du-Temple, 75004, Métro Hôtel-de-Ville or Saint-Paul. Closed Sun.*

**(see p. 147)**

**Le Repaire de Bacchus.** The flagship store of a small French-owned chain of wine shops with several branches in Paris.... *Tel 01 42 66 34 12; Le Village Royale, 12 cité Berryer, 25, rue Royale, 75008, Métro Madeleine. Closed Sun–Mon.* **(see p. 152)**

**Les 3 Marches.** Catherine B, the Sherlock Holmes of the fashion world, tracks down secondhand Chanel and Hermès accessories with an unerring eye.... *Tel 01 43 54 74 18; 1, rue Guisarde, 75006, Métro Saint-Sulpice.*

**(see p. 151)**

**Madelios.** Paris's first megastore for men—shop for YSL and Helmut Lang Jeans, or enjoy a fabulous in-store massage!... *Tel 01 53 45 00 00; 23, blvd de la Madeleine, 75001, Métro Madeleine.* **(see p. 153)**

**Malo.** His 'n' her cashmere sweaters at film star prices.... *Tel 01 47 20 26 08; 12, ave Montaigne, 75008, Métro Alma-Marceau.* **(see p. 150)**

**Marais Plus.** A treasure trove of reasonably priced, unusual gifts, toys, T-shirts, posters, and greeting cards. Also carries English-language guidebooks and has a tea salon with scrumptious desserts.... *Tel 01 48 87 01 40; 20, rue des Francs-Bourgeois, 75003, Métro Saint-Paul.*

**(see p. 153)**

**Marché d'Aligre.** Pick up perfect picnic fare at this vibrant, low-priced market near Bastille.... *No phone, place d'Aligre, 75012, Métro Ledru-Rollon.* **(see p. 152)**

**Maria Luisa.** Fashions by trendy designers like Dries Van Noten and John Galliano.... *Tel 01 47 03 96 15; 2, rue Cambon, 75001, Métro Concorde. Closed Sun.*

**(see p. 150)**

**Marie Mercié.** Flamboyant hats from the famous French hat queen.... *Tel 01 43 26 45 83; 23, rue Saint-Sulpice, 75006, Métro Saint-Sulpice.* **(see p. 151)**

**Martin Grant.** A hot favorite with the supermodels, Grant runs up Australian couture at purse-friendly prices. His wire-haired terrier Mutley is a major new runway star.... *Tel 01 42 71 39 49; 32, rue des Rosiers, 75004, Métro Saint-Paul.* **(see p. 151)**

**Mosquée de Paris.** Get the authentic hammam experience in steam bath rooms full of exotic mosaics and marble fountains.... *Tel 01 43 31 38 20; 39, rue Geoffroy-St.-Hilaire, 75005, M´tro Place Monge. Women Mon, Wed–Sat; men Tues and Sun.* **(see p. 154)**

**Muji.** The Japanese "brand with no name" that's taken Paris by storm. Shop here for kitchenware, furniture, home accessories, trendy stationery, and ultra-functional clothing.... *Tel 01 46 34 01 10; 27 and 30, rue Saint-Sulpice, 75006, Métro Saint-Sulpice.* **(see p. 154)**

**Nickel.** Hot beauty salon in the Marais for men that offers everything from Shiatsu massage to body waxing!... *Tel 01 42 77 41 10; 48, rue des Francs-Bourgeois, 75003, Métro Saint-Paul.* **(see p. 153)**

**Nicolas.** Flagship store of a chain of more than 280 wine boutiques, with bottles at all prices.... *Tel 01 42 68 00 16; 31, place de la Madeleine, 75008, www.nicolas-wines.com, Métro Madeleine. Closed Sun.* **(see p. 152)**

**Onward.** All the hip young designers under one roof, from Dries Van Noten to Helmut Lang, Jean-Paul Gaultier, and Sophie Sitbon.... *Tel 01 46 34 11 50; 147, blvd Saint-Germain, 75006, Métro Saint-Germain-des-Prés. Closed Sun.* **(see p. 150)**

**Patricia Louisor.** Bohemian chic in a party atmosphere in Montmartre.... *Tel 01 42 62 10 42; 16, rue Houdon, 75018, Métro Abbesses.* **(see p. 151)**

**Printemps/Printemps Design/Printemps Homme.** An enormous 19th-century department store in 3 buildings. Check out the fantastic stained-glass dome in the Café

Flo.... *Tel 01 42 82 50 00; 64, blvd Haussmann, 75009, Métro Havre-Caumartin. Open Thur until 10. Closed Sun.* **(see pp. 149, 153, 154)**

**Raw Essentials.** Essential rendez-vous for urban streetwear (unisex but mainly boys) and cult G-Star jeans.... *Tel 01 42 21 44 33; 46, rue Etienne Marcel, 75001, Métro Etienne Marcel.* **(see p. 153)**

**Samaritaine.** A classic French department store that's trying to enter the modern world..... *Tel 01 40 41 20 20; 19, rue de la Monnaie, 75001, Métro Châtelet, Pont-Neuf, or Louvre. Open Thurs until 10. Closed Sun.* **(see p. 149)**

**Sentou Galerie.** Spot-on selection of contemporary design—everything from minimalist Japanese lamps to tableware by hip French design duo Tsé Tsé.... *Tel 01 42 77 44 79; 18 and 24, rue du Pont Louis-Philippe, 75004, Métro Pont Marie.* **(see p. 154)**

**Sephora.** A cosmetics chain that stocks more than 10,000 brands. A must for fragrance and foundation freaks.... *Flagship store: Tel 01 53 93 22 50; 70, ave des Champs-Elysées, 75008, Métro Franklin-D.-Roosevelt.* **(see p. 153)**

**Séquoia.** Fashionable but functional bags at surprisingly purse-friendly prices.... *Tel 01 44 07 27 94; 72 bis, rue Bonaparte, 75006.* **(see p. 152)**

**Shakespeare & Co.** Funky shop for used books, frequented by recently arrived American expatriates.... *Tel 01 43 26 96 50; 37, rue de la Bûcherie, 75005, Métro Saint-Michel. Open noon–midnight.* **(see p. 155)**

**Shiseido.** Perfumes custom-designed in this beautiful boutique.... *Tel 01 49 27 09 09; 142, galerie de Valois, Palais-Royal, 75001, Métro Palais-Royal. Closed Sun.* **(see p. 153)**

**Shoebizz.** The bizz here is this season's footwear trends at unbeatable prices.... *Tel 01 45 44 91 70; 42, rue du Dragon, 75006, Métro St.-Sulpice.* **(see p. 149)**

**Shu Uemera.** This cult hangout of supermodels and make-up artists offers a stunning range of eye and lip colours as well as fab service from professionally-trained assistants.... *Tel 01 45 48 02 55; 176, blvd Saint-Germain, 75006, Métro Saint-Germain.* **(see p. 153)**

**Sisso's.** Hot new accessories boutique stocking everything from Prada accessories to Kathy Korvin jewellery.... *Tel 01 44 61 99 50; 20, rue Mahler, 75004, Métro Saint-Paul.* **(see p. 152)**

**Stephane Kélian.** Men's and women's footwear that is hip, urban, and très Parisian!.... *Tel 01 42 22 93 03; 13 bis, rue de Grenelle, 75007, Métro Sevres-Babylone.* **(see p. 149)**

**Tartine et Chocolat.** Contemporary French baby and children's wear light on the fuss and frills.... *Tel 01 47 42 10 68; 24, rue de la Paix, 75002, Métro Opéra.* **(see p. 153)**

**Tati Or.** Gold jewelry (guaranteed 18-karat) at "Tati" (read "cheap") prices, starting at about 3 euros.... *Tel 01 40 07 06 76; 19, rue de la Paix, 75008, Métro Opéra. Closed Sun.* **(see p. 152)**

**Tetes en l'Air.** Eccentric hats and headgear for those who like to be noticed.... *Tel 01 46 06 71 19; 65, rue des Abbesses, 75018, Métro Abbesses.* **(see p. 151)**

**Thierry Mugler.** The high priest of hips and bosoms is back in style with a vengeance.... *Tel 01 45 44 44 44; 45, rue du Bac, 75007, Métro Rue du Bac.* **(see p. 150)**

**Victoire.** Hip designers, from Romeo Gigli to Jin Téok, in this boutique.... *Tel 01 42 61 68 71; 10, place des Victoires, 75002, Métro Pyramides. Closed Sun.* **(see p. 150)**

**Village Voice.** The best store in Paris for English-language books, with an especially good literature section.... *Tel 01 46 33 36 47; 6, rue Princesse, 75006, Métro Saint-Germain-des-Prés. Closed Mon am, Sun.* **(see p. 155)**

**Why?.** The kingdom of kitsch—if you like inflatable plastic furniture and glow-in-the-dark tulips, this is the store for you.... *Five locations. Main store: Tel 01 44 61 72 75; 41, rue des Francs-Bourgeois, 75004, Métro Saint-Paul.*

**(see p. 154)**

**Yves Saint Laurent.** The women's couture and ready-to-wear boutique.... *Tel 01 42 65 74 59; 38, rue du Faubourg-Saint-Honoré, 75008, Métro Madeleine. Closed Sun.*

**(see p. 150)**

6

tlife

In spite of its
reputation for
being frisky after
dark, Paris is not
as naughty as one
might think, and
when it comes to

*le dernier cri*, the nightlife scene definitely plays follow-the-leader. There hasn't been a major new nightlife trend here since World War II, and during the past couple of decades, the city's club scene was barely worthy of Skokie or Saskatoon. Now, however, it does seem that most Parisians are finally starting to get over the Village People, and the music-masters of the night are taking their house and garage inspiration from London and New York, while local hip-hop, Algerian Rai, and Latin music also enjoy popularity.

There are few sights more ludicrously funny than a bunch of French people at a rave—their spastic moves barely work when they're dancing to Joe Cocker (which they still do)—but house and funk music are extremely popular with twenty- and thirtysomethings, and many clubs regularly import British and American DJs. More decorous BCBGs (yuppies with aristocratic pretensions) continue to worship at the *Saturday Night Fever* altar in expensive 8th- and 16th-arrondissement clubs where you dance with a necktie on, but even they are getting caught up in Paris's new love affair with Latino music, from the passionate precision of the tango to samba lines and salsa. Latin nights are immensely popular at clubs like **Les Etoiles** and **La Java**.

The Latin craze continues to entice Parisians back to the nightlife in huge numbers, and the bar scene is thriving, whether at bar-restaurants like **Barrio Latino** near the Bastille or at the profusion of young…eastern Paris). Though the train-blazing What's Up Bar has closed, all of the hot spots like **Café Charbon** and the **Underworld Café** in super trendy Menilmontant, a neighborhood that spans the border between the 11th and 20th arrondissements, have a human spinning their vinyl.

When the lights of the Eiffel Tower, looming over Paris in the night, are unplugged—at midnight in winter, 1am in summer—it's the signal to Paris clubgoers that it's party time. In a city that is almost fetishistically concerned with appearances, it would not do to brave the velvet ropes before 1am; 1:20am is the calibratedly cool hour to first show face.

Just getting your timing right is only step one, though, if you seriously want to sample some of the French capital's clubs. For starters, you're going to need a lot of money. Cover charges are stiff, averaging around 17 to 20 euros, and drinks tend to be very pricey—a beer will set you back 15 euros at the wildly popular gay club **Le Queen** on the Champs-Elysées, for example. Then, most crucially, there's the matter of how you look. Paris nightlife is very tribal, and your sartorial gaffes will be forgiven only if you're a stark raving beauty or show up on the arm of someone like Johnny Depp or Gwyneth Paltrow, the new face of Christian Dior. As a general rule, black is the color of choice, but no color will save you if you make the deadly fashion mistake of showing up in sweat shirts, stonewashed jeans, or *any* kind of athletic footwear.

Even if you don't do clubs, Paris still offers a huge menu of after-dark activities, ranging from pool halls to jazz bars. **Georges,** the top-floor restaurant of the Centre Pompidou and the latest offering from trend-masters the Costes Brothers, is one of the hippest places to be seen, even though it has no bar or dance floor. Instead, wouldn't-you-just-love-to-touch-me waiters and waitresses flounce in and out of three huge brushed aluminum pods that hide the kitchen toting their trays to a soundtrack of house and garage. **Le Monkey Club**, which opened in 1999 to rave reviews, is a combo bar-disco-restaurant, and this hybrid looks set to be thriving in Paris during the next few years. This place is pulling in an interesting mix of young hipsters, fashion people, BCBGs (French preppies) from the rich western suburbs, foreigners, and media execs who work in the nabe. What everyone seems to like is the California-Bauhaus decor and the idea of a one-stop night out. *Cafés-concerts* are sort of an easygoing update on the cabarets for which the city was once renowned, with patrons sitting at tables where they can drink and sometimes eat while listening to live music and, depending on the venue, dance. Certain traditional cafes are also well frequented at night, including the **Select** in Montparnasse, **Café Beaubourg** next to the Centre Pompidou (see Dining), **Café Marly** at the Louvre, and **Café de l'Industrie** near the Bastille (see below).

Most straight Parisians seem to marry young and stop going out regularly after they do, so nightlife is pretty much an under-30 scene. But don't worry, no one will give you a hard time if you're a frisky 50-year-old yearning for a bit of disco inferno. Gay clubs are age-mixed, as are almost all bars.

### Sources

Those who understand French and want up-to-the-minute information on raves and one-night-only parties can listen at 7:45pm every Friday to the 15-minute program **"Bon Plans" on Radio Nova (101.5 FM),** the hippest radio station in town. Radio Nova also publishes a monthly magazine called *Nova,* available at newsstands, that has the latest word on Paris nightlife. A handy little magazine called *Lylo,* distributed free in many clubs, has a nightlife calendar and a list of addresses.

Travelers familiar with **Minitel**, the national computer service, can find techno and rave listings at **36 15 CODA**, **36 15 FG**, or **36 15 RAVE** (Minitel terminals can be used for free at post offices). Useful alternative magazines (*Out Soon, Liquid Leva, TNT,* and *Coda*) and fliers for raves can also be found at the following "techno" record shops: **BPM**, **KGB**, **Rough Trade**, and **Techno Import**. On Mondays, the daily newspaper *Libération* publishes a hip, gay-oriented nightlife column called "Nuits Blanches" that alerts readers to weekly raves. Another good source is the **Nocturne** column by Sophie de Santis in the **"Figaroscope,"** a weekly Paris entertainment insert to the Wednesday edition of Le Figaro, the largest French daily. De Santis covers the club scene in real minutae and her column is a good source of news on weekly one-off events, raves, concerts, and club openings, and closings.

### Liquor Laws and Drinking Hours

The French have one of the highest per capita rates of alcohol consumption in the world, in part because the official drinking age of 18 is very rarely enforced. Drinking is built into daily life—especially as an apéritif before, wine with, and a digestif after dinner. Don't drive if you've had a few, though: The French are tough on drunken drivers—more than two drinks and you're likely over the limit. Drinking hours are established by the license of each establishment; some have to close at 2am, while others can remain open all night. One way or another, there's no time of the day or night when you can't find a drink somewhere in Paris.

# The Lowdown

**Dance fever...** **Les Bains Douches** is probably the best-known straight disco in town. Models and fashion folk frequent the former bathhouse not far from the Centre Pompidou. Despite a famously bitchy door policy, this place has managed, perhaps *faut de mieux*, to maintain its popularity for an amazingly long time. But you might be disappointed—where the hell's Kate Moss and did the bartender forget about the vodka in *mon cocktail*? It's your call, but depending on your style, you're probably better off in one of the yuppie party holes in the 8th arrondissement like **Le Monkey Club**, **Le Cabaret**, and **Duplex**. Le Monkey Bar, which replaced the very popular Bash, caters to a

NIGHTLIFE | THE LOWDOWN

crowd that's more likely to go on safari than to Ibiza or Aya-Napa in Cyprus, but that likes to party in spite of its good jobs and manners. Come here to play with *la jeunesse dorée* (the gilded youth) of Paris; it's actually a lot of fun and a good place to observe the phenomenon that dance ability decreases as one climbs the socioeconomic scale. **Le Cabaret** is another wear-a-suit- and-boogie spot, brimming with bankers, press attachés, counts and countesses, a smattering of models, and others who've mastered the art of perspiration-free dancing, while **Duplex** is more likely to attract the children of those who go to Le Cabaret. Of a given night, Duplex is a sea of pouting Gucci-clad *Vanity Fair* wannabes and is such an absurb place that it's actually kind of fun. You might even strike up a conversation with the odd Dutch au pair girl or a Lebanese banker trainee who studied in the U.S. If the bourgeoisie has never been your secret fascination and you want to boogie with a way-cool crowd, skip the fuss and head for **Batofar**, a club on a former lighthouse barge that's moored in the Seine. This is probably the most interesting club in Paris right now, with a really original mix of music that comes from a regularly changing cast of visiting DJs, including many passing through from other European cities. **Le Queen**, where the boy-girl ratio is about three to one—and most of the carefully coifed suburban pups here are sniffing after each other—still reigns as the disco supreme. And even though it's a gay club, it has become the cool night out for Xavier and Marie-Odile types from Saint-Cloud (the Gallic version of Teddy and Amanda types from Old Greenwich). For the very trendy and the very young, the places to go are the **Rex Club** and **Le Gibus**. The Rex Club is a feisty spot with a feisty crowd of serious club-goers who love its hardcore electronic dance music, while Le Gibus, once a famous rock venue, is now a popular and very sexy mostly gay dance club specializing in house and garage.

**Concert cafes...** The American-style bars (actually modern versions of the French wartime cabarets), known as *cafés-concerts*, have introduced two radically new concepts to Parisian clublife: live music and reasonable prices for drinks. **Cithéa**, near place de la République, hosts live bands Thursdays through Saturdays, with music ranging from salsa to funk and acid jazz. **Le Paris**, a Bastille-area cafe, stages rock and pop concerts on Saturday nights, and the **Wait & See Café**, near place de la République, features live rock and hip-hop. The Pigalle nightclub **Divan du Monde** stages shows ranging from French pop to African and Carribean music, and the cozy little **Blue Note**, near the rue Mouffetard market, mixes Brazilian, jazz, and blues into its nightly musical calendar.

**Two to tango...** *Bal-musettes* live on in Paris and have come back into vogue. These dances—where old fogies have been doing the foxtrot, polka, and tango to the strains of accordions since the 1930s—are now frequented by young people. **Le Tango**, an African disco located between the Centre Pompidou and the place de la République, becomes a *musette* on Friday and Saturday afternoons. In the Bastille area, **Balajo** does the *bal-musette* thing on weekend afternoons. **La Java**, a former Belleville haunt of Edith Piaf, becomes a "dancing," as the French call it, on Friday and Saturday nights and Sunday afternoons.

**All that jazz...** Scores of American jazz performers have left their homeland in search of a living wage in the Old World. At Paris clubs, you pay for your jazz either with a cover charge (which usually includes a complimentary first drink) or with inflated drink prices. Many cash-poor jazz fans simply nurse a single drink throughout an entire performance. The 10th arrondissement's **New Morning**, named for a Bob Dylan album, hosts top international jazz and blues performers. The setting—smoky and crowded—is perfect for that neo–Greenwich Village jazz club atmosphere, but it can choke you a bit, and the sight lines are less than ideal. David Bowie and Liza Minnelli have been known to pop in at **Bilboquet**, a Saint-Germain-des-Prés club with a penchant for New Orleans–style jazz. The tiny, crowded, and friendly **Bistrot d'Eustache**, near the Forum des Halles, brings in more modern sounds on Thursday, Friday, and Saturday nights. Jazz shares the calendar with blues and Brazilian music at the **Blue Note**, a small *café-concert* near the rue Mouffetard market. The **Petit Journal Saint-Michel** and the **Petit Journal Montparnasse** are two of the most popular clubs in the city. The first has more old-timey character and specializes in New Orleans jazz, and the latter, which has a bit of everything, scores higher in terms of stage visibility and acoustics. **Caveau de la Huchette**, near Saint-Michel, swings with big-band music, and **Sunset**, a restaurant/club in the center of town near Châtelet, hosts traditional jazz groups in its basement. The nearby **Duc des Lombards** attracts many tourists with its corner location and varied cocktail-hour concerts. **La Villa**, a basement club in a chic, modern Left Bank hotel, sometimes features top American performers. The **Jazz Club Lionel Hampton**, which six nights a week takes over the lobby of the unappealingly modern Méridien hotel, near the Arc de Triomphe, brings in a wealth of well-known artists.

**From strip to hip...** The Pigalle area still has its strip joints, sex shops, transsexual prostitutes, and tourist buses, but little by little it's being gentrified and hipped-up. The neighborhood's latest sensation is **La Fourmi**, a large, lively industrial-decor bar right next to La Cigale, one of the best concert venues in Paris—a revved up crowd oftens spills in after rock concerts. **Les Folies Pigalle**, in a former strip joint, is a disco specializing in house and garage music that attracts a mostly gay crowd. **Le Dépanneur** is a diner-like all-night bar. **Le Moloko** is a large, ultratrendy bar with red walls, papier-mâché devils, and a funky, free jukebox. **Les Noctambules** has always been what it is now—a rather sleazy Pigalle cafe with a corny three-piece orchestra—but now its high-camp appeal is a magnet for the trendy black-leather-jacket crowd. (In the staid, bourgeois world of Paris fashion, black leather jackets are *still* a rebellious fashion statement. Occasionally, the club's mean-looking, muscle-bound bouncer takes the mike and gets all mushy while crooning his off-key version of "My Way." **Le Bus Palladium** has become freshly popular as a funky night out for French prepsters who just love Motown, and it's actually sort of fun. At **Club-Club**, another small bar, you can bring your own records and play disc jockey on Wednesday nights or join the "spoken word" crowd with your newest prose or poetry at Tuesday's open mike.

**Bar-hopping in the Marais...** The Marais has become the center of the gay community in Paris (see "Where the boys are," below, for Marais gay bars), but there are also many straight or mixed nightspots in the area around the rue Vieille-du-Temple. **Petit Fer à Cheval** is a tiny but enormously popular bar and restaurant with a zinc bar, great recorded jazz, and a mixed crowd. **L'Imprevu Café** is a pleasant laid-back little spot with red-velvet movie-theater seats and a sort of Aladin's cave nook that pulls an amiable crowd of students and arty types and is less aggressively looking-for-love than some of the other local watering holes. The **Majestic** is an insufferably trendy cafe where muscle-bound waiters in tight, sleeveless T-shirts display themselves in the doorway. **Chez Richard** is more successfully hip and has a more friendly ambience. The young, pseudo-tough, Perfecto crowd lights up at **Pick-Clops**, a cafe/bar named for the sort of ne'er-do-wells who bum cigarettes (clops). Many American expats stop in at **Atmosphère**, an ordinary, unpretentious watering hole and one of two good bars in the city that go by the same name (the other Atmosphère is on the Canal Saint-Martin). The last word in hip in the area, though, is **Le Cafe du Tresor**, where ex-model Rodolphe, one of the best hosts in town, attracts an exceptionally good-looking crowd.

**Bar-hopping in and around the Bastille...** One of the best is the **Café de l'Industrie**, a large cafe with a neo-Colonial decor and with the arrival of a lot of rather brash boom-boom bars targeted at a suburban crowd, the **China Club**, an old-timer with a long bar, fumoir, (mediocre) restaurant, and cabaret has acquired a certain well-worn charm that makes its LA/Hong Kong in the '30s decor credible. **Barrio Latino** is the latest big-deal restaurant-bar to open, and if it's got a great decor created around the central atrium of a former furniture show-room, it's also a sign that the Bastille is going mainstream, since it's huge and expensive. The food's not worth it here, so pop in for a drink and a glimpse of the Paris-style pretension of hostesses wearing walk-talkie headsets. There's a VIP seating area, but it's usually tellingly empty. You can't really claim to have done this neighborhood without having popped into **Sanz Sans**, a pretty hip bar-club with a heavy-duty party crowd that likes to get ripped and dance on the tables to hip-hop, funk, Latino, and house music. The signature of this place is the big in-house video screen in back, which shows people what they're missing up front, since the action is filmed live. **Les Portes**, with its bordello decor and nuanced naughtiness, is an equally stylish but quieter option. For dancing, try **Balajo**, which is a *bal-musette* on weekend afternoons and a terrific, mixed-age disco at night, and **Chapelle des Lombards**, a disco specializing in salsa and African music.

**Where the wild things are...** Just north of the Bastille, the grandmotherly Menilmontant neighborhood has suddenly switched on, following an influx of young trendies in search of cheap apartments. What many consider to be the coolest bar in town is the gorgeous **Café Charbon**, a restored Belle Epoque dance hall where an oh-so-interesting crowd vies to set up camp for the evening in one of the leatherette banquettes. **Lou Pescalou** is a perfect reflection of the area's new young identity—hip but friendly. Plus, the stainless-steel toilets are a perfect place to indulge your fantasies of being a Russian astronaut. The supremely popular **Underworld Café** is another hip hangout, with live DJs and a laid-back crowd.

**Where the boys are...** There is no shortage of gay bars and discos in Paris. The hottest ones seem to be **Le Cox**, a Soho (London)-style cafe-bar where you can log onto the Internet for $15 an hour, and **L'Open Café,** which has become *the* meeting place for gay men before traipsing out into the night. Other popular watering holes in the Marais, the center of the gay community, include the mixed bar **Amnésia**, with its cozy armchairs; the quieter **Central**; the friendly **Duplex**; the sleazy **Mic Man**; **One Way**, which has an older crowd and an intriguing cap collection; and **Quetzal**, which has a younger, leather-clad crowd. **Le Depot** is the latest hot spot in the neighborhood, and it's a no-nonsense disco with decor of camouflage-netting and exposed ducts; there's more action in the cubicles downstairs, though, than on the dance floor. In the Bastille area, look up the raunchy **Le Keller** for serious cruising (its back room is equipped with a sling and other toys). If you're in the Châtelet area, stop in at **Banana Café,** where you might find the mixed, youthful clientele hovering around the baby grand downstairs. Châtelet is also home to **Le Mercury Bar,** an all-male disco as well as **Le Transfert,** a down-and-dirty leather bar. If you're looking for raunchy, head to Saint-Germain-des-Prés for **Le Trap,** which can get busy on Mondays for the strippers show. The immensely popular **Le Queen**, on the Champs-Elysées, is a large disco with go-go dancers, house music, and myriad "happenings" like the "bubble baths" at 2am on Tuesdays, when the room fills with bubbles and the partyers strip off their clothes and dance in surgical masks and swim goggles. **Scorp**, a campy and friendly disco between Opéra Garnier and Gare de l'Est, specializes in early-morning drag shows.

**NIGHTLIFE | THE LOWDOWN**

**For girls who like girls...** *Les filles qui préfèrent les filles* don't have as great a selection of clubs as do their male counterparts, but there are a few lesbian nightspots. The easy-going Marais bar **Amnésia** has a mixed gay and lesbian crowd; **La Champmeslé**, near the Bourse, is a tranquil spot for conversation. L'Entreacte, one of the city's more venerable lesbian clubs, has donned a flashier name, **Pulp!**, and a more upscale, lipstick image. The Wednesday lounge night is a favorite rendezvous of professional women, who love to snuggle up in arm chairs and be entertained by easy-listening music and occasional cabaret performances.

**African/West Indian clubs...** Paris has a healthy share of African dance clubs, including **Chapelle des Lombards**, upscale **Le Keur Samba**, and steamy **Le Tango**, but two of the most popular African/West Indian clubs are just outside Paris, in Montreuil: **Le Nelson** is still *the* African disco of the moment. **Cinquième Dimension** is not as chic, but its *zouk* music also keeps the crowds moving till the wee hours. Race or ethnic divisions aren't an issue, but getting back home can be. If you can't afford a taxi back to the city from the Montreuil clubs, keep dancing until the Métro starts running again at 5:30am.

**Latin fever...** Parisians of all ages are still mad for Latin music, especially salsa. Thirtysomethings pretend they are in Havana at the crowded, smoky **Chapelle des Lombards** in the Bastille area, while an intriguingly mixed crowd—Algerian busboys teamed up with swanky Versailles matrons, local yuppies, and lots of resident Latin Americans—fill the downstairs dance hall at **La Coupole** (yes, the same Coupole where Hemingway and other unspeakably tedious members of the Lost Generation hung out) for live Latin tunes on Tuesdays, Wednesdays, and Thursdays. A funky, hip-grinding crowd, including a multitude of young Latinos, gather on Thursday nights at **Les Etoiles**, a great 10th-arrondissement dive with a roughed-up rococo decor. Just slightly less feverish is the Thursday Latin night at **La Java**, a big 1930s-vintage dance hall where you would expect to hear a socialist workers anthem instead of a rhumba. The crowd is half dressed-down yuppies and half Bastille funksters. **Cithéa**, a laid-back bar and music venue near place de la Republique, also hosts salsa bands regularly.

**See-and-be-scenes...** Though it cops some of the nastiest and most pretentious attitude in Paris, the bar and restaurant at the **Hôtel Costes** are the epicenter of hip Paris nightlife. The lush 19th-century bordello decor, candlelight, perky sound-track, and celeb-studded crowd are pretty dazzling, so brave the door monsters for a peek at this inner sanctuary of chic. **Café Mabillon**, a Left Bank haunt, open 24 hours, draws a diverse crowd of prowling bachelors, as well as stylish young couples. Don't bother with Le Montana Fashion Bar, the jazz bar around the corner from the Café de Flore, unless your goal is to keep company with bewildered Japanese tourists. This bar-disco is the pitifully ersatz creation of fashion designer Paco Rabanne, and it is a horrible proof that nightlife cannot be willed into existence with a checkbook. **Le Mercury Bar**, despite its almost garish orange-and-purple decor, is a chic Left Bank place to drop into for first-rate jazz, well-mixed drinks, and a cool crowd. **Le Comptoir**, near the Forum des Halles, is a trendy place to have drinks and tapas.

**Best cozy bars...** **Chez Georges** is generally considered the most convivial bar in Saint-Germain-des-Prés, and perhaps in all of Paris. With walls painted by years of tobacco smoke and a wine list of the extremely cheap variety, it's a favorite hangout of students from the nearby Latin Quarter and a likely spot to fall into a deeply philosophical conversation with a stranger. Though most hip Parisians avoid the Latin Quarter like the plague, their bible, the magazine *Nova*, pronounced the snug, laid-back **Bob Cool** bar the only one worth frequenting on the Left Bank. It's a comfortable spot to linger after dinner or a movie. In the stately Art Deco **Hotel Lutetia**, the new red-velvet-decorated fumoir bar offers a chic option of drinks in the lobby or their darkly lit bar favored by Left Bank literati and Catherine Deneuve. The original bar, with its dark panelling and comfy armchairs, is a fine spot to linger over your favorite, invariably well-mixed tipple. As prices have soared in Saint-Germain's cafes, this has become the place where the locals troll by for a pop after dinner. The **China Club**, a spacious bar and restaurant near Bastille, is a great place to sit and chat with friends on couches and armchairs arranged in conversational groupings; upstairs, there are smaller, quieter rooms where customers play chess and other games. At **Petit Roi de la Lune**, a small Montparnasse neighborhood bar, locals play backgammon and contemplate the bar's extensive accordion collection. Try **Atmosphère** in the Marais for just-a-bar lack of pretension and the other **Atmosphère** (on the Canal Saint-Martin) for a similar study in simplicity. Both bars draw their shared name from Marcel Carné's film *Hôtel de Nord,* in which Arletty famously and disdainfully intoned, "Atmosphère, atmosphère," while standing on a bridge over the Canal Saint-Martin. Located in the heart of town, just off the place de la Concorde, **Le 30**, the bar at the new Sofitel Faubourg Hotel, is a great place to meet for drinks, since it has a fireplace, comfortable chairs, and a glamorous art-deco bar.

**All-night bars...** **Le Dépanneur**, a Pigalle bar masquerading as an American diner, is open 24 hours a day and serves food to help soak up the tequila. Near Les Halles, the **Sous-Bock** (the name means "beer mat"), modeled after an English pub (right down to the dartboard), offers *moules-frites* (mussels and French fries) and a vast selection of beers until 5am every night. The loungelike **Satellit' Café**, near place de la République, is open all night on the weekend. It doesn't really get going until around 2am, but the disc jockey has a great collection of jazz, blues, and soul records (vinyl only, please), and there are occasional live concerts. If you simply can't stop dancing when the other discos close at 5am, go to **Les Folies Pigalle**. Pigalle's ultrahip bar **Le Moloko** stay open until 6am, and if you want a nightcap or two at the crack of dawn on the Left Bank, the **Old Navy**, a raucous nightclub-bar-cafe, pulls a wonderfully strange crowd of night owls on the Left Bank and is more authentic and less posey than the nearby **Café Mabillon**, which also stays open all night.

# The Index

**Amnésia.** Gays and lesbians mingle in this relaxed Marais bar filled with armchairs arranged around low tables. A cramped basement dance floor gets hopping after midnight.... *Tel 01 42 72 16 94; 42, rue Vieille-du-Temple, 75004, Métro Hôtel-de-Ville or Saint-Paul.* **(see pp. 177, 178)**

**Atmosphère.** Much like an American bar in that it doesn't try to be anything but a bar. It is, in fact, frequented by many American expatriates.... *Tel 01 42 71 25 42; 24, rue Vieille-du-Temple, 75004, Métro Hôtel-de-Ville or Saint-Paul. Closed in Aug.* **(see pp. 176, 180)**

**Atmosphère.** Friendly, simply furnished bar alongside the Canal Saint-Martin with a youngish crowd and reasonable prices.... *Tel 01 40 38 09 21; 49, rue Lucien Sampaix, 75010, Métro Jacques-Bonsargent. Closed Mon.* **(see p. 180)**

**Balajo.** One of the best clubs in town. The clientele is mixed in age and not too pretentious, and the DJs spin tunes fromm across the decades.... *Tel 01 47 00 07 87; 9, rue de Lappe, 75011, Métro Bastille. Open Thur–Sat 11:30pm–5:30am,* bal-musette *Sat–Sun 3–7pm. Cover charge.* **(see pp. 174, 176)**

**Banana Café.** Popular, primarily gay cafe-bar near Châtelet with half-naked, male go-go dancers. A very young crowd.... *Tel 01 42 33 35 31; 13, rue de la Ferronnerie, 75001, Métro Châtelet. Open daily until 5am.* **(see p. 177)**

**Barrio Latino.** See Dining. **(see p. 176)**

**Batofar.** A showplace for alternative, often electronic concerts, which are usually followed by heavy DJ action. Come play with really cool young creative Parisians.... *Tel 01 56 29 10 00; Facing 11, quai Francois-Mauriac, 75013, Métro Bib-*

*liotheque. Closed Monday. Cover free–9.14 euros. Drinks 2.29–6.85 euros.* **(see p. 173)**

**Bilboquet.** Left Bank club offering New Orleans–style jazz and dinner in a handsome Belle-Epoque setting.... *Tel 01 45 48 81 84; 13, rue Saint-Benoît, 75006, Métro Saint-Germain-des-Prés. Open daily until 3am.* **(see p. 174)**

**Bistrot d'Eustache.** Intimate jazz bar near Les Halles that serves food until 2am. Live music Thurs, Fri, and Sat.... *Tel 01 40 26 23 20; 37, rue Berger, 75001, Métro Les Halles.* **(see p. 174)**

**Blue Note.** Cozy bar near the rue Mouffetard market that specializes in Brazilian cocktails. Live Brazilian music, jazz, or blues nightly at 10pm.... *Tel 01 45 87 36 09; 38, rue Mouffetard, 75005, Métro Monge.* **(see pp. 174)**

**Bob Cool.** The only Left Bank bar given the seal of approval by hip locals.... *Tel 01 46 33 33 77; 15, rue des Grands Augustins, 75006, Métro Saint-Michel. Open daily.* **(see p. 179)**

**Café Charbon.** The jewel of Menilmontant. Dress down (wear black) and come early to squeeze into a cushy banquette.... *Tel 01 43 57 55 13; 109, rue Oberkampf, 75011, Métro Menilmontant. Open daily until 2am.* **(see p. 177)**

**Café de l'Industrie.** Large, trendy, but relaxed cafe near the Bastille.... *Tel 01 47 00 13 53; 16, rue Saint-Sabin, 75011, Métro Bastille. Closed Sat.* **(see p. 176)**

**Café Mabillon.** Prowling bachelors, late-night couples, and kids who missed the last train gather in this 24-hour Left Bank bar for one last drink.... *Tel 01 43 26 62 93; 164, blvd St-Germain, 75006, Métro Mabillon. Daily 24 hours.* **(see pp. 179, 180)**

**Caveau de la Huchette.** Popular Latin Quarter basement jazz club.... *Tel 01 43 26 65 05; 5, rue de la Huchette, 75005, Métro Saint-Michel. Open until 2:30am weekdays, until 4am weekends.* **(see p. 174)**

**Central.** Convivial gay bar centrally located in the Marais. Cruisy, macho crowd. 8-room hotel upstairs (book well in advance).... *Tel 01 48 87 99 33; 33, rue Vieille-du-Temple, 75004, Métro Hôtel-de-Ville or Saint-Paul.* **(see p. 177)**

**Chapelle des Lombards.** Salsa and merengue reign at this 20-year-old dance club.... *Tel 01 43 57 24 24; 19, rue de Lappe, 75011, Métro Bastille. Open Mon–Sat 8:30pm–dawn. Closed Sun night. Cover charge.*
**(see pp. 176, 178)**

**Chez Georges.** Friendly, time-worn Saint-Germain-des-Prés bar with cheap drinks and lots of university students.... *Tel 01 43 26 79 15; 11, rue des Canettes, 75006, Métro Saint-Germain-des-Prés. Closed Sun–Mon.* **(see p. 179)**

**Chez Richard.** Trendy bar in the Marais, with a pleasant atmosphere but high prices. Serves food.... *Tel 01 42 74 31 65; 37, rue Vieille-du-Temple, 75004, Métro Hôtel-de-Ville or Saint-Paul.* **(see p. 176)**

**China Club.** Sit on couches or play chess in the upstairs rooms.... *Tel 01 43 43 82 02; 50, rue de Charenton, 75012, Métro Ledru-Rollin. Open nightly, until 3am Fri–Sat.*
**(see pp. 176, 179)**

**Cinquième Dimension.** A temple of West Indian dance music, in Montreuil.... *Tel 01 42 87 38 63; Centre Commerciale de la Mairie de Montreuil, 93100 Montreuil, Métro Mairie de Montreuil. Open Fri–Sun 11:15pm–6am. Cover charge (free for women on Sun).* **(see p. 178)**

**Cithéa.** A well-ventilated club with good indirect lighting. Live music Thurs, Fri, and Sat, ranging from salsa to funk and acid jazz.... *Tel 01 40 21 70 95; 114, rue Oberkampf, 75011, Métro St-Maur. Open 8pm–4am. Closed Sun.*
**(see pp. 173, 178)**

**Club-Club.** Funky little Pigalle bar with open-mike and be-your-own-DJ nights.... *Tel 01 42 54 38 38; 3, rue André-Antoine, 75018, Métro Pigalle. Closed in Aug.* **(see p. 175)**

**Divan du Monde.** Pigalle nightclub with concerts, fashion shows, and other events. Music ranges from jazz to rock, salsa, funk, and pop.... *Tel 01 44 92 77 66; 75, rue des Martyrs, 75018, Métro Pigalle. Open 10pm–dawn. Cover charge.* **(see p. 174)**

**Duc des Lombards.** Popular Châtelet-area jazz club with occasional cocktail-hour concerts (7pm or 8pm) and performances every night at 10:30.... *Tel 01 42 33 22 88; 42, rue des Lombards, Métro Châtelet.* **(see p. 175)**

**Duplex.** This club is popular with rich 20-something Euro-boppers smoking Marlboro lights and swilling whisky and Cokes. Fun for a harmlessly trashy night out.... *Tel 01 45 00 45, 2bis Avenue Foch, 75116, Métro Charles de Gaulle-Etoile. Closed Mon. Cover charge 15.24–18.29 euros.* **(see pp. 172, 173, 177)**

**Hôtel Costes.** The bar here is the spot for fashionable young Euro-trash and fashion types, who hungrily scan the scene in search of supermodels and actors.... *Tel 01 42 44 50 25; 239, rue St-Honore, 75001, Métro Concorde. Open daily. No cover.* **(see p. 179)**

**Hotel Lutetia.** There are actually 3 settings here—the dark, cozy bar, the buzzy lobby hall, and the plush new fumoir.... *Tel 01 49 54 46 46; 45, blvd Raspail, 75006, Métro Sevres-Babylone. Open daily. Drinks 7.62–15.24 euros.* **(see p. 179)**

**Jazz Club Lionel Hampton.** Swinging jazz club in the lobby of the Méridien hotel west of the Arc de Triomphe. Good music, pricey drinks.... *Tel 01 40 68 30 42; 81, blvd Gouvion Saint-Cyr, Métro Porte Maillot. Mon–Sat 10:30am–noon, Sun brunch 3pm.* **(see p. 175)**

**L'Imprevu Café.** Check out the basement for occasional jazz action at this friendly, popular cafe with an easygoing mixed crowd.... *Tel 01 42 78 23 50; 7–9, rue Quincampoix, 75004, Métro Hotel de Ville. Open daily. Drinks 7.62 euros.* **(see p. 175)**

**L'Open Café.** Corner meeting place that has become a nucleus in the gay male community.... *Tel 01 42 72 26 18; 17, rue des Archives, 75004, Métro Hôtel de Ville. Open 10pm–2am daily.* **(see p. 177)**

**La Champmeslé.** Lesbian bar with a quiet, conversational ambience.... *Tel 01 42 96 85 20; 4, rue Chabanais, 75002, Métro Bourse. Open daily, Thur–Sat until dawn.* **(see p. 178)**

**La Coupole.** The basement dance hall in this Montparnasse cafe-restaurant has become a happening nightspot, with live Latin music Tue–Thur.... *Tel 01 43 27 56 00; 100, blvd de Montparnasse, 75014, Métro Montparnasse. Open until 4am. Closed Sun–Mon. Cover charge.* **(see p. 178)**

**La Fourmi.** This Pigalle haunt is an ideal spot to strike a pose with young artists and off-hours "entertainers" from the surrounding X-rated theaters and bars.... *Tel 01 42 64 70 35; 74, rue des Martyrs, Métro Pigalle. Open daily.* **(see p. 175)**

**La Java.** *Bal-musette* where you can dance the waltz or tango on Fri and Sat nights or Sun afternoons. Live salsa groups Thursdays... *Tel 01 42 02 20 52; 105, rue du Faubourg-du-Temple, 75010, Métro Republique or Belleville. Open Thur–Sat 9pm–5am, Sun 2–7pm. Cover charge, free on Sun afternoon.* **(see pp. 174, 178)**

**La Villa.** Basement club in the modernized Left Bank hotel of the same name. Quality jazz acts.... *Tel 01 43 26 60 00; 29, rue Jacob, 75006, Métro Saint-Germain-desPrés. Open Mon–Sat 10pm–3am.* **(see p. 175)**

**Le Bus Palladium.** Rock 'n' roll is here to stay with the young crowd at this reincarnated Pigalle disco.... *Tel 01 53 21 07 33; 6, rue Fontaine, 75009, Métro Pigalle. Open Tue–Sun 11pm–dawn. Cover charge (free entry for women on Tue).* **(see p. 175)**

**Le Cabaret.** This disco pulls in people-column-wanabees, and the surly staff cater to their every whim, which may include excluding you at the door. In spite of everything, it's a good time.... *Tel 01 42 89 44 14; 68, rue Pierre Charron, 75008, Métro Franklin-D.-Roosevelt. No cover.* **(see pp. 172, 173)**

**Le Cafe du Tresor.** The stylish young Marais bar/restaurant run by former Kenzo model Rodolphe.... *Tel 01 44 78 06 60; 5, rue du Tresor, 75004, Métro Saint Paul. Daily until 2am.* **(see p. 176)**

**Le Comptoir.** A mixed crowd frequents this chic Les Halles tapas spot. A DJ plugs in Thur–Sat.... *Tel 01 40 26 26 60; 37, rue Berger, 75001, Métro Les Halles.* **(see p. 179)**

**Le Cox.** Spacious and attractive cyber gay bar with an arty, international crowd that spills out onto the sidewalk.... *Tel 01 42 72 08 00; 15, rue des Archives, 75004, Métro Hôtel-de-Ville.* **(see p. 177)**

**Le Dépanneur.** One of the few places in Paris where you can drink at any hour of the day or night. American-diner decor, trendy late-night crowd.... *Tel 01 40 16 40 20; 27, rue Fontaine, 75009, Métro Pigalle. Open 24 hours daily.* **(see pp. 175, 180)**

**Le Depot.** The latest Marais gay hot spot is a disco with a dimly lit basement that's busier than the dance floor. Homoerotic video walls get the crowd in the move and a heavy-duty sound system prevents idyll chatter.... *Tel 01 44 54 96 96; 10, rue aux Ours, 75003, Métro Rambuteau. Open daily. Cover charge 6.86–8.38 euros.* **(see p. 177)**

**Le Gibus.** A serious urban dance club with a large gay following, this place really moves to mostly house and garage music. Wed are popular with trance music.... *Tel 01 47 00 78 88; 18, rue du Faubourg-du-Temple, 75011, Métro Republique. Closed Mon–Tues. Cover charge 7.64–15.24 euros, drinks 7.62 euros.* **(see p. 173)**

**Le Keller.** Put on your leather before visiting this rough, tough, raunchy gay bar near Bastille. Women not admitted.... *Tel 01 47 00 05 39; 14, rue Keller, 75011, Métro Bastille. Open nightly from 10pm.* **(see p. 177)**

**Le Keur Samba.** Upscale African nightclub near the Champs-Elysées, with a very selective door policy.... *Tel 01 43 59 03 10; 79, rue La Boétie, 75008, Métro Franklin-D.-Roosevelt. Open daily midnight–7am. Cover charge.* **(see p. 178)**

**Le Mercury Bar.** Highly popular, 4-level gay bar with a good-looking young crowd. Women rarely admitted.... *Tel 01 40 41 00 10; 5, rue de la Ferronnerie, 75001, Métro Châtelet. Open daily, until 4am Fri and Sat.* **(see pp. 177, 179)**

**Le Moloko.** Funky, popular Pigalle bar with good recorded music.... *Tel 01 48 74 50 26; 26, rue Fontaine, 75009, Métro Blanche. Open daily until 6am.* **(see pp. 175, 180)**

**Le Monkey Club.** The latest hot spot for young bourgeois professionals and the fashion and media crowd near the Champs-Elysees. A pretty good, and pretty expensive, time.... *Tel 01 58 56 20 50; 65–67, rue Pierre Charron, 75008, Métro Franklin-D.-Roosevelt. Closed Mon. No cover.*          **(see p. 172)**

**Le Nelson.** Popular African disco in Montreuil.... *Tel 01 42 87 31 85; place Jean-Jaurès, Centre Commercial Terminal 93, Mairie de Montreuil, 93100 Montreuil, Métro Mairie de Montreuil. Open Thur–Sun midnight–dawn. Cover charge.*
**(see p. 178)**

**Le Paris.** Ordinary-looking cafe near Bastille, with live music on Sat.... *Tel 01 47 00 87 47; 24, blvd Richard-Lenoir, 75011, Métro Bréguet-Sabin. Open 6am–1am. Closed Sun.*          **(see p. 173)**

**Le Queen.** Largest, happeningest gay disco in Paris. Women admitted selectively. Go-go dancers set the pace.... *Tel 01 42 89 31 32; 102, ave des Champs-Elysées, 75008, Métro George-V. Open daily midnight–dawn. Cover charge Fri and Sat.*          **(see pp. 173, 177)**

**Le Tango.** The ambience is hot at this African club and the dancing intimate, to say the least. On weekend afternoons, the club turns into a *bal-musette*.... *Tel 01 42 72 17 78; 13, rue au Maire, 75003, Métro Arts-et-Métiers. Open Fri–Sat 11pm–5am.* Bal-musette *open Sat 2–7pm, Sun 2–8pm. Cover charge (free for women before midnight).*
**(see pp. 174, 178)**

**Le 30.** This bar off the lobby of this new hotel is a peaceful, pleasant spot for a *têtê a tete* over cocktails.... *Tel 01 44 94 14 14; Hotel Sofitel Le Faubourg, 15, rue Boissy d'Anglas, 75008, Métro Concorde. Open daily. Drinks 7.62–15.24 euros.*          **(see p. 180)**

**Le Transfert.** Acts, not words, count in this hot, friendly gay bar frequented by tough, raunchy leather men. Women not admitted.... *No telephone; 3, rue de la Sourdière, 75001, Métro Tuileries. Open daily 11pm–dawn.*     **(see p. 177)**

**Le Trap.** The action takes place upstairs in this Saint-Germain-des-Prés gay bar, one of the city's oldest and raunchiest.

NIGHTLIFE | THE INDEX

Women not admitted.... *No telephone; 10, rue Jacob, 75006, Métro Saint-Germain-des-Prés. Open daily 11pm– 4am. Cover charge.* **(see p. 177)**

**Les Bains Douches.** Star-studded disco in a former bathhouse near the Centre Pompidou. Hard to get into but easy to leave.... *Tel 01 48 87 01 80; 7, rue du Bourg-l'Abbé, 75003, Métro Arts-et-Métiers. Open nightly 11:30pm–dawn. Restaurant 8:30pm–1am. Cover charge.* **(see p. 172)**

**Les Etoiles.** Live Latin music is the draw at this club, also known for its wild rococo decor, near Strasbourg-Saint-Denis.... *Tel 01 47 70 60 56; 61, rue Château-d'Eau, 75010, Métro Château-d'Eau. Open Thur–Sat 9am–4am. Cover charge (includes a main course).* **(see p. 178)**

**Les Folies Pigalle.** A 2-level disco featuring progressive house and techno music, go-go dancers, and a gay crowd. Turns into an after-hours club Sat and Sun.... *Tel 01 48 78 25 56; 11, place Pigalle, Métro Pigalle. Open Thur–Sat, midnight–5am. Cover charge.* **(see pp. 175, 180)**

**Les Noctambules.** Pigalle nightspot that hasn't changed since the 1950s, except the clientele is now younger and hipper.... *Tel 01 46 06 16 38; 24, blvd de Clichy, 75018, Métro Pigalle. Open Mon–Thur 10pm–4am, Fri–Sat 10pm–5am. Closed in Aug.* **(see p. 175)**

**Les Portes.** This popular Bastille bar has a coy 1920s bordello ambience and decor that appeals to a young clientele who'd never dream of "paying for it."... *Tel 01 40 21 70 61; 15, rue de Charonne, 75011, Métro Bastille. Open daily until 2am.* **(see p. 176)**

**Lou Pescalou.** The draw at this unpretentious but very hip Menimlmontant bar is the pool table.... *Tel 01 46 36 78 10; 14, rue des Panoyaux, 75020, Métro Menimlmontant. Open daily until 2am.* **(see p. 177)**

**Majestic.** A too-trendy cafe in the Marais. Light meals are served.... *Tel 01 42 74 61 61; 34, rue Vieille-du-Temple, 75004, Métro Hôtel-de-Ville or Saint-Paul.* **(see p. 176)**

**Mic Man.** Videos and live action are in the basement of this rather seedy Marais gay bar. Women not admitted.... *Tel*

*01 42 74 39 80; 24, rue Geoffroy l'Angevin, 75004, Métro Rambuteau. Open daily, until 4am Fri–Sat.*
**(see p. 177)**

**New Morning.** A 10th-arrondissement club attracting some of the best international jazz, blues, African, and South American groups.... *Tel 01 45 23 51 41; 7, rue des Petites-Ecuries, 75010, Métro Château-d'Eau.* **(see p. 174)**

**Old Navy.** Soldiers on leave, party girls, stumped writers, habitual local sozzlers—the gang's all here at this funky, frisky café-bar that gets harmlessly stranger as the night wears on.... *Tel 01 43 26 88 09; 150, blvd St-Germain, 75006, Métro Mabillon. Daily non-stop.* **(see p. 180)**

**One Way.** An older gay leather crowd frequents this Marais bar. Women not admitted.... *Tel 01 48 87 46 10; 28, rue Charlot, 75003, Métro République.* **(see p. 177)**

**Petit Fer à Cheval.** Friendly Marais bar-restaurant. Always packed.... *Tel 01 42 72 47 47; 30, rue Vieille-du-Temple, 75004, Métro Saint-Paul or Hôtel-de-Ville. Food served until 12:30am. No credit cards.* **(see p. 175)**

**Petit Journal Montparnasse.** Jazz club with good sightlines, good acoustics, and excellent musicians.... *Tel 01 43 21 56 70; 13, rue du Commandant-Mouchotte, 75014, Métro Montparnasse. Open Mon–Sat 9pm–2am.* **(see p. 174)**

**Petit Journal Saint-Michel.** Latin Quarter club with New Orleans–style jazz.... *Tel 01 43 26 28 59; 71, blvd. Saint-Michel, 75005, RER Luxembourg. Open Mon–Sat 10pm–2am.* **(see p. 174)**

**Petit Roi de la Lune.** An accordion collection distinguishes this Montparnasse bar-cafe where it's hip to play backgammon.... *Tel 01 45 43 45 96; 11, rue Francis-de-Préssensé, 75014, Métro Pernety. Closed Sun.* **(see p. 180)**

**Pick-Clops.** Smoking is *de rigeur* for the cool, young clientele of this Marais cafe-bar.... *Tel 01 40 29 02 18; 16, rue Vieille-du-Temple, 75004, Métro Hôtel-de-Ville. Open daily 8am–2am.* **(see p. 176)**

**Pulp!** Formerly L'Entreacte, one of the city's most popular lesbian clubs now has a flashier, more lipstick image. Mixed crowd during the week and ladies only on the weekend.... *Tel 01 40 26 01 93; 25, blvd Poissonière, 75002, Métro Rue Montmartre. Closed Mon–Tues. Cover charge on weekends.* **(see p. 178)**

**Quetzal.** One of the cruisiest gay bars in the Marais where cute young leather boys go to scowl at each other.... *Tel 01 48 87 99 07; 10, rue de la Verrerie, 75004, Métro Hôtel-de-Ville.* **(see p. 177)**

**Rex Club.** A brash and packed-out club with a frisky and devoted following of regulars who live for its electronic dance music.... *Tel 01 42 36 83 98; 5, blvd Poissoniere, 75002, Metro Bonne-Nouvelle. Closed Sun–Mon. Cover charge 9.15–12.20 euros, drinks 4.57–7.62 euros.*
**(see p. 173)**

**Sanz Sans.** Well-mixed drinks and well-spun Latin, funk, hip-hop and house.... *Tel 01 44 75 78 78; 49, rue du Faubourg-St-Antoine, 75012, Métro Bastille. Open daily. No cover. Drinks 4.57–7.62 euros.* **(see p. 176)**

**Satellit' Café.** Lounge lizards will feel at home in this bar, where a DJ plays old jazz, blues, and soul, and there are occasionally good live shows.... *Tel 01 47 00 48 87; 44, rue de la Folie-Méricourt, Métro Oberkampf. Open daily, until dawn Sat and Sun.* **(see p. 180)**

**Scorp.** Gay/mixed disco with camp decor and even campier drag shows at 4am. Friendly atmosphere.... *Tel 01 40 26 28 30; 25, blvd Poissonnière, 75002, Métro Sentier. Open daily 11pm–dawn. Cover charge Fri and Sat.*
**(see p. 177)**

**Sous-Bock.** Large, English-style pub with wide selection of international beers.... *Tel 01 40 26 46 61; 49, rue Saint-Honoré, 75001, Métro Pont-Neuf or Les Halles. Open daily until 5am.* **(see p. 180)**

**Sunset.** Agreeable basement jazz club where you can dine while listening to some of France's best jazz talents.... *Tel 01 40 26 46 60; 60, rue des Lombards, 75001, Métro Châtelet. Open daily until 4am.* **(see p. 174)**

**Underworld Café.** A popular bar-club on the thriving Menil-montant nightlife circuit, this place rocks to different tunes nightly.... *Tel 01 55 28 33 28; 25, rue Oberkampf, 75011, Métro Oberkampf. Closed Sun. No cover. Drinks 1.52–6.86 euros.* **(see p. 177)**

**Wait & See Café.** Concert cafe near place de la République, with live rock and hip-hop.... *Tel 01 48 07 29 49; 9, blvd Voltaire, 75011, Métro République. Open until 5am Fri–Sat. Closed Mon.* **(see p. 173)**

# 7

# inment

Though the first
image most folks
have of Paris
entertainment is
the age-old tits-
and-feathers
revues, these days

the city's legendary cabarets are more can't-can't than can-can. Unless your idea of a great night out is to be surrounded by heavy-breathing Japanese businessmen, take the hundred dollars a person you save by skipping these sorry spectacles and spend it on tickets to an opera, a ballet, or a concert.

Due mainly to lavish government subsidies, Paris remains one of the great arts centers of the world, and even if France hasn't been producing a lot of native talent recently, it can afford to import the very best performers and companies from other cities. Unfortunately, despite government largesse, ticket prices are stiff; your best bets are the Ballet de l'Opéra de Paris, any opera, and, for French speakers, a production at the Comédie Française or the Théâtre de L'Odéon. The mainstream French theater has lost its way in febrile but feeble attempts to imitate Broadway and London's West End, but good productions of French classics, à la Molière, are generally available.

Interested in local stars? Keep your eyes peeled for performances by American soprano Jessye Norman (she lives in Switzerland but Paris is her regular performing venue); concerts by Les Arts Florissants—a wildly popular Baroque chamber music group directed by American William Christie; plays by Alfedo Arias, an avant-garde Argentine playwright and resident of Paris; and cabaret recitals by Ute Lemper, the German singer who lives in Paris and performs often at the Bouffes du Nord theater, one of the city's most atmospheric locales.

## Sources

*Pariscope* and *L'Officiel des Spectacles* come out every Wednesday with complete listings of films, theater, music, dance, and art exhibitions. *Pariscope* includes **"Time Out Paris,"** a 12-page, English-language insert that also gives instructions on how to decipher the French listings. French speakers should also pick up the *Figaro* newspaper on Wednesdays because its weekly supplement, the **"Figaroscope,"** provides not only the same listings, but restaurant reviews, an excellent nightlife column, and a lot of general information about the trendiest places and faces. The hip monthly magazine *Nova* is another good source.

## Getting Tickets

The major ticket outlets in Paris are **Virgin Megastore** (tel 01 49 53 50 00; 52, ave des Champs-Elysées, 75001) and the book/record stores **FNAC** with outlets everywhere; its main location is in the Forum des Halles (tel 01 40 41 40 00; 1–7, rue Pierre-Lescot, 75001, Métro Les Halles) and The **Office du Tourisme** (tel 01 49 53 53 56; 127, ave des Champs-Elysées, 75008, Métro Etoile; open daily 9am to 8pm) can also make theater and exhibition reservations.

Half-price theater tickets are available on the day of the performance from **Le Kiosque Théâtre** on the place Madeleine (Métro Madeleine) and in the RER station at Châtelet-Les-Halles. No information is given by telephone, and a small commission is charged. Most major theaters participate, but tickets to *cafés-théâtres* are not sold. And although selection varies according to availability, it's generally fairly good.

Opera, classical music, and dance performances are often sold out well in advance, but don't despair. You can show up an hour or so before a performance, line up at the ticket window, and pray for cancellations—unclaimed tickets are put on sale a half-hour before the curtain goes up at most stages. This is risky, however, and there's a much more efficient local custom: Scrounge up a scrap of paper and pen, and make a little sign that says "Cherche une place" (or "deux places," as the case may be). People often arrive with tickets for

friends who couldn't make it, and they'll be happy to sell the extras to you, usually at face value. This might also work at a rock concert, but there you're more likely to encounter professional scalpers. By the way, *sans visibilité* (impaired visibility) tickets

**Dancing in the streets**

On June 21, the summer solstice, all of Paris celebrates the **Fête de la Musique**. Just step out the door and you'll hear music—anyone who wants to can perform in the street without a permit. More organized events range from rock concerts at the place de la Bastille to classical music in the place de la Concorde. Not surprisingly, it's often cacophony—imagine a classical quartet competing with a heavy-metal band a block away. You might stumble on a brilliant blues group in a back street or Renaissance choristers in the place de Furstemberg—or you might see a gyrating horde of samba dancers on the rue de Rivoli at 2am, trailing a truck blaring salsa music. Since 1937, the city's firemen (pompiers-sapeurs) have observed **Bastille Day** with shindigs in their fire-station courtyards on July 13 and 14. Anyone can come, so long as you make a small donation. There's usually either a live band (most fun are the corny ones with an accordion player) or a disc jockey, and everyone—from the oldest granny to the youngest toddler—joins in the dancing. The best parties are at the Sévigné, Vieux-Colombier, Montmartre, and Château-Landon firehouses. Watch out for flying firecrackers.

are often available at very low prices. About half the stage can usually be seen from these seats and sometimes the whole stage if you stand. There's also the possibility of moving to better seats that are unoccupied. It's worth a try.

# The Lowdown

**The play's the thing...** The **Comédie Française**, established by Louis XIV in 1680, is the granddaddy of French theater and still the best place for classics, with top actors playing on its stage in works by Molière, Racine, Feydeau, et al. If your French isn't tip-top, however, there's little point in going to a performance. The same recommendation and warning apply to the small, handsomely renovated **Théâtre du Vieux-Colombier**, a branch of the Comédie Française that presents both contemporary and classic plays.

   **Bobigny/MC93**, located on Lenin Boulevard just outside of Paris in the "Communist Belt" (many Paris suburbs have elected Communist administrations), presents international productions of works by the likes of Robert Wilson and Peter Sellars, as well as homemade productions and a yearly visit from London's Royal Shakespeare Company. English-language productions are often staged at the lovely **Odéon-Théâtre de l'Europe** and at the **Bouffes du Nord**. The latter is British director Peter Brook's theater in a lovely Italianate structure once damaged by fire and purposefully left scarred despite renovations. (It's art statement.) The seating there is highly uncomfortable, but the productions, often in English, are top-notch. Other small theaters that offer at least occasional English-language productions—usually of the Sam Shepard or Harold Pinter variety—are the Left Bank's **Théâtre de Nesle** and the **Théâtre du Tourtour**, near the Centre Pompidou.

   Not to be overlooked for its French-language avant-garde productions is the **Cartoucherie**, the home, in eastern Paris, of Ariane Mnouchkine's acclaimed Théâtre du Soleil, a troupe known for daring productions of classic Greek plays and even Molière. **Nanterre/Théâtre des Amandiers**, located in the western suburb of Nanterre, is known for excellent productions of contemporary plays in French; sometimes it hosts English-language companies like England's acclaimed Nottingham Playhouse.

**Classical sounds...** Classical concerts are held at a wide variety of venues all over Paris. The **Théâtre du Châtelet** recently reopened after a year-long renovation that has modernized the technical workings of one of the great Parisian halls. Originally built by Baron Haussmann, who wanted to create a grandiose theatre worthy of his massive 19th-century urban renewal of Paris, this house seats 3,000 and is looking splendid with new carpeting, lighting, and seats. In addition to a well-deserved reputation for opera and dance productions, Châtelet has earned acclaim in recent years as an innovative music venue, complenting its classical music program with a special series of concerts for young people, as well as lunchtime salon recitals featuring the stars of current major productions. At the **Maison de Radio France**, the headquarters of the national radio network located near the Seine's Statue of Liberty, the good-but-not-great **Orchestre National de France** and the **Orchestre Philharmonique** stage concerts, many of them free. Composer/conductor Pierre Boulez's Ensemble InterContemporain offers a heady alternative to the classics—its avant-garde sounds can often be heard at the **Centre Pompidou**. Concerts at the **Cité de la Musique** in the La Villette complex in northeastern Paris present a grab-bag of musical styles, from North African sounds to chamber music. The **Salle Pleyel**, near the Arc de Triomphe, was the site of Chopin's last public performance, but it doesn't live in the past: It's still one of the top venues for classical concerts and recitals. The big names also pop up for recitals at the **Salle Gaveau**, off the Champs-Elysées.

Many Parisian churches regularly hold concerts, from the Sunday evening organ recitals at the magnificent **Notre-Dame** to the chamber groups and quartets that play beneath the justly famed stained-glass of the more intimate **Sainte-Chapelle**. The **Madeleine**, on the place de Madeleine, often presents choral music, but the church is too immense to do justice to the voices. The **Saint-Eustache**, a strange mixture of Gothic and Renaissance architecture next to the Forum des Halles, presents organ recitals on Sunday evenings. The **Cathédrale Américaine**, located off the Champs-Elysées, sometimes hosts visiting American gospel choirs or accomplished organists; don't confuse it with the **Eglise Américaine** on the quai d'Orsay, which holds less ambitious vocal recitals and one-man or one-woman instrumental programs. The

**Saint-Germain-des-Prés**, the oldest church in Paris, may overdo Vivaldi's *Four Seasons,* but when the trumpets of the Orchestre Bernard Thomas sing in this lovely 12th-century church, it can bring tears to your eyes. Almost as ancient is the smaller **Saint-Julien-le-Pauvre** in the Latin Quarter, which offers many of its concerts by candlelight. Nearby **Saint-Séverin**, considered one of the city's most beautiful Gothic churches, presents frequent concerts by its in-house vocal ensemble.

**What's opera, doc?...** The grandest opera of all will be found at the **Opéra National de Paris-Bastille**, a massive 1989 building that has thrived despite attacks on its bland architecture, the dismissal of internationally renowned directors and conductors, orchestra strikes, constant political meddling, and frequent breakdowns of one of the most technologically advanced stages in the world. Prices are very high for what the Socialists wanted to be "the opera of the people," but you still have to book far in advance to avoid being shut out of its 2,700-seat hall. The Opéra Bastille's predecessor, the wonderfully ornate **Opéra Garnier** (where the Phantom of the Opera hung out), was decreed to be used exclusively for ballet after the unpopular new opera opened, but after a total renovation of its main theater, it's now technically just as up-to-date as the Opéra National de Paris-Bastille.

Both full-scale and light operas can also be seen and heard at the charming **Opéra Comique**, which has staged Puccini's *La Bohème,* as well as works by Offenbach, Mozart, and Gounod. More daring is the **Théâtre du Châtelet**, which has hosted many acclaimed productions, including Wagner's *Ring Cycle* and William Christie's fabulous rendering of Purcell's *King Arthur.* The **Théâtre des Champs-Elysées**, normally a dance venue, stages operas by the likes of Tchaikovsy, Rimsky-Korsakov, and Handel.

**Men in tights...** Parisians flock to dance performances, whether they be *Swan Lake,* flamenco, Tibetan dance, or the weirdest experimental modern contortions. The **Opéra Garnier** is now the official home of the **Ballet de l'Opéra de Paris,** considered by many to be the world's best ballet. If you don't take in a performance, you should still try to visit this bring-on-the-gilt hall, commissioned in 1875 by Emperor Napoléon III (see Diversions). Ballets are also staged at the **Opéra National de Paris-Bastille**.

Presenting works by troupes like La-La-La Human Steps, Trisha Brown, or Pina Bausch, the **Théâtre de la Ville**, on the place du Châtelet, may be the city's most important modern dance venue. Baryshnikov, Mark Morris, the Kirov Ballet, and many other famous dance companies have tripped across the stage of the handsome and historic **Théâtre des Champs-Elysées**, where Nijinsky's 1917 première of *The Rite of Spring* is said to have started riots. The **Théâtre National de Chaillot** reserves its stage between theater productions for troupes like the *Ballet Béjart Lausanne*. Busy **Théâtre du Châtelet** is the Paris home of William Forsythe's Frankfurt Ballet. The **Théâtre de la Bastille** showcases new companies on their way up to the big time. Just outside of Paris is the **Maison des Arts de Créteil**, known for the unbearably pretentious production of Maguy Martin; you have to be a modern-dance die hard to get through one of these shows. For something more exotic, check the program of the **Rond Point Théâtre Renaud-Barrault**, which often hosts ethnic dance troops from other countries.

**Pop and rock concerts...** The mega-venues for rock concerts are the **Zénith**, an immense concert hall in the Parc de la Villette, and the **Palais d'Omnisports de Paris-Bercy**, a 16,000-seat stadium in Bercy, with grass-covered walls. Both places book the likes of aging French rocker Johnny Hallyday and such international names as Chris Isaak. Some stars also show up at the **Olympia** or the **Grand Rex**, two real theaters near the **Opéra Garnier** that are small enough that you can actually see the stage without binoculars. Edith Piaf and Jacques Brel sang at the Olympia, and today you might see French chanteur Claude Nougaro, blues singer Paul Personne, or big-time rock acts who "want to get back in touch with their audience." Alternative and local rock groups perform at **La Cigale** and **Elysées Montmartre**, smaller theaters in the Pigalle area. The handsome, 19th-century, one-ring circus building, the **Cirque d'Hiver**, sometimes hosts concerts by French stars like pop singer Jacques Higelin (one of the best of an uninspiring bunch). Parisians are delighted by the revival of **La Boule Noire**, the intimate venue next to La Cigale in Montmartre that was a popular rock venue in the sixties.

**Life is a cabaret...** If you like to pay outrageous prices to watch topless Las Vegas–style showgirls and eat mediocre food while surrounded by busloads of tourists, by all means go to the **Moulin Rouge** (yes, they still do the can-can), the **Folies-Bergère**, the **Crazy Horse Saloon**, or the **Lido**. The Moulin Rouge, up in Montmartre, goes in for spectacle, boasting 1,000 costumes and 100 artists; save yourself some money by avoiding the uninspired dinner. Dancers at the Crazy Horse, just off the Champs-Elysées, have the sexiest names: Kismy Patchwork, Looky Boob, and Pussy Duty-Free.

There is another world of French cabaret. For smaller-scale shows that might feature stand-up comedy (in French), singers, sketches, or plays, try the *café-théâtres*, some of which also serve dinner. The **Blancs-Manteaux** concentrates on comedy, as does the popular **Point Virgule**. **Café de la Gare** offers cabaret acts, and the **Double-Fond** has magic acts. All four are in the Marais.

**Comedy tonight...** **Laughing Matters** is the name of a regular series of English-language comedy gigs held upstairs at the legendary Hotel du Nord (yes, the one where Arletty breathed "Atmosphere, atmosphere". This can be a fun night out, since you'll likely meet a full cast of local anglophone expats and might run into some really good contemporary British stand-up comedy like Eddie Izzard, who's become a cult success in London. With his rasp voice and drag costume, he's screamingly funny. Of the French comedians you see around, Valerie Lemercier is probably the one who's mostly likely to get a giggle out of you, while the appeal of mainstream stars like Smain and Bigard often escapes those who are perfectly fluent in French.

**On the fringe...** Keep an eye on the "Scenes" section of *Pariscope* for performances by the immensely popular **Zingaro,** a wild and weird circus in which muscleman Bartabas wrestles and writhes with his company, which consists mainly of horses.

**The sporting life...** Emotions run high when the Paris Saint-Germain football (soccer) team plays on its home turf at the **Parc des Princes**, and if Parisians had often been blasé about the sport in the past, France's dramatic World Cup victory in 1998 brought the sport a new influx of high-profile fans—*le foot, c'est chic*. The sleek **L' Stade de France**, which looks like a high-tech layer cake and seats

25,000 around a field the same size as the place de la Concorde, is pretty stunning and can be visited even when there's nothing going on there. Rugby matches are also held at the **Parc des Princes,** with the Five Nations Tournament from January to March and the French national championships in late May and early June. The **Stade Roland Garros**, out in western Paris near the Bois de Boulogne, hosts the **French Open** tennis championship at the end of May and the beginning of June. At the **Palais d'Omnisports de Paris-Bercy**, events range from rock concerts to martial arts tournaments to the Paris Open tennis tournament and even an indoor windsurfing competition. For horse-racing fans, the Bois de Boulogne has two tracks, the Hippodrome de Longchamp for flat-track racing and the Hippodrome d'Auteuil for steeplechase, while the Hippodrome de Vincennes in the Bois de Vincennes is a trotter's course (see Getting Outside for all three).

# The Index

**Ballet de l'Opéra de Paris.** See **Opéra Garnier.**

**Blancs-Manteaux.** One of the best-known cafés-théâtres, this venue in the Marais has two small theaters presenting plays and comedy sketches in French.... *Tel 01 48 87 15 84; 15, rue des Blancs-Manteaux, 75004, Métro Hôtel-de-Ville.*
**(see p. 200)**

**Bobigny/MC93.** Impressive modern theater in one of Paris's Communist-run suburbs, where productions tend toward the experimental and international.... *Tel 01 41 60 72 72; La Maison de la Culture, 1, blvd. Lénine, Bobigny, Métro Bobigny-Pablo Picasso.* **(see p. 196)**

**Bouffes du Nord.** British director Peter Brook puts up top-notch productions at this arty, quasi-ruined theater in northern

Paris.... *Tel 01 46 07 34 50; 37 bis, blvd. de la Chapelle, 75010, Métro La Chapelle.* **(see p. 196)**

**Café de la Gare.** Plays and comedy acts in French keep 'em laughing at this *café-théâtre* in the Marais.... *Tel 01 42 78 52 51; 41, rue du Temple, 75004, Métro Hôtel-de-Ville.*
**(see p. 200)**

**Cartoucherie.** Home to Ariane Mnouchkine's Théâtre du Soleil and four lesser-known companies.... *Tel 01 43 74 24 08; route du Champ-de-Manoeuvre, 75012, Métro Château-de-Vincennes, shuttle bus available from Métro for performances.* **(see p. 196)**

**Cathédrale Américaine.** Sponsors concerts ranging from American gospel to organ and choral music.... *Tel 01 47 20 17 92; 23, av. George V, Métro George-V.* **(see p. 197)**

**Centre Pompidou.** Composer Pierre Boulez's Ensemble Inter-Contemporain performs its experimental music, as well as works by other modern composers.... *Tel 01 44 78 48 43 or 01 44 78 12 33; rue Rambuteau and rue Saint-Merri, 75004, Métro Rambuteau or Hôtel-de-Ville.* **(see p. 197)**

**Cirque d'Hiver.** More likely to host a French pop singer or a Jean-Paul Gaultier fashion show than a circus these days.... *Tel 01 47 00 28 81; 110, rue Ameloqt, 75011, Métro Filles-du-Calvaire.* **(see p. 199)**

**Cité de la Musique.** A music conservatory, musical archives, and a theater that regularly hosts classical concerts.... *Tel 01 44 84 44 84; 211, av. Jean-Jaurès, 75019, Métro Porte-de-Pantin.* **(see p. 197)**

**Comédie Française.** The historical home of the French dramatic arts, near the Palais-Royal.... *Tel 01 40 15 00 15; 2, rue de Richelieu, 75001, Métro Palais-Royal.*
**(see p. 196)**

**Crazy Horse Saloon.** Home of the most erotic cabaret show in Paris.... *Tel 01 47 23 32 32; 12, av. George V, 75008, Métro Alma-Marceau.* **(see p. 200)**

**Double-Fond.** A Marais cafe that stages magic acts.... *Tel 01*

*42 71 40 20; 1, place du Marché Sainte-Catherine, 75004, Métro Saint-Paul.* **(see p. 200)**

**Eglise Américaine.** Vocal recitals and guitar concerts are some of the musical offerings at this American church on the quai d'Orsay.... *Tel 01 47 05 07 99; 65, quai d'Orsay, 75007, Métro Invalides.* **(see p. 197)**

**Elysées Montmartre.** Pigalle rock concert venue that presents groups like Boyz II Men, as well as French and world music.... *Tel 01 44 92 45 49; 72, blvd. Rochechouart, 75018, Métro Anvers.* **(see p. 199)**

**Folies-Bergère.** Music hall in Montmartre where the shows are perhaps more clever than the flesh-and-feathers norm.... *Tel 01 44 79 98 98; 32, rue Richer, 75009, Métro rue Mont-martre.* **(see p. 200)**

**French Open tennis.** See **Stade Roland Garros.**

**Grand Rex.** A proper theater with good acoustics, near the Opéra Garnier, that attracts some big names, Bob Dylan and Ry Cooder among them.... *Tel 01 45 08 93 89; 1, blvd. Poissonnière, 75002, Métro Montmartre.* **(see p. 199)**

**L' Stade de France.** This state-of-the-art stadium in the Métro accessible suburb of Saint Denis is a tour de force of Star Trek style modern architecture.... *Tel 01 55 93 00 00; Le Stade de France, St. Denis, Métro St-Denis-Porte-de-Paris. Admission 5.79 euros, Entrance through Porte H.* **(see p. 200)**

**La Boule Noire.** A renovated, atmospheric performance space in Montmartre for emerging talent and one-night dance par-ties and cabaret events.... *Tel 01 49 25 89 99; 120 blvd. Rochechouart, 75018, Métro Pigalle.* **(see p. 199)**

**La Cigale.** Reasonably sized Pigalle theater for rock concerts by both new and well-known acts.... *Tel 01 42 23 15 15; 120, blvd Rochechouart, 75018, Métro Pigalle.* **(see p. 199)**

**Laughing Matters.** A regular series that showcases the best of mostly British young comedians passing through Paris.... *Tel*

*01 53 19 98 88, www.anythingmatters.com; Hotel du Nord, 102, quai de Jemmapes, 75010, Métro Republique. Shows on Sun, Mon, Tues. Tickets 15.24 euros.*

**(see p. 200)**

**Lido.** Cabaret where the dancing Bluebell Girls and even ice-skating acts entertain tourists over dinner or champagne.... *Tel 01 40 76 56 10, www.anythingmatters.com; 116 bis, av. des Champs-Elysées, 75008, Métro George-V.*

**(see p. 200)**

**Madeleine.** Massive 19th-century church where choral recitals are often held.... *Tel 01 44 51 69 00; place de la Madeleine, 75008, Métro Madeleine.* **(see p. 197)**

**Maison de Radio France.** Orchestre National de France and the Orchestre Philharmonique perform here.... *Tel 01 42 30 10 45; 116, av. du Président Kennedy, 75016, Métro Ranelagh or Passy.* **(see p. 197)**

**Maison des Arts de Créteil.** Choreographer Maguy Marin's innovative dance company draws Parisian audiences to its base in this eastern suburb.... *Tel 01 45 13 19 19; place Salvador Allende, 94000 Créteil, Métro Créteil-Préfecture.*

**(see p. 199)**

**Moulin Rouge.** The birthplace of the can-can is still going strong in Montmartre, though its topless extravaganza is seen primarily by tour groups.... *Tel 01 53 09 82 82, 82 bd de Clichy, 75018, Métro Blanche.* **(see p. 200)**

**Nanterre/Théâtre des Amandiers.** Theater in a Western suburb that sometimes hosts visiting English-language troupes.... *Tel 01 46 14 70 00; 7, av. Pablo Picasso, Métro La Défense, then bus 159, or RER Nanterre-Préfecture, then free shuttle bus.* **(see p. 196)**

**Notre-Dame.** The landmark cathedral has free organ concerts Sundays at 5:30pm and choral music on the fourth Tuesday of each month.... *Tel 01 42 34 56 10; place du Parvis-Notre-Dame, 75004, Métro Cité.* **(see p. 197)**

**Odéon-Théâtre de l'Europe.** Classic Left Bank theater, with a few plays in English every season, including works by

Shakespeare.... *Tel 01 44 41 36 36; place de l'Odéon, 75006, Métro Odéon.* **(see p. 196)**

**Olympia.** Excellent concert theater because of its smallish size. A place you might see big-time rock acts who are sick of arena shows.... *Tel 01 47 42 25 49; 28, blvd. des Capucines, 75009, Métro Opéra.* **(see p. 199)**

**Opéra Comique.** Lovely restored theater in the Opéra Quarter, presenting light opera and an occasional play.... *Tel 01 42 44 45 45, reservations 01 42 44 45 46; 5, rue Favart, 75002, Métro Richelieu-Drouot.* **(see p. 198)**

**Opéra Garnier.** This opulent 19th-century landmark is now the home of the Ballet de l'Opéra de Paris.... *Tel 01 40 01 25 14; place de l'Opéra, 75009, Métro Opéra. For info and showtimes, log onto www.opera-de-paris.fr.* **(see pp. 198, 199)**

**Opéra National de Paris-Bastille.** The city's controversial new opera house. Dance too.... *Tel 01 44 73 13 99 (information), 01 44 73 13 00 (reservations); 2 bis, place de la Bastille, 75012, Métro Bastille. For info and showtimes, log onto www.opera-de-paris.fr.* **(see p. 198)**

**Orchestre National de France.** See **Maison de Radio France.**

**Orchestre Philharmonique.** See **Maison de Radio France.**

**Palais d'Omnisports de Paris-Bercy.** Rock concerts, exhibitions, and sporting events.... *Tel 08 03 03 00 31; 8, blvd. de Bercy, 75012, Métro Bercy.* **(see pp. 199, 201)**

**Parc des Princes.** National team soccer and rugby matches.... *Tel 01 49 87 29 29 (soccer) or 01 42 30 03 60; 24, rue du Commandant-Guilbaud, 75016, Métro Porte-d'Auteuil.* **(see pp. 200, 201)**

**Point Virgule.** *Café-théâtre* in the Marais featuring comedy acts and sketches.... *Tel 01 42 78 67 03; 7, rue Saint-Croix-de-la-Bretonnerie, 75004, Métro Hôtel-de-Ville.* **(see p. 200)**

**Rond Point Théâtre Renaud-Barrault.** Plays and ethnic

ENTERTAINMENT | THE INDEX

dance performances from around the world are held in this round, 19th-century building off the Champs-Elysées.... *Tel 01 44 95 98 15; 2 bis, av. Franklin D. Roosevelt, 75008, Métro Franklin D. Roosevelt.* (see p. 199)

**Saint-Eustache.** Free organ recitals are held Sundays in this Gothic church.... *Tel 01 42 36 31 05; 2, impasse Saint-Eustache, 75001, Métro Les Halles.* (see p. 197)

**Saint-Germain-des-Prés.** The oldest church in the city hosts frequent classical concerts.... *Tel 01 43 25 41 71; 3, place Saint-Germain-des-Prés, Métro Saint-Germain-des-Prés.* (see p. 198)

**Saint-Julien-le-Pauvre.** Sweet, ancient little Left Bank church that often holds candlelight classical concerts.... *Tel 01 48 01 91 35; 79, rue Galande, 75005, Métro Saint-Michel.* (see p. 198)

**Saint-Séverin.** A gorgeous Gothic church in the Latin Quarter, with a choral group that performs regularly.... *Tel 01 43 25 96 63; 1, rue des Prêtres-Saint-Séverins, 75005, Métro Saint-Michel.* (see p. 198)

**Sainte-Chapelle.** This jewel of a chapel is the site of frequent classical concerts.... *Tel 01 48 01 91 35 or 01 45 45 65 77; 4, blvd. du Palais, 75001, Métro Cité.* (see p. 197)

**Salle Gaveau.** A hall off the Champs-Elysées for classical recitals and small concerts by both renowned international stars and lesser-known talents.... *Tel 01 45 62 69 71; 45, rue La Boétie, 75008, Métro Miromesnil.* (see p. 197)

**Salle Pleyel.** Top-level classical concerts and recitals in a hall near the Arc de Triomphe.... *Tel 01 45 61 53 00; 252, rue du Faubourg-Saint-Honoré, 75008, Métro Ternes.* (see p. 197)

**Stade Roland Garros.** The star-studded French Open tennis tournament takes place at this stadium in late spring. Write or fax well in advance for tickets.... *Tel 01 47 43 48 00, fax 01 47 43 04 94; 2, av. Gordon-Bennet, 75016, Métro Porte d'Auteuil.* (see p. 201)

**Théâtre de la Bastille.** Theater known for taking chances on young dance and theater companies. The spring is for theater, the fall for dance.... *Tel 01 43 57 42 14; 76, rue de la Roquette, 75011, Métro Bastille.* **(see p. 199)**

**Théâtre de la Ville.** Top venue for modern dance, chamber music, and recitals, in the heart of the Right Bank.... *Tel 01 42 74 22 77; 2, place du Châtelet, 75004, Métro Châtelet.* **(see p. 199)**

**Théâtre de Nesle.** Small Left Bank theater that sometimes produces English-language plays.... *Tel 01 46 34 61 04; 8, rue de Nesle, 75006, Métro Odéon.* **(see p. 196)**

**Théâtre des Champs-Elysées.** Many famous dance companies have appeared at this handsome, historic theater. Also hosts opera productions.... *Tel 01 49 52 50 50; 15, av. Montaigne, 75008, Métro Alma-Marceau.* **(see pp. 198, 199)**

**Théâtre du Châtelet.** Fine opera, classical music, and occasional dance performances are staged in this beautiful theater.... *Tel 01 40 28 28 40; 1 place du Châtelet 75001, Métro Châtelet.* **(see pp. 197, 198, 199)**

**Théâtre du Tourtour.** A basement theater near the Centre Pompidou that occasionally stages English-language plays.... *Tel 01 48 87 82 48; 20, rue Quincampoix, 75004, Métro Rambuteau.* **(see p. 196)**

**Théâtre du Vieux-Colombier.** A branch of the Comédie Française in a small, handsomely renovated Left Bank theater.... *Tel 01 44 39 87 00; 21, rue du Vieux-Colombier, 75006, Métro Saint-Sulpice.* **(see p. 196)**

**Théâtre National de Chaillot.** Plays by Edmond Rostand, Marguerite Duras, Bertold Brecht, and occasional dance performances.... *Tel 01 47 27 81 15; 1, place du Trocadéro, 75016, Métro Trocadéro.* **(see p. 196)**

**Zénith.** A mega-rock-concert venue in the Parc de la Villette.... *Tel 01 42 08 60 00; 211, av. de Jean-Jaurès, 75019, Métro Porte de Pantin.* **(see p. 199)**

**Zingaro.** An amazing circus. Look for announcements of appearances in *Pariscope* or *L'Officiel des Spectacles.* **(see p. 200)**

# hotlines & other basics

**Airports...** Two international airports serve Paris: **Roissy-Charles-de-Gaulle** (referred to as Roissy, pronounced "rwah-SEE" by natives) and **Orly**. Orly is closer to town than Roissy and is increasingly used for domestic flights. Roissy is enormous but fairly easy to get around; signs tend to be clearly marked and easy to understand, even for first-time visitors. For flight information call **Orly** at 01 49 75 15 15 or **Roissy** at 01 48 62 22 80.

**Airport transportation into town...** A taxi is usually the most convenient way to travel, but it can be a nightmare if traffic is a mess (which it often is). Avoid taxis like the plague if you are in a rush, if it is raining or snowing, during daily rush hours, and on Friday evenings, when most Parisians are trying to get the hell out of town. (The ride from Orly will cost 15.25–22.87 euros; the ride from Roissy costs an average of 30.48 euros, plus .91 euros for each piece of luggage you put in the trunk.) The **RER** suburban train line (see "Trains," below) has a Roissy stop, connects to the Métro (subway) at the Châtelet, Gare du Nord, Saint-Michel, and Denfert-Rochereau stations, and costs 7.62 euros. It's great if you are arriving at Terminal 20, but to get to or from any other terminal you have to schlep your baggage onto a shuttle bus. That may be a bit of a hassle, but the shuttle is free and the trip takes only about 40 minutes on one of the RER trains that runs nonstop to Roissy from the Gare du Nord station. The **Rois-sybus** costs 6.86 euros and leaves from rue Scribe (Métro Opéra) and terminals 2A (Gate 10), 2C, 2B (Gate 12), 2D, T9 (Gate A), and 1 (Gate 30, arrival level) every 15 minutes.

Getting to and from Orly is even more complicated. By public transportation, you can take the **Orlybus** (4.57 euros) from Gate H, Platform 4, at Orly Sud; or Gate J, Level O, at Orly Ouest, which leaves you at the RER station at Denfert-Rochereau in Paris, from which you can take the Métro. Going to the airport, the Orlybus leaves from outside the Denfert-Rochereau RER station every 13 minutes. The train line to Orly, **Orlyval** (8.69 euros), seems designed to be inconvenient. The airport stations are on the first floor of Hall 2 in Orly Ouest and gates E/F on the ground floor of Orly Sud; trains take you to the Antony-Orly station, from which you must take RER line B to Paris, then the Métro to your destination. From Paris, take RER line B in the direction of St.-Rémy-les-Chevreuses and get off at Antony-Orly, where you pick up Orlyval to Orly Sud or Ouest. Air France provides bus service to Roissy and Orly from several locations around the city (10.67 euros to Roissy; 7.62 euros to Orly, both one-way). The buses may be used by anyone, and they are more convenient than public transport—if you are located near one of the stops—but more expensive. For details in English, call 01 41 56 89 00.

**Baby-sitters...** Home Service (tel 01 42 82 05 04), **Kid Service** (tel 01 47 66 00 52), and **Ababa** (tel 01 45 49 46 46) provide English-language baby-sitting services. All claim to have experienced, reliable tot wranglers.

**Buses...** Paris has a good bus system that's easy to use and much more pleasant than the Métro because you can watch the city go by while you travel. (You can also watch it sit still if you get stuck in a traffic jam.) At each bus stop there is an easy-to-understand diagram of the routes served and the time schedule, and bus shelters also display a city-wide map of the bus system. Tickets are the same ones used on the Métro (see "Subways," below) and can be purchased on board from the bus drivers. (They even make change!) One-use tickets must be validated by punching them into the apparatus behind the driver's seat. Most passes (see Subways, below) are good for bus travel. Simply show your pass to the driver.

There is no free map that includes all of Paris's labyrinthine streets, but bus maps are included in the *Plan de*

*Paris par Arrondissement,* and similar street guides are available at all newsstands and bookstores. A handy little book called *Le Guide Paris Bus,* some of which is in English, will tell you everything you need to know about the bus system.

The major drawback to taking the bus is that you often can't. Many do not run after 8:30pm or on Sundays. The late-night **Noctambus** service doesn't start until 1:30am, and it runs just once an hour (until 5:30am) from rue Saint-Martin and avenue Victoria at Châtelet. In theory, you can flag down any Noctambus and the driver will pick you up and let you off anywhere along the route, as long as you're willing to pay more than daytime fare and share the bus with a variety of drunks and unsavory looking characters.

The **Balabus** is a sightseeing bus that runs between the Gare de Lyon and La Défense on Sundays and bank holidays. It runs from noon to 9pm, from the beginning of April until the end of September. Métro tickets can be used to pay fare, which varies according to how far you go (maximum three tickets).

**Car rentals...** Renting a car is expensive in France. You can save money by booking a car from home; ask your travel agent about fly/drive packages. If you end up renting in France, you can go through **Avis** (tel 01 55 38 68 60) or **Hertz** (tel 01 39 38 38 38), which have counters in the airports and train stations. Reliable companies with lower prices include **Ada** (tel 01 45 54 63 63 or 08 36 68 40 02) and **Europcar** (tel 01 30 43 82 82).

**Consulates and embassies...** U.S. Consulate: tel 01 43 12 22 22; 2, rue Saint-Florentin, 75008, Métro Concorde. **Canadian Embassy:** tel 01 44 43 29 00; 35, ave Montaigne, 75008, Métro Franklin-D.-Roosevelt. **British Consulate:** tel 01 44 51 33 01 or 01 44 51 33 03; 16, rue d'Anjou, 75008, Métro Madeleine.

**Currency...** The euro became the country's only recognized currency on February 17, 2002, making the franc obsolete. True, the new currency isn't as ornate or fanciful as the franc notes were (in fact, the euro borders on downright ugly), but visiting Americans will find it easier to convert prices since the euro and U.S. dollar are almost evenly exchanged ($1USD=1.08 euro). Like the dollar, the euro is divided into 100 centimes, but is distributed in coins of 1, 2, 5, 10, 20, and 50 cents. The euro also comes in coins of 1 and 2 euros, and notes of 5, 10, 20, 50, 100, 200, and 500.

Don't fret if you have leftover French francs from

a previous trip. Most banks will exchange your francs for euros at the fixed tariff rate of 6.55957F to 1 euro—however, they might charge you a commission.

There are commercial currency exchanges—*bureaux de change*—in train stations and airports, and all over the city, especially in areas frequented by tourists such as Champs-Elysées and rue du Rivoli. Many, but not all, banks will exchange currency. Look for the sign: "Change." A commission is usually charged. The **Banque de France** (tel 01 42 92 42 92; 31, rue Croix-des-Petits-Champs, 75001; Métro Palais-Royal) usually has the best exchange rate. You can also make cash withdrawals against your credit card at banks and currency exchanges. The **American Express** office (tel 01 47 14 50 00; 11, rue Scribe, 75009, Métro Opéra) has a currency exchange, plus special services for cardholders. If you have an international **credit card** or **ATM card** with a PIN number, you can withdraw cash at any time from any ATM at banks or post offices. If you lose your **Visa** card, call 08 36 69 08 80; for **American Express**, call 01 47 77 72 00; and for **MasterCard**, call 01 45 67 84 84. Ask your lender if you will be charged extra when you use your card abroad.

**Dentists...** SOS Dentaires has dentists available 8pm–11:40pm and on weekends and holidays (tel 01 43 37 51 00; 87, blvd de Port-Royal, 75013, Métro Gobelins). Call first for an appointment the same day. **Dr. Marc Shulman** is a well-established American dentist whose staff also speaks English (tel 01 45 61 06 42; 38, ave Hoche, 75008; Métro Etoile). The **American Hospital** (tel 01 46 41 25 25; 63, blvd de Victor-Hugo, Neuilly, Métro Pont de Levallois or Pont de Neuilly, bus 82) has 24-hour bilingual emergency dental services.

**Doctors...** If you need a doctor to make a house call, call **SOS Médecin** (tel 01 47 07 77 77). For an **ambulance**, call 15 or 01 45 67 50 50 (see "Emergencies," below, for police and fire numbers). Hospital emergency rooms (*urgences*) will treat you with no questions asked, but you should check your health-insurance policy before you travel to be sure you'll be covered for treatment abroad. The **American Hospital** (tel 01 46 41 25 25; 63, blvd de Victor-Hugo, Neuilly, Métro Pont de Levallois or Pont de Neuilly, bus 82) has English-speaking doctors and 24-hour emergency services, including dentistry, but it can be expensive.

**Driving around...** If you can avoid driving in Paris, do. Traffic is extremely heavy and French drivers aren't known for their patience or *politesse*. You can drive legally in France with an American or Canadian driver's license for up to a year—no international license is required—however, it is strongly recommended and can be purchased through the American Automobile Association for $10. The most important rule of the road is that the car coming from the right in an unmarked intersection has the right of way, so always slow down at intersections and let any car coming from the right pass ahead of you. Seat belts are required for every passenger, even in the back seat.

**Drugstores...** French law requires that each neighborhood have at least one pharmacy open all night; look in drugstore windows for the address the nearest *pharmacie de garde,* which is open that night. Two or three pharmacies in each neighborhood are open on Sunday. **24-hour Pharmacie les Champs-Elysées** (tel 01 45 62 02 41; 84, ave des Champs-Elysées, Métro George V) is centrally located.

**E-mail...** Almost every arrondissement is home to at least one cybercafe, whether it be a mom-and-pop establishment or a conglomerate such as **easyEverything,** which now has three locations in Paris, all of which never close (31–37, blvd de Sébastapol, 75001, Métro Les Halles; 6, rue de la Harpe, 75005, Métro Saint-Michel; 66, ave de Champs-Elysées, 75008, Métro Franklin-D.-Roosevelt or George V.). Each easyEverything location is equipped with more than 300 PCs and offers services such as Microsoft Office and Webcams. Connections start for as little 1.52 euros for 40 minutes. If you're looking for more specialized services (not to mention a Mac format) hop on over to **Clickside** (14, rue Dormat, 75005, Métro Maubert Mutualité). This cybercafe is fired up with programs including PhotoShop, Dreamweaver, Quark Xpress, and Microsoft Office as well as services such as printing and CD burning. Expect to pay 1.52 euros for 10 minutes and up to 4.57 euros for an hour of log-in time.

**Emergencies...** For an **ambulance**, dial 15 (or 01 45 67 50 50). For **police emergencies**, dial 17. In case of **fire**, dial 18. In case of **poisoning**, call 01 40 05 48 48. **SOS Help** (tel 01 47 23 80 80; open 3pm to 11pm) is an English-language crisis line.

**Festivals and special events...**

For exact dates and locations, consult the weekly events rag *Pariscope* or the Office du Tourisme (tel 01 49 52 53 54; 127, ave Des Champs-Elyséeses, 75008, Métro Etoile).

January **La Grande Parade de Montmartre** (tel 01 43 65 10 10), Montmarte; Jan 1, American-style parade complete with pom-pom girls.

March: **Salon de l'Agriculture** (tel 01 49 09 60 00), Parc des Expositions, Porte de Versaille; farm animals and machinery on display and farm-fresh foods to eat. **Banlieue Bleues** (tel 01 49 22 10 10), Saint-Denis; jazz festival. **Foire de Trône**, Métro Château de Vincennes; late March–May, amusement park.

April: **Poisson d'Avril** (April Fool's Day), all over town; Apr 1, fish images and practical jokes rooted in the Middle Ages tradition of poking fun at a particularly infrequent bather by pinning a fish to his back and letting it stay there until it reeked worse than the wearer (today they use paper fish). **Martial Arts Festival** (tel 01 44 68 44 68), Palais d' Omnisports de Paris-Bercy, 75012; competition and demonstrations of various techniques. **Paris Marathon** (tel 01 41 33 15 68); 26.2-mile footrace through the streets of the city, ending on the Champs-Elysées.

May: **French Open Tennis Championship** (tel 01 47 43 48 00), Stade Roland Garros, Métro Porte-d'Auteuil; professional tennis championship tournament. **Fêtes de Versailles** (tel 01 39 59 36 22), Château de Versailles; every Sun through Oct, musical fountains at Louis XIV's château. **Braderie de Paris** (tel 01 42 97 52 10), Parc des Expositions, Porte de Versaille; gigantic garage sale.

June: **Grand Steeplechase de Paris** (tel 01 49 10 20 30), Hippodrome d'Autoteuil; famous horse race. **Grand Prix de Paris** (tel 01 43 57 21 47), Hippodrome de Longchamp; another famous horse race. **Fête de la Musique**, throughout the city; summer solstice music free-for-all on the streets, in restaurants and cafes, including major rock concert on the place de la République (festival guides available at newsstands). **Course des Garçons de Café**; midmonth, waiters and waitresses race through the streets of Paris wearing their uniforms and balancing a bottle and a glass on a tray as they run. **Gay Pride Parade** (tel 01 40 50 69 69, bilingual); annual parade, party, and expo for lesbian, gay, and bisexual celebrants.

July: **La Villette Jazz Festival** (tel 01 44 84 44 84), Parc de la Villette; July 1–10, live jazz in a huge park right next to Métro Porte-de-Pantin. **Festival du Cinéma en Plein Air** (tel 08 03 30 63 06), Parc de la Villette; mid July–end Aug, free outdoor films nightly at 10 (go early and bring a picnic). **Bastille Day**, in fire stations and public squares all over Paris; July 13–14, the French equivalent of America's Fourth of July celebration. **Paris Quartier d'Eté** (tel 01 44 83 64 40), various venues throughout the city; mid-July–late Aug, a cultural festival including concerts, dance, circus, and theater.

August: **Tour de France** (tel 01 41 33 15 00), Champs-Elysées; final leg of the world's oldest and most prestigious bicycle race.

September: **Festival d'Automne** (tel 01 53 45 17 00), various locations; mid Sept–late Dec, cultural festival including dance, theater, music, cinema, and plastic arts. The **Techno Parade** (tel 08 36 68 91 99), modeled on Berlin's famous Love Parade, started in 1998 and held annually in mid-September. It's basically a giant celebration of night clubbing, with an emphasis on techno music; last year it attracted 200,000 revelers, plus 25 floats from various Parisian and provincial French night clubs. **Journée de la Patrimoine**; third weekend, monuments and historic buildings are open to the public. **Biennale Internationale des Antiquaires** (tel 01 47 20 31 87), Carrousel du Louvre; antiques show.

October: **Paris Auto Show** (tel 01 43 95 37 00), Parc des Expositions, Porte de Versaille; new cars on display. **Fêtes des Vendanges à Montmartre** (tel 01 46 06 00 32), Montmartre; first week, grape harvest parade. **Women's ready-to-wear fashion shows** (tel 01 42 66 64 44), various locations.

November: **Festival d'Art Sacre** (tel 01 44 70 64 10); Nov–Dec, Christmas music concerts in churches throughout the city. **Mois de la Photo, the Month of Photography** (tel 01 44 78 75 01), is staged every other year (2000, 2002, etc.) and features themed photography exhibits at the Maison Europeenne de la Photographie in the Marais and museums and galleries all over town.

December: **Braderie de Paris** (tel 01 42 97 52 10), Parc des Expositions, Porte de Versaille; gigantic garage sale.

**Gay and lesbian services...** SIDA Info Service (tel 08 00 84 08 00, toll-free) is an AIDS hotline, and **SOS Homophobie** (tel 01 48 06 42 41; open Monday through Friday, 8pm to 10pm) provides assistance to victims of antigay aggression. The **Centre Gai et Lesbien** (tel 01 43 57 21 47; 3, rue Keller, 75011, Métro Bastille; open Mon–Sat 2pm–8pm, Sun 2pm–7pm) provides information on activities and events in the gay community.

**Newspapers...** Most newsstands carry the *International Herald Tribune, USA Today, The Wall Street Journal Europe,* the

*Financial Times,* and some carry other major British dailies. The major French dailies are *Libération* (left-wing and hip, but much more mainstream now than at its Maoist beginnings); the highly conservative *Le Figaro;* and the staid, well-written, left-leaning *Le Monde.*

**Opening and closing times...** Cafes open early, at around 7am, and stay open until at least 8pm and in some cases until 2 in the morning. Restaurants are usually open from noon to 3pm and 7:30 to 11pm. Boutiques open at around 10am and close at 7 or 7:30pm. Smaller shops may close at lunchtime, usually between 1 and 2:30. Many boutiques are closed Monday mornings. Major department stores are open from about 9:30am to 7pm, and most stay open until 10pm one night of the week. Most banks are open from 9am to 4:30pm, except on Friday when they stay open an extra hour in the afternoon. Small branches are often closed between 1pm and 2pm. Many businesses close during all or part of August.

**Parking...** On-street parking is almost impossible to find, and you're in for a nightmarish experience if you're unlucky enough to have your car towed (if that happens, go to the nearest police station to find out where it's been taken). Parking lots are marked by a square blue-and-white "P" sign; just a few of the large in-town hotels have their own. Centrally located lots include **Parking Notre-Dame** (place Parvis-Notre-Dame, 75004), **Parking Saint-Germain-l'Auxerrois** (1, place du Louvre, 75001), and **Parking Saint-Sulpice** (place Saint-Sulpice, 75006). All three charge around 2.13 euros per hour or 15.24 euros per day.

**Passports and visas...** Visas are not required for citizens of the United States or Canada for visits of less than 90 days. If your passport is lost or stolen, report to the consulate of your embassy immediately to have it replaced (see "Consulates and embassies," above).

**Radio stations...** There are no all-English radio stations in Paris, though the airwaves are full of British and American pop hits. Foreigners love the commercial-free station **FIP (105.1 FM),** which mingles rock with classical and jazz and has soft-spoken female announcers. **Radio Nova (101.5 FM)** plays hip-hop, funk, acid jazz, and reggae. **France-Info (105.5 FM)** has 24-hour news in French. **Skyrock (96 FM)** plays mainstream pop music, and **RFM (103.9 FM)** specializes in rock 'n' roll. **Radio Classique (101.1 FM)** has classical music. **Radio Montmarte (102.7 FM)** airs French oldies.

**Restrooms...** The self-cleaning streetside toilets of Paris are the envy of the Western world—for .30 euros, you get the use of consistently clean facilities. Be sure to accompany small children, though, or they may be undetected by the sensors and swept along when the entire toilet-sink apparatus, including the floor and wall, lifts up and disappears into a separate area to be cleaned and sanitized. Large department stores generally have non-life-threatening public restrooms. At cafes, most French people order a coffee at the bar and then leave it there while they run to the toilet (usually downstairs). All eating establishments are required to have restrooms, but the law doesn't say they have to be clean, so they usually aren't. Don't be shocked to discover a squat toilet, little more than a porcelain-covered hole in the ground; they're still common in cafes.

**Smoking...** If you're bothered by smoke, ask for a table in the *zone non-fumeur* at a restaurant—but don't be surprised to find neighboring diners puffing away on their Gauloises or Marlboros. Except in some of the large, expensive restaurants, the law is widely ignored. In the Métro, on the other hand, most people respect the ban against lighting up.

**Sports hotlines... Allo Sports** (tel 01 42 76 54 54) provides dates and ticket information on sporting events in the Paris area. **Paris Guide Direct** (tel 08 36 69 90 83) has info in English.

**Standards of measure...** The metric system is used in France. Hand gestures are often more useful for indicating what you want in a shop, but here are some basic conversions: 1 inch = 2.54 centimeters, 1 mile = 1.61 kilometers, 1 ounce = 28 grams, 1 pound = .45 kilograms, 1 quart = 0.95 liter, 1 gallon = 3.8 liters. In the other direction: 1 centimeter = 0.4 inch, 1 meter = 3 feet 3 inches, 1 kilometer = 0.62 miles, 1 gram = 0.04 ounces, 1 kilogram = 2.2 pounds, 1 liter = 1.06 quarts.

For clothing, *taille unique* means one-size only. T-shirts and knitwear are often sized 1, 2, 3 (small, medium, large). Children's clothes are sized by age. Otherwise, follow these conversions:

Women's clothing

| French | 36 | 38 | 40 | 42 | 44 | 46 |
|---|---|---|---|---|---|---|
| American | 6 | 8 | 10 | 12 | 14 | 16 |

Women's shoes

| French | 36 | 37 | 38 | 39 | 40 | 41 |
|---|---|---|---|---|---|---|
| American | 5 | 6 | 7 | 8 | 9 | 10 |

Men's suits

| | | | | | | | |
|---|---|---|---|---|---|---|---|
| French | 44 | 46 | 48 | 50–52 | 54 | 56 | 58–60 |
| American | 34 | 36 | 38 | 40 | 42 | 44 | 46 |

Men's shirts

| | | | | | | | |
|---|---|---|---|---|---|---|---|
| French | 35 | 36–37 | 38 | 39–40 | 41 | 42–43 | 44 |
| American | 14 | 14½ | 15 | 15½ | 16 | 16½ | 17 |

Men's shoes

| | | | | | |
|---|---|---|---|---|---|
| French | 42 | 43 | 44 | 45 | 46 |
| American | 9 | 10 | 11 | 12 | 13 |

**Subways...** The Paris subway, the **Métro**, is easy to use, with maps in every station. Métro lines are numbered but are also known by the end stations; line 1 is the La Défense-Château de Vincennes line, for example. Métro service begins at 5:30am, and the last trains leave either end station at 12:30am. The cost of an individual ticket is 1.22 euros, but you can save by buying in bulk: a carnet (10 tickets) is 9.14 euros. The **RER** suburban train network is sometimes handy for getting around Paris more quickly than by Métro because it has fewer stops. Most RER stations are also Métro stops, so transferring from one to the other is easy. Within the city, you can use a Métro ticket or the RER. Unlike the Métro, you'll need your ticket to both enter and exit the turnstiles of an RER station. A **Carte Orange** provides an unlimited number of trips on the Métro, on buses, and on RER within the city for one month (43.45 euros) or one week (12.96 euros; weeks run Mon to Sun). These passes require a passport-sized photo; most stations have photo machines. Don't try to validate the Carte Orange on buses (the *cartes* look a lot like the regular tickets); just show your card to the driver. The **Paris Visite card** (8.38 euros, 13.72 euros, 18.29 euros, 26.68 euros) is good for one, two, three, or five days in Paris and the Ile-de-France (the surrounding region) on all forms of Paris public transportation; Paris Visite also makes you eligible for discounts at certain sightseeing attractions. The one-day **Mobilis** card (5.03 euros) works on the same principle but doesn't include sightseeing reductions. Tickets can be purchased in any station or at tobacco shops (*tabacs*). Validate your ticket by inserting it in the turnstile, which will spit it out again; hold onto your ticket until you've left the Métro—if a *controlleur* asks to see your ticket and you don't have a valid one, you'll be fined on the spot, though, tourists can sometimes avoid fines by playing dumb and understanding only English.

**Taxes...** France's VAT (value-added tax) is now 20.6 percent, levied on all goods and services except for books and newspapers, which carry a VAT of only 5.5 percent. See Shopping for information on reclaiming this tax on purchases of more than 182.93 euros. For customs information, call 01 49 28 54 55.

**Taxis and limos...** Except during rush hours, finding a taxi is fairly easy, unless it's raining or there is a Métro strike. Taxis can be hailed on the street, or you can line up at one of the many *stations de taxi*, clearly marked with a large "T." A taxi is available if the entire light on its roof is glowing; if just the bulb in the center is lit, the cab's occupied. Don't get angry if a driver refuses to take you after asking where you are going. A half-hour before the end of a shift, a homeward-bound cabbie has the right to turn down any passenger who's trying to catch a ride in the opposite direction. Drivers expect about 10-percent tip; there are extra charges for pickups at train stations or other transportation terminals, for luggage weighing more than 5 kilograms, for a fourth person in the cab, and for an animal. Drivers can refuse to take more than three people or an animal (except a seeing-eye dog). Fares are higher at night and outside city limits (marked by the *périphérique*, or ring road circling the city). Radio-dispatched taxis turn on their meters when they receive a call, so don't be surprised when yours arrives with a hefty sum already on its meter. For a radio-dispatched taxi, call **Alpha-Taxis** (tel 01 45 85 85 85), **Artaxi** (tel 01 42 03 50 50), **G7 Radio** (tel 01 47 39 47 39), **Les Taxis Bleus** (tel 01 49 36 10 10), or **Taxi-Radio "Etoile"** (tel 01 42 70 41 41). Chauffered limousines are available from **Carey Limousine** (tel 01 42 65 54 20) or **Prestige Limousines** (tel 01 42 50 81 81). Both have multilingual drivers. **SP2**'s (tel 01 55 65 19 99) motorcycle taxis, complete with driver and sanitary helmet, will get you through traffic fast, but will cost more.

**Telephones...** There are hardly any coin-operated phones left in Paris, except in cafes. You have to buy a Télécarte in a post office or tobacco shop to use a pay phone. Follow the instructions on the phone's screen: *"Décrochez"* means "pick up the receiver"; *"insérez votre carte"* means "insert your card"; *"numerotez"* means "dial the number"; *"raccrochez"* means "hang up." In some cafes, you have to ask at the bar for the use of the phone and then pay the cashier when your call is completed. The first thing you'll hear after dialing is rapid clicking sounds, followed by long rings when the connection is made, or a faster signal if the line is busy.

France is now divided into five regions with different area codes. All Paris region numbers begin with 01. The other codes are 02 for the northwest, 03 for the northeast, 04 for the southeast, and 05 for the southwest. All numbers have ten digits.

For international calls, dial 00, followed by the country code (1 for the United States and Canada), the area code, and the number. To reach American long-distance operators, dial 08-00-99-00-11 for **AT & T**, 08-00-99-00-19 for **MCI**, and 08-00-99-00-87 for **Sprint**.

For French directory assistance, dial 12. For international directory assistance, dial 00-33-12, followed by the country code or 11 for the United States or Canada. Toll-free calls begin with 0800. Other numbers beginning with 08 carry an extra charge.

**Tipping...** A service charge of 15 percent is included in all restaurant and hotel bills. If you are happy with the service, leave some change for the waiter or the hotel maid. Many French people never leave anything extra, so service people won't be shocked (though they might not be pleased) if you don't. Give taxi drivers about 10 percent of the fare if they've been agreeable and helpful.

**Trains...** The **SNCF** is the national train system. There are six major train stations in Paris: the **Gare de Lyon** (trains going to the southeast of France and to Italy), the **Gare du Nord** (Brussels, London via the Eurotunnel, and other northern destinations), the **Gare de l'Est** (destinations to the east), the **Gare Saint-Lazare** (the northwest, including Normandy), the **Gare d'Austerlitz** (Spain and the southwest), and the **Gare Montparnasse** (the west, including Britanny). Suburban trains also leave from these stations. Each station has a Métro stop with the same name. For train information and reservations, call 08 36 35 35 35 from 7am to 10pm. For suburban lines, call 01 53 90 20 20. Always remember to *composter* (validate) your ticket in the orange machines near the quays in the station before boarding your train. If you don't, you'll be fined by the conductor.

The RER is the suburban train network. Inside Paris, it can be used almost as an express Métro line (see "Subways," above). For destinations outside the city, purchase RER tickets at the ticket counters or vending machines in each station.

**Travelers with disabilities...** Paris is not easily accessible for those who have difficulty moving around. All Métro stations have stairs; only bus line 20 (between Gare Saint-Lazare and Gare de Lyon) has wheelchair-accessible buses. Though most hotels have elevators, they're often too small to accommodate a wheelchair, and bathrooms can be extremely cramped. The large, modern hotels are the best bet for anyone in a wheelchair, and taxis (whose drivers are required to help with a wheelchair) offer the only convenient way to cover a lot of ground. Thankfully, the sidewalks have ramps at every street corner. More attention has been paid to the needs of the blind. There are bumps on the edge of the quays in the Métro, and elevator buttons have tactile numbers.

The **Comite National de Liason Pour la Readaptation des Handicapes** (tel 01 53 80 66 63, 236 bis rue Tolbiac, 75013) publishes *Paris Ile de France Pour Tous*, which is a good general guide for the disabled; it's available in English and costs 9 euros if you buy it in Paris, 12 euros if you order from overseas. The **Office du Tourisme** (tel 49 52 53 54; 127, ave des Champs-Elysées, 75008; open daily, 9am–8pm) has information on the accessibility of transportation, museums, and monuments. A pamphlet published by the national railway, the SNCF, is available in train stations. *Paris-Ile-de-France for Everyone*, an informative book on the accessibility of hotels, museums, etc., in the Paris area, is available by mail for 12.20 euros (tel 01 53 80 66 66; CNRH 236 bis, rue de Tolbiac, 75013).

**TV stations...** If your hotel room has TV but no cable, you will be able to watch **channels 1, 2, 3, 5**, and **6**. You may get a kick out of seeing reruns of some old American series in French, especially on **Channel 6**. **Channel 5** is Arte, a highbrow French-German collaboration with obscure films, documentaries, and musical programs. On cable, you may or may not have **Canal+**, a movie channel, but you probably will get **CNN Europe**, **BBC Prime** (a mix of BBC programming), **MTV Europe** and **MCM** (music videos), **Eurosport**, **Planète** (nature and science documentaries), **RAI Uno** (Italian), **TVE 1** (Spanish), and **Euronews** in both English and French on different channels. **Canal J** has children's programming until 8pm.

**Visitor information...** The main branch of the **Office du Tourisme** at 127, ave des Champs-Elysées, 75008 (tel 01 36 68 31 12, recorded information in English 01 49 52 53 56, Métro Etoile; open daily, 9am–8pm) has several agents to answer your questions. There are also branches at airports and train stations.